Memoirs of a Left Hander

Vern Schultz

authorHOUSE®

AuthorHouse™
1663 Liberty Drive
Bloomington, IN 47403
www.authorhouse.com
Phone: 1-800-839-8640

First published by AuthorHouse   4/18/2011

ISBN: 978-1-4567-3305-6 (sc)
ISBN: 978-1-4567-3304-9 (e)

Printed in the United States of America

Any people depicted in stock imagery provided by Thinkstock are models, and such images are being used for illustrative purposes only. Certain stock imagery © Thinkstock.

This book is printed on acid-free paper.

PROLOGUE

Most biography's I've read are of famous politicians, sports heroes, historical figures or successful financiers. It's always interesting to learn their secrets to success and fame. This book, which I suspect falls under the heading of a biography, is about a person who really did nothing extra special, didn't win any fancy awards, never made a lot of money, and certainly was no sports hero. It's probably best described as a biography about a mid-western, middle class, average citizen who found being left handed much more fun and challenging than being another run of the mill right hander. This story is about the mundane life of Vern Schultz…that's me! Now wait just a minute. Don't be so quick to put this book back in the bookcase and look for something more exciting. I think it's only right that you learn a bit more about the life of a middle class, left handed, average American citizen. Remember, everyone can't be famous!

When my wife Toodie and I completed writing our Will in 2005 the lawyer made a suggestion. She said that it's an excellent practice to write up a narrative about our lives that could be shared with our children, grand children and even great-grand children after we pass away. She indicated that this type narrative or article would be an excellent supplement to our Will. I didn't think much about her suggestion until the winter of 2008 while vacationing in Puerto Vallarta, Mexico. I was sitting by the beach with little to do and thought that maybe this would be a good time to jot a few notes about my life; as dull as it may be. Well, I'm afraid I got carried away and spent the next couple of years writing notes here and there whenever I had a free moment. This book is a culmination of those notes.

Looking back, I feel I've lived a full life and learned a few things worth sharing with others. My parents offered a sound foundation for my future and provided the stability and genetics that have allowed me to reach the ripe old age of 80. I've got nothing to lose, so why not open my soul to the world and tell all. I hope those who read these memoirs will understand that my life was simple, with no great accomplishments or lifetime achievements. For me, however, it was a wonderful life and I thank God for each day. Writing these memoirs proved to be a fun exercise for me. It provided an opportunity to brush away a few of the cobwebs in my brain and remember back to what I consider to be, "the good old days. At least I thought they were!"

CONTENTS

SECTION I
THE GOOD OL' DAYS
(1929 – 1944)

1929 ---One of the most devastating years in America. The stock market crashed, rich folks went broke, the suicide rate leaped, employment dropped off the map, banks closed, the hobo ranks grew, and soup lines became the restaurant of the day. America was truly in crisis! But all was not lost. Fleurine Schultz, with the aid of Arthur Schultz, made a significant contribution to America on December 1st, 1929. A contribution that would hopefully play a part in bringing our Country back to normalcy…it was the day Vernon (that's me) entered the world!

Back in 1929, Arthur and Fleurine Schultz lived at 1034 Edmund Street in St. Paul, Minnesota. This city was gaining fame in those days as a key railroad center, a leader in grain processing and as a safe hiding place for John Dillinger and his Chicago mobsters. My folk's home was on the very western border of the Frogtown District, the area of St. Paul populated predominantly by German and Austrian immigrants. The St. Agnes Catholic Church stood proudly, like a beacon, in the center of 'Frogtown' and served as the focal point of this community. It also served as the home church for our family, both sets of grandparents and numerous German relatives. When my dad enrolled at St. Agnes grade school in 1905, the nuns would slap your hands with a ruler if you spoke any language but German. Wow, and I had trouble learning English!

There are many explanations given as to why this neighborhood of St. Paul was called 'Frogtown'. One old timer explained to me that in the early days this area of town had a very high water table with numerous ponds and lots of frogs. In time, the ponds were drained, homes were built

1

and the frogs disappeared, but the 'Frogtown' name remained. At the very northern point of 'Frogtown' were the large railroad barns that offered employment for many of these Austrian and German immigrants. These immigrants would, in turn, write home telling about the employment opportunities that St. Paul offered. In these letters they referred to their home community as 'Frogtown'. These letters brought new German and Austrian immigrants to St. Paul where they also settled in 'Frogtown' close to friends and work. Although there were other European immigrants in this neighborhood, the German and Austrian population predominated with the St. Agnes Catholic Church serving as the community gathering location. I've been told that Irish or Italian Catholics might even be turned away at the front door and told to go to their own church. In those times you were expected to know your place and stick with your own nationality group!

As a youngster, I remember attending church at St. Agnes each Sunday with either my parents or my grandparents. In those days you had to be careful where you decided to sit, because folks actually paid for a particular church seat. If you made the fatal mistake of sitting in another person's seat, the usher was there to escort you away. I found this out the hard way on more than one occasion. Frankly, I would have much rather spent my dime attending a Saturday movie then for that church seat. I thought those movies at the Faust theater a few blocks away were much more exciting!

My Grandma Schultz (later Wahlberg), in her early-married years, lived on the corner of Thomas and Kent Street directly across the street from the St. Agnes Church. After my grandfather Schultz died in 1907, she opened a small confectionary store at this site with the help of my dad and his older sister, Laura. My dad was just 7 years old when his father died. From what I understand they made a very meager living from this store. Fortunately my Grandma's family owned this building so I suspect there was little rent charged and their residence on the second floor was probably free. My Grandma's maiden name was Fritz and if you stripped off the new façade added to that building in the 1960's you would see the name "Fritz" imbedded in the original stone structure right above the main entrance. The Fritz families were some of Frogtown's original German settlers. Let's face it, when my Grandma Fritz married August Schultz they were simply destined to live in that German settlement of Frogtown. It's amazing, with such a strong German background; I never learned one word of German.

I mention our family's association with St. Agnes and the Frogtown area because this tight knit German based community played an important role in my family's early life in St. Paul and has left me with many fond memories. I can remember taking saxophone lessons from a nun at St. Agnes School. This remains vivid in my memory because at 8 or 9 years old that saxophone case got mighty heavy walking that mile to the school for my music lesson and back home. By the way, St. Agnes Church is also known for an unusual occurrence that occurred in the 1930s. Pallbearers were carrying a casket up the long series of front steps at the church for a funeral mass, when the bottom of the casket broke open, and the body proceeded to roll back down the steps. What a way for a church to be remembered. Back in the 1930's this was probably considered just an unfortunate event. Today however, a multi- million-dollar lawsuit settlement would most likely be cause for celebration by the family of the deceased!

Who would ever have guessed that after graduating from the University of Minnesota in 1952, my first full time teaching/coaching job would be at St. Agnes High School? I truly was returning to my roots. To be perfectly honest, it was the only real job offer I had!

From The Beginning

I understand my dad played a key role in designing my parents' home at 1034 Edmund Street in St. Paul sometime in the late 1920s. Apparently the lot was very narrow so some adjustments had to be made in room size to meet city building codes. The first floor contained a fairly small but adequate kitchen, a dining room and living room. There were three bedrooms and one bathroom on second floor. It sounds like a perfect setting for a family of four back in the 1930s. It would have been if my parents hadn't decided to gain some additional income by renting out one of the bedrooms. Having a renter meant that Loren, my older brother, and I had to share a bedroom. My folks used the large bedroom, which, in truth, wasn't any larger than the other two. I guess that rent money during those depression years was more important than providing me with a private bedroom. It would appear that Loren and I came second in their priorities.

It's kind of ironic that this home had just one bathroom. Apparently that's all my folks felt was needed for the four of us and our renter (actually five, when a few years later my young brother Ronny arrived). They must have had stronger bladders in those days. Today, there are four bathrooms in our home for just my wife and me. In fact at one time we considered a fifth bathroom, just adjacent to the back entrance. I predict that my mother's first reaction to us having four bathrooms would be, "That's three to many to clean!"

A Mr. Enter was our first roomer. He had immigrated to America from Europe and needed a place to live until he could afford to bring his family to St. Paul. He worked at the Farwell, Osman & Kirk Company in downtown St. Paul during the two or three years he lived with us. My memory of him is quite faint but do remember him as a kind gentleman with a heavy German accent. After he left, a Mr. Lennon became our new roomer. He stayed for many years until my folks sold the house in 1944 and moved to the more affluent Como Park area. Mr. Lennon was a barber and a great sports fan. He became almost a part of the family. I remember spending many evening hours talking about local sports and in particular our local St. Paul Saints Professional Baseball Team. Mr. Lennon really helped stimulate my early interest in baseball. I always wondered why my folks didn't include free haircuts as part of the rent!

My Dad worked at the St. Paul Fire Department Repair Shop on Edmund and Rice Street all the while we lived on Edmund Street. In the 1930s he drove an old model T Ford shop truck back and forth to work. He would park this truck in a vacant spot next to our garage located in the back alley. This shop truck was really something. It was fire engine red in color with a crank in front to get it started. I remember sitting in the driver seat pretending I was a fireman going to a fire. I'd give anything to own that truck today! Just think, my dad drove just 8 miles round trip to work each day in a company car. Years later when I moved to Prior Lake and worked in St. Paul, I drove 50 miles round trip each day wearing out one car after another. Think of the money I could have saved with a company car. I wonder if my Dad realized what a great deal he had.

A black 2 door 1938 Chevrolet was the first car I remember in our family. My Dad built a garage off our back alley especially for this car. This garage was unique because he had dug out a large pit at least 6 feet deep in the center of the garage. This pit allowed him to work under the car when repairs or an oil change was needed. He used a short homemade ladder to get in and out of this pit. Not many folks in those days had this kind of homemade hoist, or in fact knew anything about repairing a car. My Dad was an expert, in fact he was an expert at fixing just about anything. I may have inherited his eye color but certainly not his technical skills… or his brains.

I remember asking my Dad how he ever learned to repair cars and qualify for a mechanic's job at the Fire Department Repair Shop. I knew he had only attended St. Agnes grade school through 6th grade and had no formal auto repair training. He explained that he began working at a company called Auto Engine Works located right behind Montgomery Ward's in St. Paul's Midway District during his early Teens. This Company actually made the parts for cars. Apparently there were no Amoco Parts

Stores in those days. His answer really opened my eyes to the early years of the Automobile era. After retiring, he explained that when cars became computerized, his days as a mechanic ended. He just wasn't ready for the computer era!

A Perfect Neighborhood

Looking back to those 14 years on Edmund Street was a blast! That neighborhood had everything that Loren and I could have ever wanted or needed as kids. Let me describe what it's like to live in a perfect neighborhood.

The Hamline/Cherokee streetcar line ran on Thomas Street just one short block north of our home. This streetcar would take you anywhere you wanted to go in the St. Paul/Minneapolis area. Once the Hamline/Cherokee streetcar arrived downtown you could transfer to any of the other lines heading in various directions. Using a simple transit token, the streetcar was the perfect vehicle for traveling throughout the entire twin cities area. Unfortunately in the 1950s the decision was made to scuttle the streetcar system completely. Now, 60 years later, plans are being made to construct a light rail transit system from downtown St. Paul to downtown Minneapolis. This route has become very controversial and extremely expensive to build. Would you believe that the University streetcar line operated for years on this exact route and served as the primary connection between these sister cities. What an expensive, absolutely devastating mistake to let the streetcar system go defunct. Remember, this is an 80 year old foggy talking who made use of the streetcar system as his major mode of transportation and served as my cheapest travel route when attending the University. To be totally honest, hitchhiking was actually cheaper but a little more unpredictable!

At least twice a week my grandma's major social outing was to take the streetcar down town, meet her daughter Laura, and browse through the Golden Rule and Emporium Department Stores. According to my mother they seldom bought anything. They would then have the 75 cent lunch at Kresge's or Woolworth's dime store and end the afternoon people watching on the mezzanine floor at Schuneman's Department Store. The streetcar had them home in plenty of time to make the family supper. That fun outing cost my grandma Schultz the sum total of two streetcar tokens and a 75 cent lunch. Lunch with my cronies today (with a tip) costs a minimum of $10.00 plus an average of $4.00 in gas. Who the #$%#$% decided to get rid of those streetcars anyway!

The Centre Theater was just a short three blocks south of our house. For just ten cents you could attend a Tom Mix or Gene Autry cowboy movie in addition to what was called 'cliff hangers.' These were 20 minute movie shorts always ending with someone hanging from a cliff, falling from a plane or three seconds away from sure death. You had to attend next Saturday's movie to see the outcome and we rarely missed a Saturday. I did miss one Saturday and I'll tell you why. When you reached 13 years of age the movie price went up to a quarter. I had just turned 13 and hoping to save 15 cents told the ticket taker I was 12. I was actually born in 1929 and when she asked my birthday I got flustered and said I was born in 1928. That actually made me 14. I paid the quarter and went to confession the next Saturday instead of to the movie!

Desnick Drugs was located on the SE corner of University Avenue and Lexington Parkway and their ice cream fountain had every flavor imaginable. Directly across the street, next to the Pure Oil filling station was my absolutely favorite restaurant, 'White Castle'! On the South West corner was the National Tea Grocery store. Directly south of this store was the famous Coliseum Roller Rink. What a fantastic place! Right in the center of this roller rink, on Lexington Ave., was an open viewing area where you could watch the skaters and listen to that wonderful organ music. We spent many hours at that site checking out those pretty female skaters.

The Coliseum was a very significant building because it served as the left field home run fence for Lexington Baseball Park, home of the American Association St. Paul Saints professional baseball team. Just think, a short four blocks away, I could watch the likes of Duke Snyder, Roy Campenella, and many other future major league baseball stars play ball on their way up to the major leagues. Let me tell you, this corner of Lexington and University and its surrounding area was a virtual recreational center for our neighborhood. A lot of pretty sharp looking gals also hung around that corner; but of course, that didn't interest me.

Just across the alley from our home, on Charles St., was Rohweders

Confectionary Store. We never had far to go for a nickel ice cream cone or penny candy. Right next door, on the corner of Charles and Oxford, was Schillers Food market. I remember when you entered Schillers you were individually waited on by either Mr. or Mrs. Schiller. They offered a very personalized service even though Mrs. Schiller was kind of a grump!

A block to the north on Thomas Street, right off of Lexington Ave., was our friendly neighborhood shoemaker. Next door to him was a mini-drug store. On the corner of Oxford and Thomas, a short block away, was another small mom and pop grocery store. It was a store we seldom used. Why walk blocks away when everything we needed to buy could be purchased just a few steps away; right behind our house. In the winter we didn't bother even wearing a coat to the store. It was worth getting a little cold for the possibility of a free piece of candy.

What really made this neighborhood super for us kids was a vacant land area just three houses east that we kids called 'the dump.' It was a large excavated hole that covered about a four-house area and ran from Edmund Street to Charles Street. This was our playground! It's where my friends and I (Frances Doyle, Jack Paddock, and others, whose names I can't remember) played those great adventure games by the hour. You know the games; cops and robbers, pirates, war battles and every conceivable game we could imagine. This was the perfect playground, without any swings, sand boxes, or a fancy clubhouse. It was better than any playground or park operated by the St. Paul City Parks and Playgrounds Department. I drove by 'the Dump' years later and it had simply vanished. In its place were four new homes on Edmund Street and another four on Charles Street. I feel sorry for kids living in my old neighborhood. Those house builders actually destroyed their playground!

Three short blocks north of our home was a large hill that served as our sled and toboggan slide each winter. I should add that right next door to this hill was a walled in fortress called the 'House of Good Shepard'. The rumor was that this building housed all the 'bad' girls in Minnesota. Let me tell you, we never went very close to that place. When I became older, I did develop more of an interest in that facility!

We had our own private football field that was a narrow grassy area located between the Casket Company and a large Printing Company four blocks East on University Avenue. You just had to be careful about getting 'building burns' when you ran too close to the sidelines. Immediately south of these buildings was a large field called 'Circus Hill'. Each spring the Ringling Brothers Barnum and Bailey Circus would do their shows on this field. We kids would help them with their setup in return for free tickets to the show. For a few days each year we were 'circus' people.

Immediately south of Circus Hill were the largest group of baseball and softball fields in St. Paul called Dunning Field. I can't tell you the number of pickup games and competitive games I played on those fields. As a kid we played mostly fun and unorganized baseball games; one a cat, two a cat or anything that resembled baseball. As I grew older it was the home site for Pee Wee League, Midget League, Grade School, Capitol League, American Legion, High School and later City League games. This was also home of the fast pitch softball lighted field. My Dad and I attended many of those softball night games, in addition to watching the premier baseball games at the Dunning 4 field. We didn't have TV in those days but we sure had lots of activities available to us right within walking distance of our home. Best of all, we could do all this without a neighborhood watch committee!

About seven blocks West on University Avenue was the popular Montgomery Wards Store. Everyone in our area shopped at 'Monkeys' for everything from clothes to hardware, appliances, and just about anything you can imagine. They even had a major auto repair shop. This store also offered a huge mail order department where you could order just about anything out of the Wards catalog. You could actually buy a house or car from the mail order department. I remember the Wards warehouse being so large that the clerks used roller skates to get around. Wards also had a massive front entrance where you walked up about ten steps to enter into the main lobby. Located right in the center of this lobby was a huge candy department. They had every type of candy imaginable and a penny would always get you something. To our amazement, Montgomery Wards went out of business in the mid 1990's. It apparently couldn't compete with the Wal-Mart's, Home Depots, Best Buy's and other similar stores that offered new approaches to shopping. I miss going to Wards; the original one-stop shopping center. Apparently their management got complacent and didn't keep up with the times… what a loss!

A Special Bonus

Like I said, my neighborhood had it all! There was something else, however, that made this neighborhood even more special. How would you like living right next door to your Grandma and Grandpa? Well, that was another luxury I had. My Grandma and Grandpa Wahlberg owned the duplex on the corner of Edmund and Oxford. (My Grandpa Schultz had died when my Dad was just 7 years old and later in life my Grandma married Martin Wahlberg). He had come to America from Sweden and worked for a time at Schuneman-Manhiemer's Department Store (later known as Schunemans, eventually Dayton's and currently Macy's). My Dad told me that once Martin Wahlberg married my grandma he decided to retire at the ripe old age of 50. My grandma's income by that time came from some interest she and her (Fritz) family had in building and apartment rentals. My grandpa's early retirement decision didn't set well with my dad who had an extremely strong work ethic. I remember my grandpa spending most of his time sitting in their living room or on the front porch. I was on friendly terms with him, but there are those who labeled him a 'grouch'. I can't recall him smiling very often and, come to think about it, I never did see him laugh, but what do you expect from a Swede!

Before I was born, my folks lived for a time in my grandparent's upper duplex so they had lots of experience living in close proximity to my grandma and grandpa Wahlberg. For me it was a wonderful new experience. I could run over to their house just about any time I wanted and get a cookie or two, a sugar sandwich or a variety of other treats. There was one condition however. I had to sit on the kitchen floor right by the pantry and eat my treat. No way was my grandma going to allow crumbs or sugar all over her house. Now that I look back, I've come to the realization that all of my relatives, including my parents, were spotless housekeepers. 'Clutter' was not in their dictionary. Fortunately or unfortunately, I appear to have inherited that trait. My wife Toodie says, if nothing else, I would always make a good housekeeper…never a cook. I haven't figured out if that is a complement or not!

I remember on one occasion eating a sugar cookie at my Grandma's house when I was five or six years old. For some reason, I was laughing and crying at the same time and managed to swallow my tongue. I was near unconsciousness when my mother, a nurse, rushed over and saved the day by reaching in and pulling my tongue out. According to my mother, my grandma froze on the spot. Aren't mothers wonderful?

My grandparents didn't own a telephone and we did. My dad rigged up a wire between our homes with a buzzer. When someone called my grandma at our house my mother would buzz their house and she would rush right over. Everyone thought this was an ingenious move on my dad's part, with exception of my mother. She told me later in life that my grandma would never go home after she received her call, but would stay and visit by the hour. I remember my mother saying that she could never come up with a really good way to solve this problem without hurting grandma's feelings. I told her that she should have just cut the wire. By the way, her advice to me was, "Never live next door to relatives". To be perfectly honest her real advice to me was never live within five miles of relatives (or was it 50 miles?)

Sugar Cookies – Within Walking Distance

The original LaRose clan emigrated from France and settled on the Canadian side of the St. Laurence Seaway in the 1700's. In the early 1900's they moved to Faribault, Minnesota. It was in Faribault, that my grandmother Melena Tatrault married Peter LaRose. My grandfather worked in a combination furniture/mortuary business while living in Faribault. According to my mother, it was common practice in those days to have this type of combined business. The sale of wooden caskets worked hand in glove with the furniture business… at least it did in those days. You know, I really don't think selling caskets along side of bedroom sets at HOM Furniture would be a successful business today!

My mother was the eldest of five children. She apparently was given major responsibility in caring for her younger brothers and sisters. I got the impression from my mother that being the oldest child presented more negatives than positives. After leaving high school she worked in the Faribault shoe factory for a time. This was not a very challenging job with a limited future. She then made the major decision to leave Faribault and attend Ancker Hospital Nursing School, located on West 7th Street in St. Paul. Ancker hospital served as the 'General' hospital in St. Paul with the Nursing School located right on the hospital campus overlooking the Mississippi River. I remember her saying that nursing school was a glorious experience and that she absolutely loved being a nurse. What made attending the Ancker Nursing School even better was the fact she had no brothers and sisters to care for, had no meals to prepare and there was indoor plumbing! Just the indoor plumbing makes it sound like a great move to me!

There was something unique about Ancker Hospital back in those days. There were railroad tracks running right next to this hospital. If an ambulance or any emergency vehicle was traveling with a patient to Ancker Hospital and a train was on those tracks, they had no choice but to wait until the train passed by. I believe it was in the 1950s that the City finally built a bridge over the RR tracks to resolve this dilemma and also to allow for a free flow of traffic on West 7th Street. They tell me that quite a few babies were born on the wrong side of those railroad tracks to mothers who just couldn't wait for one of those long freight trains to finally pass by!

My LaRose grandparents moved from Faribault to St. Paul after their family had left home and my grandfather had retired. At least three of their children, along with many relatives had moved from Faribault to the Capitol city so they decided to follow suit. They also settled in the Frogtown area on Charles Street about 4 or 5 blocks away from our home, and walking distance to St. Agnes Church. It was close enough for me to walk or ride my bike to their house. Grandma LaRose also made great sugar cookies…a good reason for a bike ride!

I remember my Grandma LaRose as being short, kind of big around the middle and having bird like legs. She was a real 'fun' lady who laughed a lot and, I suspect, pretty much ran that household. My Grandpa LaRose was a tall thin gentleman with a St. Frances head of hair, bald in the middle and hair around the sides. He was a very friendly but extremely quiet man who apparently did everything my grandma told him to do. At the time, my mother's youngest sister, Mary Louise, lived with them. Their son Bernard and his wife Toots moved right next door, in the upper duplex, after they were married. If I remember right, Bernard also told me never to live within 5 mile, or preferably fifty miles, from relatives!

Like I said, Grandma LaRose made the greatest sugar cookies you could imagine. I remember my mother asking for the recipe and my grandma would laugh and say, "Just put a pinch of this and a handful of that". This may not have been a very scientific recipe, but believe me, they were really great cookies. Their house was a little bit unusual in that it had, what I considered, two living rooms. No one ever sat or entered the front living room that I can remember. All the socializing, card playing and visiting took place in the middle living room. Just off of this room was a small room, like a den or sewing room. It was separated from the living room by long strings of beads that tingled when you passed through. Those beads intrigued us kids and more than once we were told to sit down and quit that 'tingling'. In fact in those days we were told to sit-down and be quiet most of the time!

I will never forget the day we visited Grandpa and Grandma LaRose on December 7th, 1941. Music was playing on the radio when the announcer cut in with the announcement that Pearl Harbor was being bombed and we most likely were heading to war with the Japanese. That turned out to be a somber day for us and, I am sure, everyone in America. I had just turned 12 years old and perhaps too young to understand all the ramifications of this event. I remember my grandfather saying that our lives would be dramatically changed in the months and years ahead... Wow, was he right!

A favorite hobby of my LaRose grandparents was fishing on Bass Lake, a lake just north of St. Paul. I can't recall how often they went fishing but I know it was frequently. On certain occasions they would invite me to join them. It was an exciting experience for me at first, but as I got older it lost some of its luster. They followed a very rigid fishing routine that never varied. You would row out to a certain point and then drop the anchor and not move for the rest of the day. This 'point' was measured as being directly west of the Tuberculosis Sanitarium and north of a specific gray boathouse. Trolling, moving from this key fishing location or talking was not on the agenda. Apparently fish have superior hearing!

I can still visualize my grandma as an ungodly sight to behold. She wore this large straw hat, an old house dress and nylon stockings that covered her arms to protect her from the sun, horse flies or God knows what. Her appearance in this fishing garb is hard to imagine. I honestly believe her appearance scared the fish away. With each fish outing, the afternoons began to get longer and longer. I would fish with a simple drop line and once did catch a large Northern Pike that was a source of family conversation for years to come. I always felt that the fish in that lake had wised up to my grandparents' never changing routine and simply developed a new travel route. Don't get me wrong, those fishing expeditions will always be one of the highlights of my youth...but not of my adulthood.

Who Needs School

A memory that has stuck with me over these years was my dramatic entry into grade school. Most people I know look back on their first day of school with fond memories. My son Tom just couldn't wait for that first day of school as did Casey his younger brother. Patty, our daughter, was so anxious that at three years of age she packed a lunch to attend school with her brother Tom on his first day in third grade. It was a hard sell to convince her she would have to wait a couple more years. Ask anyone you know, and invariably they will tell you that the first day of school was an exciting anticipated event in their life. Well, this was not true for 'Vernon'. On my first day at Galtier Grade School I had to be carried kicking and screaming from home into my grandpa's 1939 Chevrolet. He then physically carried me from the car to my kindergarten classroom. Guess who ends up an educator in the family?

My second day of school wasn't much better. My mother let me take a small toy truck from home to play with at school. Shortly after class began the school Principal entered our classroom and told the teacher that a police boy accused me of stealing the toy truck from a yard on the way to school. I denied this, so the principal called my mother who informed her that it really was my toy from home. The principal made the police boy come into our classroom and apologize to me in front of the whole class. I still remember the funny look he gave me as he left the classroom… like, I'll see you later kid! I may not have been the smartest kid in my class but I wasn't the dumbest either. I was smart enough to know it would be wise to avoid that police boy. I remember running all the way home that afternoon. The last person I wanted to see was that police boy!

In time, school turned out to be a much better experience than I ever thought. It's hard to admit but before long I really looked forward to attending. I remained at Galtier Grade School for just my kindergarten year and then transferred over to St. Columba Catholic School where I attended from first through eighth grade. St. Columba was just two blocks away from Galtier so over the years I ended up friends with students from both schools. The only difference between schools was how the teachers dressed. The teachers at Galtier all wore colorful house dresses, but at St. Columba they all dressed alike with long flowing black dresses and a matching black hood. My mother told me they dressed like this because they all were sisters. I figured their mother must have got a heck of a good buy on that black cloth!

These St. Joseph nuns lived downtown at St. Agatha's conservatory, right between the downtown YMCA and World Theatre, and each morning would arrive in cabs and return home in cabs. I recall no male teachers or lay women teachers at St. Columba. I should also note that the church had Father Casey as pastor and at least three priest assistants. How times have changed. Today our St. Michael parish in Prior Lake has just the Pastor plus a half time deacon and the St. Michael grade school has a male lay principal and a mixture of male and female lay teachers…absolutely no nuns. It's interesting that we still call them Catholic schools!

I remember two specific situations where it was necessary for my mother to come to my rescue while attending school at St. Columba. The nun teaching sixth grade apparently was not pleased with my ability to write legibly using my trusty left hand. She thought that, with practice, I could improve this skill by using my right hand. Apparently this caused considerable anxiety on my part seeing that my right hand was about as useless as a shovel without a handle. My mother very politely, but firmly, informed this nun that I had been left handed for the past eleven years and I would continue to be left handed for my future lifetime. The nun reluctantly agreed with her. My mother could be very convincing…thank God!

I was having considerable difficulty with arithmetic in seventh grade… actually in every grade. The nun teaching seventh grade was concerned with my progress and tried everything to upgrade my arithmetic skills. She kept me after school each day so I would keep up with the other students. Looking back, I can really appreciate her dedication. This created a problem, however. I was playing on the school basketball team and the good sister's after school tutoring kept me from practicing basketball. Again, my mother saved the day. She informed this nun that she wanted a well-balanced son and that bouncing the basketball would provide this balance. My tutoring ceased and I apparently became better 'balanced'. By the way, I did get a passing grade in arithmetic…but just barely. I think it was the nun's prayers that did it!

Baseball…More Fun Than Arithmetic

I really credit Mr. Lennon, our roomer, and my dad with fostering my interest in baseball. From the time I was just a little kid, until the day we moved to Como, my dad played catch with me in front of our home on Edmund Street by the hour, almost every day. We lost more baseballs down that sewer on the corner of Edmund and Oxford than you can ever imagine. He would have me pitch to him; always trying to improve my form. One of my dad's idols was Johnny Vandermeer, a major league left handed pitcher with two no-hitters under his belt. Johnny Vandermeer was known for kicking his leg high in the air to gain more speed on his fastball. I can still hear my dad say over and over again, "Vern, kick your leg higher and it'll come faster." He may well have been right, but I am convinced that high leg kick resulted in my need for two hip replacements in later life. I'm not complaining at all. The fun I had playing baseball would have been worth four hip replacements. It's just those metal detectors at the airport that I hate! Years later my Dad told me that Grandpa Wahlberg would sit on his porch watching us play catch. He thought all that playing ball was a real waste of time. My dad told me he had a dramatic change of attitude after he learned I was getting paid to play baseball. I'll say it again…what can you expect from a Swede?

I remember asking my Dad if he played a lot of baseball when he was a kid. He said that he had to work most of the time just to keep bread on the table, which left no time to play sports. He left school after the sixth grade and worked from that time on. I do remember my Dad as being very well coordinated and I'll bet if circumstances had been different he would have been an excellent athlete. After he retired and moved to Texas he took up golf and did extremely well. I couldn't beat him…but that really doesn't say much. As I've found out on numerous occasions in my lifetime…life isn't always fair!

The first organized baseball of my career took place in the sixth grade at St. Columba grade school. Clarence Coleman was the coach and he was having tryouts for the school team. My Dad encouraged me to try out but being kind of shy I said I didn't think I was good enough. He said, "You try-out anyway." I learned very early in my life that when my German father told me to do something I'd better do it. Reluctantly I did try out and to my surprise I not only made the team but ended up as the starting first baseman and as a relief pitcher. I'll always thank him for being persistent with me. This was just one of many occasions in my life where his 'encouragement' allowed me to realize that I could compete in many areas of life. Without his 'kick in the butt' I may never have entered the mainstream of life in sports, music or education. Being shy is like an addiction…you must fight to overcome it or end up going absolutely nowhere!

The real baseball magnet for us neighborhood kids however, was Lexington Ball Park, home of the Saint Paul Saints American Association Baseball Team. The 'Saints' were the farm club for the Brooklyn Dodgers. At first we would attend games as members of the 'Knothole' gang. For ten cents we could sit in the left field bleachers and see many of America's future big league stars. At about 12 or 13 years old a number of us kids got jobs at Lexington Park employed as groundskeepers. If my memory is correct I worked each summer at the ballpark until I was 16 or 17 years old. This job involved sweeping the stands in the morning followed by a break till about 2:30. At that time our work got serious and we cut the grass, dragged the infield, put clay in the pitching mound, raked the batting box and marked the field with a white lime material. We would head home for dinner then back to the park where we donned white coveralls with "Saints" stenciled on the back and went to our assigned locations to retrieve baseballs that left the playing field. Believe me; those coveralls with "Saints" stenciled on the back made me a pretty important guy in my neighborhood. If you treated me right, I might just know how to sneak you into the game free!

Each groundskeeper was assigned a set location during the game. Our job was to retrieve the baseballs hit in the stands or that flew out of the park. The best assignments were in the right field stands, in the bleachers, on the roof to the right of the press box, or to the left of the press box. The best assignment of all was on the coliseum roof to retrieve those homerun balls. There were two really bad assignments. 1. Sitting in the parking lot of the Prom Ballroom and 2. Sitting in the parking lot on University Avenue. These last two assignments were really boring. Can you imagine, sitting outside the ballpark an entire evening just waiting to retrieve a foul ball or two. We rotated assignments so everyone faced at least one of these outside the park assignments every week. The Prom Ballroom assignment however did have one plus. It allowed you to listen, from a distance, to some of the greatest big bands of the era. The sounds of Woody Herman's band and so many others, would just escape through the walls of that fantastic ballroom. The saxophones sounded exceptionally sweet…Oh, to play like them!

Just think how different professional baseball games are today. We were responsible for retrieving every baseball that left the playing field, and expected to fight for the ball if necessary. The reward we offered was a free ticket to a future ball game. The balls we collected were put right back into play. Today if a ball just touches the ground or has a slight blemish it's tossed out of play. Players and even umpires regularly throw practice and game balls into the stands. Any ball hit out of the playing field is automatically given up to the person retrieving it. No wonder tickets to professional baseball games are so expensive today. Heck, if we didn't retrieve every ball in our assigned area we were in trouble. They nicknamed me 'Butch' because I never got in trouble! In my final years of working at the Ballpark, I did advance to running the scoreboard and to the really plum assignment of bringing balls to the umpire and catching fouls off of the backstop screen. A good catch might even bring a round of applause from the fans. It was just like show biz!

I believe we received the sum total of $1.80 a day, which was a fairly good salary in those days for a kid. Unfortunately, after eating five White Castle hamburgers, a full pint of ice cream and drinking a big bottle of Pepsi each and every day, little cash remained. My Dad, till his dying day, could never figure out where my pay was going. I was afraid to tell him that I ate it away. Even today White Castle sliders remain one of my very favorite foods. I figured out one day that if I ate five White Castle hamburgers, 300 days a year, that would total 1500 White Castle's. In my teen-age years I probably put away closer to 2000 White Castle's a year. Us ground keepers were serious hamburger eaters!

It didn't take me long to get used to folks calling me 'Schultzie'. That greeting is still very common today. During my ballpark years however, the nickname 'Butch' became my handle. This stuck with me for at least five years all during my ballpark career and into high school. Later, in my post high school years I became 'Lefty'. Still today, when I meet someone from that ballpark era his or her greeting will be, 'Hi Butch'. It will draw a strange look from Toodie or my friends. Maybe I got this nickname because I was so tough…or ugly!

The real benefit of this ballpark job was the opportunity to play ball on this professional field when our work was done and when the Saints were on the road. A fun game we regularly played was called 'clubhouse ball' that even the professional ball players enjoyed playing. The clubhouse roof was divided into designated areas; one area for a single, another for a double, another a triple and a homerun area. A pitcher would throw the ball and the skill was hitting it into the right area. We played this game by the hour. We also shined shoes for free baseballs and, let's face it, it was just a thrill to socialize with the players. What a great job. I must confess, however, that if my mother knew the kind of language that floated around the ballpark, she would have dragged me home by the ear. I don't know why but swearing and baseball seem to go hand in hand. Some guy once told me that the more you swear the better your batting average. Now I know why I had all that trouble hitting!

When the St. Paul Saints were on the road there was still plenty of activity occurring at Lexington Park. Teams from the old Negro baseball league regularly played at the Park. I remember watching the immortal Satchel Paige with his blazing fast ball pitch more than once. The Bearded Giants were a popular draw because all the players had beards. This was really different because no one in the American Association was allowed to have any facial hair. I remember Jesse Owens racing a horse, Jacky Price performing a baseball trick show and professional girl's baseball games. Heck, we had just as much fun when the Saints were out of town!

There's an old song titled, 'Out behind the Barn.' This song talks about all the crazy things a young farm hand learned out behind the barn. Well, I can tell you I got my practical education, 'Out behind the Ballpark'. Let me share a few bits of baseball park knowledge that has stuck with me over the years:

1. To keep cool in the summer wear long underwear. That's right; all the umpires working at Lexington Park wore long underwear while working their games. I know, because after each game they would hang their underwear out to dry under the stands. Apparently when you sweat in long underwear it keeps you cool. I don't think anyone follows that logic today.

2. If you want to date girls, be a baseball player. Girls would hang around the front gate of Lexington Park each evening just waiting to meet the players. At the time I just didn't understand… but I do now!

3. To be a good baseball announcer all you really needed was a western union ticker tape machine. For road games, Dick Seibert the twins' announcer, would read the ticker tape as it came in and pretend he was right there at the ballpark. Dick had a wonderful imagination so he was great at fooling all those fans listening to the game. Fans had their ear glued to the radio thinking the game was right at Lexington Park and Dick was on site describing every play. Remember there was no TV…radio was the real communicator.

4. When the baseball management really wanted to play a game (like the season opener) and the weather was rainy, you still could play the game. Just pour gasoline on the wet dirt infield and set it on fire. It's amazing just how fast that dirt infield could dry out. The opening game was always a sellout which meant big money, so the game gets played no matter what!

5. The ballpark was an absolute magnet for drawing 'characters' to the park. It was a dream location to set up a special education classroom. Some of these folks worked on our ground crew, others worked in the concession department selling hotdogs or beer in the stands, and others just hung around the park for something to do. In a way the ballpark was a great social learning opportunity for me. I kind of learned what the real world was like. Looking back, I wouldn't have missed this opportunity for the world.

6. If you have the desire to be a professional baseball player and just have average ability, I can offer you a sure-fire solution to making the team roster. Decide to play when there is a War on and all the good players are in the service. In 1943–45, during the peak years of World War II, teams needed to bring in local players to fill out a roster. I remember a number of local athletes who were recruited to play for the St. Paul Saints. They were good players but probably not up to usual professional league standards. You still had to have nine players on a team, so this was a workable solution. When the war ended all the really good players returned. Thank God for the Kenny Mauers,

Gene Kellys, Dick Fureys and other local players who made it possible for professional baseball to continue during those challenging war years.

7. There is usually a simple way to resolve most baseball problems. George Washington (no, not the one you read about in your history books) was a ball player who played for the St. Paul Saints back in the early 1940s. He had short stubby fingers making it difficult for him to maintain a firm grip on the bat when he would swing at the ball. On a fairly routine basis he had the bad habit of releasing the bat, in one of his mighty swings, sending it sailing in the direction of fans sitting in the expensive first base box seats. Those fans quickly found out they were in dangerous territory. In an effort to protect these fans, and to avoid pending lawsuits, the team management got their heads together and came up with a winning solution. They constructed a portable backstop screen that was wheeled out and placed in front of the box seats where George's bat usually landed whenever he was playing. When George was traded to another team they stored this portable backstop right under the first base grandstand never to be used again. The rumor was that George could throw his bat farther than he could hit the ball!

8. Devour as many White Castle hamburgers as your stomach can handle prior to attending ball games. They are far less expensive then those over priced ball park hot dogs… and I guarantee they'll keep you regular!

Two major events occurred on April 12th, 1945 that I recall very vividly. President Franklin Roosevelt died at 3:35 P.M on that date and on a more positive note Howie Schultz received the call to join the Brooklyn Dodgers major league baseball team. I was fourteen years old at the time and was playing for the St. Columba grade school baseball team. I'm not sure I understood the significance of President Roosevelt's death but I sure understood the significance of Howie Schultz making it to the big leagues. Howie was one of my baseball hero's. We lived at 1034 Edmund and he also lived on Edmund Street just a block and a half west of our house. He was over 6 feet 6 inches tall and starred in both baseball and basketball at Central High School. He was by far the best first baseman in the city and could hit the ball a mile. I watched him play whenever I could and could quote his batting average on any given date. I loved it when my friends would ask if he was my brother, after all his name was Schultz and we both played first base. So, what if I did imply to a few friends that he was my older brother…Wouldn't that have been something!

As it turned out Howie Schultz also played professional basketball for the St. Paul Lights and later for the Minneapolis Lakers. He was one of a relatively few athletes with the natural skills to play two professional sports and he was outstanding at both. After retiring from professional sports Howie returned to St. Paul and taught and coached at Mechanic Arts High School, then at Hamline University and later Murray High School. I officiated a number of his basketball games and found Howie to be a real gentleman and outstanding coach. One day, with a smile on his face, he shared a story describing the important role he played in helping to enhance the integration movement while playing for the Brooklyn Dodgers. He said, "Branch Rickey, General Manager for the Brooklyn Dodgers, wanted the first black ball player (Jackie Robinson) to play for the Dodgers. I couldn't see Jackie replacing Peewee Reese at shortstop or those other outstanding infielders so I felt it was only right for me to give up my first base position to Jackie Robinson so baseball could be integrated." Well, maybe there was just a little bit more to it than that but what a great story, what a great individual and Howie Schultz remains one of my hero's even today!

Playing The Xylophone

I was about 7 years old when my folks informed me that I was going to be taking music lessons and, by the way, would I like to play the saxophone? To play the same instrument Xavier Cugot played in his Latin Band sounded great. I also remember seeing a saxophone in the music section at Montgomery Wards and even tried a few notes with those funny looking paddles. My dad saw this advertisement for a used saxophone in the want adds of the St. Paul Dispatch paper and we went to check it out. When the owner opened the case I saw this strange instrument that I had never seen before. That's when I realized that a saxophone wasn't a xylophone. I was intrigued with this unusual instrument and my dad bought it. I never told my dad that this wasn't the instrument I was expecting. In later years I realized there were many more opportunities playing the saxophone in local bands then the xylophone. Anyway, I had no interest in wearing those funny Cugot costumes I saw in the movies or moving to South America where Latin music thrived. Can you even imagine carrying that bulky xylophone from job to job...you'd need a truck!

It was probably 1937 when Loren and I began our music career taking lessons from a Mr. Paul Lau. He was a cello player with the Minneapolis Sympathy Orchestra and obviously a highly skilled musician. It was in the heart of the depression so I suspect his pay with the orchestra was minimal and giving music lessons was good supplemental money. But just think about it for a moment. Here was this highly trained musician who would drive to our house each week to give beginning music lessons to two punk kids. I have no idea the actual amount he received for these lessons, but my dad was pretty frugal so I guarantee he wasn't getting big money...maybe a dollar a lesson. What a humbling experience this must have been for this talented musician, but like everyone else at that time, his family had to eat. Can you imagine, a cello player giving me lessons on the saxophone…he must have really needed the money!

Mr. Lau, being of German ancestry, was a no nonsense man, who expected us to practice and to know our weekly lesson. I think he was satisfied with my progress, and with my folks paying the bill you better believe that I practiced. I hesitate to rank Loren's progress on his trumpet lessons, except to say that he could always play louder than me. I know that Loren didn't like it one bit when Mr. Lau would ask me to play Loren's trumpet lesson on the saxophone so he could see how it should be played. It's really fun any time you can show up your older brother! To be perfectly honest, music was probably the only thing I could do better than Loren. A few years later I took lessons from a nun at St. Agnes School and that completed my musical training. She was a piano teacher who didn't know a thing about the saxophone. I wish I could have taken lessons from a skilled saxophone player who could have helped provide certain practical tips and playing techniques unique to this instrument. I would have given anything to take lessons from that fantastic sax player in the Whoopee John Old Time Band…he was my music idol.

In 1939 I was invited to participate in a music contest held at Cretin High School. I didn't think my skills were good enough and pleaded with my folks to not participate. Apparently they didn't share my opinion. I remember shedding a few tears and spending a few hours in my room. That 'time out period' may have had something to do with me changing my mind and agreeing to perform. This is when I found out my folks were smarter than I thought. They must have known something I didn't, because to my surprise and amazement, I won first prize in the Saxophone category. I still proudly possess that gold medallion. This experience made me realize that maybe my folks weren't as dumb as I thought. Winning that contest did absolutely wonders for bolstering my temerity.

I enjoyed playing the Sax but hated it with a passion when my folks had company and my mother would invariably say, "Vernon, get your Saxophone and play a song for these folks." I later wised up and learned to 'take off' when my folks had company. I remember little else about my budding music career until I entered high school. You can bet I kept practicing…my folk's saw to that. No way was that money for lessons going to be wasted. In later years, I often thought about my early music experiences and realized that without my folk's encouragement (that's a polite term) I would have most likely quit taking lessons after a couple of weeks. My dad held to the philosophy that when you started something you didn't quit. You stuck it out. This same philosophy held true when you attended sporting events with him. You stay in your seat till the game is over because you never know what might happen…you just don't quit. Gosh, that's the same thing my high school and college coaches preached to me. "You never quit!" Apparently they were all taught by the same professor!

The People I grew Up With

The Boss - My dad was a really clever guy. There were very few things he couldn't do. He could make just about anything, and fortunately worked in a Shop that had every piece of equipment and tool needed. That Fire Department Repair Shop on Edmund and Marian Street had a full machine shop, a complete array of automobile repair and maintenance equipment, a battery shop, a leather shop and machines I never did understand. He was also the most honest man I ever knew and would never use any of this equipment for personal use during the workday. He made much of our home furniture, kept our automobiles in top condition and made numerous items we used in our home and yard. Much of this was done at home but many an evening was spent at the shop. The Public Safety management gave full approval for shop staff to work on personal projects after work hours. Believe me; he made good use of this privilege!

My dad was very clever and inventive, always looking for a new solution to a problem. For example, he worked closely with a pilot from Northwest Airlines in designing the strobe light now used by all airplanes. He received no credit for his input but told me he enjoyed seeing its ultimate success. He also came up with an innovative idea of dropping sand in front of the back tires of police cars to avoid getting stuck in winter driving. It worked, but never to his liking. The sand had a tendency to drop slightly in front of the back wheels. He said they needed to install a small blower that would force the sand right under the wheels. That project was never pursued. About the time Ronny was in high school he began working on an airboat concept but put it aside when he retired. I wish he had spent time working on a gas free vehicle for me to use, when I lived 25 miles from work!

What I remember most, however, is the work that he and my brother

Loren did in making gas operated motor 'Chugs'(motorized racing cars). These chugs turned out to be the envy of every kid in the neighborhood. My brother and Dad built these Chugs but I had the really important job of being the designated driver. The first Chug they built was scheduled to compete in the Soap Box Derby races held in Highland Park. This was really a classy racing machine but had no motor. Loren drove this chug in a pure gravity race down the steep Highland Parkway hill. Unfortunately he failed to win this Soap Box Derby race but did end up with first prize for the best upholstered Chug. It may not have been the fastest racer, but it certainly was a great looker with that leather upholstery.

Loren and My dad then decided to build a racing Chug driven by a Briggs-& Stratton gas-operated motor. The motor was located right behind the driver seat with a drive belt that connected the motor to the rear axel. You pulled a handle that tightened the belt and away you would go. It may sound simple in today's world but it was a real innovative invention back in the 1930s. No other kid had one of these Chugs. Let me tell you, when I drove this chug down Edmund Street, at the blinding speed of 20 miles per hour, took a sharp turn onto Chatsworth, and circled the block to return home, every kid in the neighborhood was running after me just dying for a ride. What a wonderful way to get popular. I hate to say it, but I have Loren to thank for all this neighborhood prestige I was getting. Without question, I became the most popular kid in the neighborhood. There are some benefits in having a big brother…who made racing chugs!

The second Chug that Loren and my dad built was even more refined, with a fancy drag brake. To stop the chug, you would push really hard on a foot pedal. This action would at least slow you down… coming to a quick stop was actually never mastered. You may wonder what my role was in the construction of these Chugs. My role might best be listed under the heading of 'Driver and Consultant'. At times, I would go with Loren and my dad to the shop during the construction phase of these Chugs. When I wasn't needed, which was generally always the case, I would spend hours scooting around the shop on one of those little carts that mechanics use to work under cars. This allowed me to practice my driving skills in preparation for the day the Chug would be completed and I would be at the wheel. No one seemed to mind that my engineering skills were not put to better use.

My Dad always talked about the automobile of the future having just three wheels. He and Loren decided to build our next Chug using this three-wheel model. Believe me it was a beauty. I remember when they brought it home. It was red, sleek in appearance and really something to behold. They decided to park it under my Grandma Wahlberg's back steps. Well, somebody else must have also thought it was something special because it was stolen the first night we had it home. We were all heartsick about this loss. It was the last Chug Loren and my dad ever built. With no more chugs to drive, my popularity in the neighborhood took a severe nosedive!

Loren later built a motor scooter to get around the neighborhood. We apparently had a disagreement of some kind and I ended up being banned from using this scooter. I remember him planning this big adventure of driving his motor scooter all the way to Willmar, Minnesota. I recall my mother in no way endorsing this trip but my dad thought it was a great idea. Are you aware that mothers generally are far more conservative than fathers? Loren actually made it to Willmar but I remember his phone call asking my Dad to come to Willmar and take him home. Apparently it had something to do with failing to put springs on the scooter. I seem to remember he had trouble sitting for the next week!

When homes were built in our neighborhood, in the 1920's and 1930's, the City made one serious mistake. They constructed a sewer system with sewer pipes too small to handle heavy rainstorms. Two things would occur with each rainstorm; first, the corner of Oxford and Sherburne (two blocks South) was the low point in the neighborhood and a good size lake would suddenly appear on this corner. Basements of every home in that area would be flooded. For a few days that lake ended up being our neighborhood swimming pool. The homeowners hated this flooding but we kids loved 'Oxford Lake'. Second, the laundry tubs in the basement of most neighborhood houses would back up and water would shoot up from the tub drains just like a geyser. My Dad solved this problem by rigging up a wooden post that would screw down on the drain and seal it water tight. No water backed up in our basement. Like I said, there wasn't much my Dad couldn't do!

My dad was one who believed in exploring new ideas. He learned of an innovative approach to growing strawberries when you only had limited space...our small back yard would come under the heading of 'limited space.' This approach involved growing strawberries in a barrel. He proceeded to secure a large old whiskey barrel and filled it with a special dirt/fertilizer recipe. He then drilled about 20 three-inch holes all throughout the barrel and planted the strawberry seeds in these holes. As

I recall, the strawberries flourished and the birds really appreciated every berry they ate. Another great idea that needed a bit more research!

My dad followed the rules in everything that he did. I wish I could say the same. I don't think he ever exceeded the speed limit or ran a stop sign. If he bought ice cream cones for the family, he would park the car until we were finished. He was a true German to the core in that he believed in following the rules. I know of more than one relative that had him labeled as stodgy or a real square. At the time, I must admit that maybe it was my opinion as well. Today, I see it all so different. He was teaching us values, respect and honesty. He did his job well and after we grew up he relaxed, laughed a lot more, let his hair down and had a good time enjoying the fruits of his labor. The older I get, the more I realize how really smart my dad was!

I don't want to give the impression Art Schultz lacked a sense of humor. I remember him hooking up a rocking chair in the basement recreation room with a battery and Ford coil. When a metal tab in the seat of the chair would contact the Ford Coil it produced a significant shock. He would invite his friends to sit in the chair and literally shock the Hell out of them. Everyone including my dad would die laughing…except the guy who got shocked. He rigged up the same mechanism in what looked like a gift-wrapped candy box. He would hand the box to someone and a similar shock would occur. You could certainly tell who had a sense of humor and who didn't after they grabbed the box. There were those who didn't think this was so funny and even accused him of having a warped sense of humor. I thought it was funny!

Jim Griffin, my referee partner and St. Paul policeman, was a good friend of my dad and often stopped at the fire department repair shop. He told the story of a policeman who would stop by the shop on a regular basis and steal my Dad's lunch. He thought it was really funny. After this happened a few times Jim said my dad fixed a fake lunch with sandwiches laced with car grease. I remember Jim saying that there are folks who think it's funny when they pull a trick, but lack a true sense of humor when the trick is reversed on them. Apparently this policeman was one who lacked a true sense of humor. My dad's lunch was never stolen again! Who said my dad didn't have a sense of humor?

Alcohol was definitely not one of my Dad's favorite beverages. On a really hot day or at a family affair he might down one beer but never two. When he drank that beer it was literally 'in one gulp'. Down the hatch it went; there was no horsing around. He absolutely had no time for drinkers.

I can't recall even one occasion that I saw him frequent a bar. On the other hand, my Grandpa Wahlberg would drive his 1939 Chevrolet two blocks down to Herges Bar on Chatsworth and University with some frequency and spend the afternoon. I know my grandma wasn't in favor of this adventure to Herges Bar and my Dad liked it even less. I guess everyone in the family can't be perfect!

How times have changed. The fire station right next to my dad's shop was designated as the 'black' station. Only Black firemen were ever assigned to this station. My dad got along great with these fellows as he did with Jim Griffin who was one of just a few Black policemen. I can recall some less than complementary comments he made about some of the Black folks living on Rondo Street which was in the predominantly Black neighborhood of St. Paul. I remember asking him how he got along so well with those black firemen and Jim Griffin but seemed to be somewhat critical of certain of the black folks he really didn't know. His answer was simply, "Well, those other folks are just different!" Apparently when you get to know people of color as friends and co-workers, then they're OK, and if you don't know them personally it's easy to generalize that "They're different." I didn't buy his logic but feel his comments helped me see diversity from a much broader perspective and probably made me less judgmental. Labeling people as being different when you really don't know them is a lot like the baseball pitcher who figures a batter is an easy out because he struck out his last time up. After he proceeds to blast a homerun the second time up the pitcher sees him differently. It's like "Now I respect him because he's' different' than those other run of the mill players. Unfortunately, everyone can't hit home runs…but it doesn't mean they're different!' Who knows, maybe the guy hitting singles is every bit equal to the home run hitter!

You have to remember in those days there were no Black baseball players or Black professional athletes in general, few Black politicians, still a number of segregated facilities, and limited job opportunities for minorities. When it comes to having biases toward different racial groups back in those early years, I suspect my dad was more liberal than most but still had built in biases based on his upbringing. To his credit, he bought all his suits from Jake Jules clothing store in Minneapolis because he knew he could barter with the Jewish clerks and he loved to barter. We bought our shoes from Mintz Shoes down on the levee in St. Paul for the same reason. He bought his Television sets and had them repaired by Officer Turpin a Black local policeman my dad liked and knew he could trust. If my dad had any racial biases he never let them stand in the way of getting "A good deal!"

The Real Boss - I was told my dad's older sister, Laura, introduced my mother to my dad while she was attending Ancker Hospital Nursing School. I know little about their courtship but understand they went on many dancing and long blade ice skating dates. They continued these activities well beyond middle age. They loved to go to the Hippodrome at the fairgrounds to long-blade skate with that wonderful waltz music as background. My folks also continued to dance on a regular basis during their retirement years in McAllen, Texas. My dad had a special dip step in his dancing that I never could master. Believe me, they were a handsome couple. I remember attending one of their Minnesota Club dances in McAllen and realized at the time that Toodie and I were the youngest dancers on the floor, and having trouble keeping up with all those old smoothies.

My mother probably wouldn't agree with me, but I feel she inherited her mother's sense of humor. I noticed this much more as she got older and was easier for me to compare with the memory of my Grandma LaRose. In many ways my mother and father were very different in the way they saw life. My mother had an excellent awareness as to individual differences in people, she was a good personal diagnostician, and she listened. She was willing to look at both sides of any issue. I'll bet she was an outstanding nurse. I would have hired her as a Rehabilitation Counselor in a heartbeat!

My dad, on the other hand, saw issues more as black and white, seemed less flexible in his approach to issues, more direct and to the point. You put these two personalities together and you had a winning combination. Over 55 years of marriage proves that fact. Their relationship kind of reminded me of our St. Paul Superintendent of Schools in the 1970's who was a very nice, kind, loveable man. The Assistant Superintendent on the other hand was tough as nails, called a spade a spade, and served as the Superintendent's hatchet man. They worked beautifully together. Who says opposites don't attract!

My mother pursued her career in Nursing at the Bethesda Hospital in St. Paul after her marriage. Loren and I were both born in this hospital, which was located just two blocks north of the State Capitol. She gave up Nursing when Loren came along and became a full time homemaker. When we reached high school age she then resumed her Nursing career on a part time basis. She went to work Monday and Tuesday evenings at the Northern Pacific Hospital in the Midway District, just a few blocks away from Wilson High School, where both Loren and I attended. My mother told me she enjoyed nursing as a career because it gave her a feeling of accomplishment and purpose; not necessarily for its monetary rewards. I loved the fact that she worked because on those Monday and Tuesday evenings either Loren or I would drive her to work at 7:00 and pick her up at 11:00. We had the car with all its freedom for that four-hour period. Loren and I would battle for the car on those two evenings. When Loren entered the service I no longer had any competition. I would have loved it if she had decided to work five days a week!

Interestingly enough, some of my mother's lady friends thought it was wrong for her to return to her nursing career. They felt that, as a woman, she should be happy and satisfied with her job as a homemaker. My mother was one of those pioneer women in the 1940s who decided there was a role for women out of the home as well as in the home; and she was going to prove it. She felt she could juggle a career along with being both a good mother and homemaker. She did a great job at both. I certainly supported her view completely; after all, I wanted to use that car on Monday and Tuesday evenings!

My dad did all the shopping in our family and my mom did all the cooking. He bought the best food in town and especially the meat he purchased from Pioneer Sausage Co. located on Rice Street, a few blocks from his shop. This meat was really top drawer. He would purchase these great wieners that contained little appendages of meat where the casement had erupted. They were considered seconds and probably cost less but we kids loved them because these appendages tasted so good. I don't think I ever saw my dad do one bit of cooking. Why should he when my mother was an outstanding cook and an absolute expert at using the right spices. She took pride in her cooking and if guests were coming, she wanted to know ahead of time to prepare the best meals possible. In other words... no surprises! Her fried steaks were outstanding, I can still taste her special recipe for chicken and dumplings, and those hot dishes were indescribably delicious. She must have liked peas because we had lots of them, but never had spinach. I had spinach at Toodie's house and loved it. I learned later that she didn't like spinach...so...what the cook doesn't like...you don't get!

My mom's deserts were outstanding! I remember the caramel cake, cream puffs, fruit salads (they were desserts to me), every kind of pie and chess pies. Fortunately, I married another great cook...just how lucky can a guy get. I remember on one occasion my folks asked me to check on their house when they were on vacation. My mother baked a caramel cake just for me. Each time I checked on the house I took just one piece of cake hoping it would last a long time. What a mistake! After a week it was covered with mold. How dumb can you get?

My mother loved playing cards and always belonged to at least a couple of card clubs. I'm not absolutely sure but believe many of the women she played cards with were her ex-nursing classmates. I remember one lady in particular who, in the middle of the card party, would go up to my folk's bedroom and pray. I always wondered why she was praying while the other ladies were laughing and having a great time. Who knows, maybe she was praying for a better hand of cards. My mother's card clubs would rotate from house to house. This meant that the host had to have a neat and clean house and come up with some new and innovative luncheon dish. My mother was really good at this. On one occasion my Aunt Laura came to the card party, walked into the living and proceeded to take her finger and run it across the top of the door ledge, apparently to check my mothers housekeeping skills. My mother never forgave my Aunt Laura for that insulting act. By the way, there was no dust! If you think about it, the women raised during this period of time took real pride in their profession; being a good homemaker and cook. Don't kid yourself, they checked out each other's housekeeping skills and tried to top each other's cooking skills. Just like fellows in the building trades who took pride in their work, these ladies took just as much pride in their occupation. My Aunt maybe went just a little bit too far!

Speaking of clean houses, Loren and I had housekeeping chores. We rotated on washing and drying dishes along with a variety of other cleanup duties. My special job each week was to dust those wooden mopboards that served as the border between the walls and floor. It didn't seem to matter if they were dusty or not. Our house was always spotless, but unlike some of our friends, we actually were allowed to sit in the living room. Apparently if no one sat in the living room it could never get dirty. I guess that makes sense, but maybe not very practical! One evening, when my mother was 97 years old and living in the North Ridge Retirement Center, she looked me in the eye, smiled, shook her head and said, "Vernon, all that cleaning." What she was really saying; "was it all worth it?"

Both my mother and dad periodically played cards in the evening with friends. My mother just loved to play Bridge and I understand she was quite good. My dad didn't seem to care much for cards but I think he played pretty much to satisfy my mother. They played cards and visited most often in the evening with fellows my dad had worked with and their wives. Most evenings, however, my folks spent at home with us kids. I can see them now sitting in the living room listening to the radio, my mom knitting and crocheting and my dad reading the paper, with naps thrown in for good measure. My time at home was spent practicing my saxophone, lots of house projects, listening to the radio, playing catch with my dad in the early evening and playing in ball games or attending them. I'd say we were a busy family that did a lot together. Can you imagine, we lived in a home without TV or a computer and survived!

In the early 1940's we were probably the first in our neighborhood to have Television. There was a policeman named Turpen who had a radio and TV repair business as a side job. My dad and he were good friends so he sold my dad a Setchell Carlson TV set at a much reduced price. Actually most everything my dad bought was at a reduced price because he liked to bargain and was darn good at it. Being one of the first to get a TV, we became awfully popular in the neighborhood and with our close relatives. When the 'Show of Shows' or Milton Berle was on TV we invariably had company drop in. Pretty soon every one was buying a TV, but for a lot more money than my dad paid. I'm convinced that my dad believed buying a product at its listed price was sinful!

I can't say our family life was exciting or extra special in any way. What I can say however, is that our lives were stable, secure, loving and safe. Let me set the record straight, we didn't have a lovey, huggy, kissy type upbringing. Heck, we were German. A good handshake was all we needed. We left all that lovey kissy stuff to the Italians and Irish!

The Smart Kid - My brother Loren was two years older than me, very mechanically inclined and, I hate to say it, was gifted with the brains in the family. How fortunate for me that I was so much better looking than him (just kidding, of course), was blessed by being 'left handed', loved sports and cared little about how things worked. We were opposites in so many ways but somehow managed to survive together. After all, when you have to share a bedroom with your brother for all those years, it's wise to get along. We had a couple of skirmishes, as most brothers do, but all in all it was nice to have a big brother around when you needed a little support or advice. At about 12 years old I could hold my own with Loren in one of our skirmishes, and by the time I was 14 I could take him!

Loren had a great relationship with my Dad especially when it came to building, designing and making things, especially those outstanding chugs they built together. Loren was the kind of guy who always asked, "Why does it work that way?" or "How did you do that"? He had an inquisitive mind that never stopped. On the other hand, I was more interested in the finished product and "When is it going to be ready to run?" I could care less as to how something was made. We would have made a great NASCAR team. Loren would build and maintain the fastest race car in the country and I would be the world famous driver; and of course take all the glory!

The relationship I had with my dad, on the other hand, was focused more around sports and athletics. It's interesting how, as brothers, we could have such diverse interests. The truth is, if I didn't get along with Loren he might not let me ride one of his motorized chugs. I could never take this chance so I made sure we got along. It helps to see the big picture!

I was kind of a wimp when it came to arguing with my folks. I pretty much did everything they told me to do, even though I may not have liked it. Loren, on the other hand, had more of a mind of his own and wasn't willing to give in if he thought he was right. I'll never forget the time I was talking with my mother when she was in her 90's and living in the Retirement Center. I said, "Do you remember the time you had an argument with Loren about something or other. You told him that if he ever did that again he would end up in Reform School?" She got absolutely livid and denied ever saying that. I said that I remembered it vividly and thought it was a pretty good idea. She became really upset and it sort of spoiled our visit. By the way, she really did say it! In case you're wondering, Loren never did end up in Reform School…even though he maybe should have!

While living in our Como home, Loren had a big party in our basement recreation room for his friends from Wilson high school. It was a boy-girl affair and I remember sitting on the basement steps during the entire party keeping an eye on everyone. According to Loren I really squelched his party. What really made Loren furious was when the time came for him to drive some of the girls' home. I asked to go along, or maybe 'demanded' is a better term. I can still remember the 'look of hate' that Loren gave me, but fortunately for me, my mother couldn't see any reason why I couldn't ride along. I don't think he has ever forgiven me for screwing up that party and playing chaperone. If my young brother Ron had done that to me, I would have killed him on the spot!

One Friday, Loren surprised us and came home from the Navy on a very short weekend leave. He asked permission to use the car for a date. I had already asked and received permission to use the car. My mother, being true to her word, said," I'm sorry Loren, but I told Vernon he could use it." Believe me, this caused quite a scene. That was a decision my mother really wished she could have changed. More than once, in her later years, she expressed to me her regret for that decision. She said that she lay in bed that evening unable to sleep worrying about Loren walking across Como Lake on that frigid evening wearing just his lightweight Navy 'P' coat. She told me, "Loren was home for just a short time on leave, and I didn't have the sense to let him have the car. I don't know what I was thinking." Sometimes mother's get too emotional…of course she made the right decision!

For many of our early-married years, Loren and I drifted in different directions as we began our careers, got married, had children, and made new friends. Loren eventually made a major career move, in the 1950's. He left his position with the Univac Company in St. Paul to become plant manager of their Univac facility in Utica, New York. This was a major promotion requiring his family to relocate. A few years later Loren returned to the Twin Cities for a work related visit. It so happened that I was planning a driving trip to a conference in New York City at the same time he planned to return to Utica. I invited him to ride with me in my VW Beatle and said that I would drop him off on my way to New York City. He agreed, and the two of us spent 24 hours together in that cramped little Beatle. We alternated driving and sleeping in the back seat only stopping to grab a bite of food. It was a wonderful trip that allowed us to get re-acquainted and develop a sincere interest in each other's work. I credit that Beatle with fostering a wonderful relationship with Loren that has grown over the years. Thank God for my VW Beatle, even though I could never get that @%$^& heater to work.

The Come Along Kid - That 10-year age difference between Ron and me made it more difficult to develop a really close relationship as kids. When you think about it, he was just 12 years old when I had already left home to get married. I do remember that he became the best skater and hockey player in the family making good use of the ice on Como Lake. His Mutt Race championship run with our dog Ginger at Como Lake was an event I will always remember. I often thought how strange it would have been to coach or be his teacher during the time he attended St. Agnes High School. Fortunately for him I was in the process of leaving St. Agnes by the time he arrived. Was he lucky!

I also have a vivid memory of the year that Rudolph Moeller came from Germany to live with my folks, and Ron, as part of an Exchange Student program. How could you forget a kid who spoke just minimal English when he arrived in St. Paul in September, and ended up the top student in his class at St. Agnes High School, by June? If that didn't put some undue pressure on Ron, I would be mighty surprised. Although I was already married while Rudolph was living with my folks, we became good friends. We still communicate each year at Christmas time. He recently retired after a successful career with the Department of Labor in the German Government. Rudolph was an extremely bright young man who certainly exemplified the high caliber of youth taking part in this exchange program. I can say with some certainty that, as a student, I most likely would not have made the cutoff for acceptance into this exchange program. But give me some credit… I was smart enough not to apply!

After getting married I often wondered if Ron was assigned to take over my cleaning responsibilities of dusting off the mopboards, cutting the lawn, doing the dishes plus all those other mundane household tasks. Actually, by the time Ron came along our folks had mellowed to the point that he was probably excused from all yard or household chores. Research points out that the last child in the family really has it made. Ron lucked out! After high school Ron went on to graduate from St. Cloud State University. Not only did he manage to graduate but also had the good fortune of meeting his future bride, Ann, while in St. Cloud. After their marriage Ron entered the Air Force and was stationed in a number of exotic locations. His Air Force Classification was as a weatherman. I don't know if it's true or not, but word has it that he was reassigned from Libya back to the States after predicting a July snowstorm in the desert!

There is one thing I never could understand about Ron. He was an avid hockey player, seemed to love the Winter Carnival, raced his dog in the middle of winter, and then makes his home in the heat and humidity of Texas. When I asked him about this decision he said that he hated all that cold and snow of winter. Maybe getting hit in the head with that hockey stick back in 1955 scrambled his brain a bit!

Family Togetherness

Our family vacations would be wherever our 1938 Chevrolet would take us. The most frequent vacation destination was to Faribault, Minnesota, my mother's hometown. Once or twice a year we would all pile in the car and travel through Rosemount, Farmington, Northfield, and Dundus before we arrived in the bubbling town of Faribault. We would seldom stay more than one night but for me, this was a real adventure. My mother had two prominent relatives in Faribault. Andy Keller, a cousin, owned a confectionary store and was the town Mayor. Another relative, (Och's) owned the major Department Store. There were cousins, aunts and uncles, and friends of my mother that would make these visits exciting. One vivid recollection I have of these visits is listening to certain of my mother's relative's jabber in French. I also remember that the French had difficulty talking without using their hands. I'm certainly glad I didn't inherit that trait!

Another annual get-away was that summer drive to Marshfield, Wisconsin to visit My Aunt Genevieve and Uncle Ron Fulwiler and their two children Margie and Rick. Genevieve was one of my mother's younger sisters. I just loved this visit because my Aunt would always play the piano and sing. She was such a warm, personable lady who made you feel so welcome. She was one of my favorite people. I well remember, she started a Merle Norman Cosmetic business from scratch in downtown Marshfield. She had this dynamic personality that everyone loved. Her business flourished and even my mother became one of her regular customers. My Aunt Genevieve claimed she had a Merle Norman cream that would clear any case of acne. This interested me because they didn't call me 'Mr. Pimples" for nothing. I just couldn't imagine putting any type of cream on

41

my face. Finally my mother talked me into trying out this special Merle Norman product. Remember the saying, 'Mothers are always right.' My pimples slowly disappeared and I became pretty again! Apparently Aunt's also are always right!

My Uncle Ron Fulwiler was so much fun and always had a smile on his face. Away from his regular job he was sort of an amateur inventor who made unique kid toys, yard ornaments, plus an assortment of other things. I'll never forget the time he gave us a pair of toy elephant shoes he had constructed. These were small colorful boxes that fit on our shoes and made noises when we walked. We used these shoes for many years. I don't think my dad cared very much for my Uncle Ron but more or less put up with him. My dad was a little more on the conservative and stoic side which was in direct contrast to this fun loving, happy-go-lucky, crazy inventor uncle. Frankly I loved this guy and wanted to grow up and be like him. Another dream that never came true.

Our trip of the century, however, took place in 1939 when our family decided to attend the New York World's Fair. Can you imagine the challenge it must have been for my folks to pile five people into our 1938 Chevrolet and take off for New Your City? That's right, five people. My folks actually agreed to take one of Loren's friends, Pat Bailey, with us. Geez, the car wasn't cramped enough. I recall this trip taking six to seven days of grueling travel in the heat of summer just to make it to New York City. Our only air conditioning was turning those front window side vents as far as they would go. This brought a flow of fresh air into the car but unfortunately it was more hot air. Being just nine years old I have no recollection of where we stayed or ate along the way. In those days, there were no freeways, few motels and even fewer restaurants. I just remember we would travel day after day right through the heart of those huge cities like Chicago and Detroit. After a few days it seemed like we would never reach our destination. Apparently my folks were ready for this challenge because we made it all the way to New York City, enjoyed every day at the Fair, and returned home no worse for wear. My Dad may have had the reputation of being conservative, but no one could say he wasn't adventurous!

We stayed in a private home in Flushing, New York right near the Fair site. This World's fair offered a tour of what modern science was to bring us by the year 1960. Even at nine years old, I found it exciting. My Dad loved new and exciting things and this fair offered a glimpse at what the future was to offer. My dad wasn't going to wait till 1960 to find out what the future had in store for him!

Another of my dad's favorite local interests was the St. Paul Winter Carnival. He would take us to many of the events during Carnival week. We saw every Carnival parade, every ice castle, and most ice-skating events. Each year we also went on those special toboggan slides that were constructed in front of the State Capitol. Of course all that activity brought on those hunger pangs and invariably my dad would buy us hot dogs, which I absolutely loved. Believe me, eating those hotdogs in that biting cold was worth the frozen hands and toes. Only a White Castle hamburger might have tasted as good!

Another exciting event for us kids was to visit Battle Creek Park located just east of the Mississippi River on the way to St. Paul Park. This park was the site of the huge Battle Creek ski jump that seemed to hang right from the sky. In the winter we attended many of the Sunday afternoon ski jumping events that were absolutely thrilling. On one summer visit to the park, my brother and I decided to climb to the top of the jump and check out the view. I got half way up and decided, with fear of heights taking over, that half way was far enough for me, but my brother was right below me and refused to turn back. I reluctantly reached the top and froze on the spot. I stayed on my knees and immediately commenced that treacherous climb down. My dad asked how the view was, and I replied that I was too scared to look. That climb allowed me to make a major decision in my life. I would neeeeeveerver ever be a ski jumper!

One of our favorite senior citizen activities in retirement is going out to dinner maybe two or three times a week. I hardly can recall an occasion, when I was growing up, when my folks took us kids out to a restaurant for lunch or dinner. They probably figured there was no sense paying for restaurant food when it was less expensive and better tasting at home. I did however frequent the White Castle every chance I could get and my dad loved ice cream so we did stop off at Bridgeman's ice cream parlor for treats quite often. I vividly remember those famous Bridgeman malted milks with that tall glass filled with ice cream topped with whipped cream and a cookie. If that wasn't enough, the metal malt container still contained more ice cream. There was no question in our mind that Bridgeman's ice cream was the very best. For some unknown reason those Bridgeman ice cream parlors bit the dust in time, like so many other revered institutions. I guess we'll just have to settle for Dairy Queen Blizzards!

Instead of going out to a restaurant, my dad would drive downtown to the New Kin Chew Chinese restaurant and bring Chow Mein home at least once a month. This was a special treat that we all looked forward to. Like I said, my mother was a great cook and taking the family to a restaurant was expensive so why go out? Being frugal (some call it being cheap) is a Schultz hereditary trait passed on to me…just ask my friends!

The Saturday morning Farmers Market in Prior Lake couldn't hold a candle to the large Farmers Market in downtown St. Paul where my dad enjoyed shopping. This market was huge with a permanent cover to protect against the elements. There were hundreds of venders with every type of vegetable imaginable, plenty of live poultry, flowers and garden supplies. During the holiday season the market is where everyone came to buy their Christmas tree. What a place for us kids to visit and explore. This is where my dad would regularly buy a live chicken to take home for butchering. It was quite a sight to watch him chop the chicken's head off in the back yard and watch the headless chicken hop around the yard for a minute or so. It was a show in itself. The chicken and dumplings dinner that followed was a meal that could not be duplicated by anyone but my mother. Just writing about it makes me hungry. It was those trips to the Farmers Market and downtown to pick up Chow Mein that made life exciting for us kids. So what if we didn't hit the fancy restaurants…who cared?

Special Things I'll never Forget

My Grandma Wahlberg had an icebox in the small-unheated hallway leading to her kitchen. I remember the 'ice man' carrying a block of ice over his shoulder (wearing a black rubber cape) then dropping the ice in her icebox. This is how she kept her meat and dairy products cold. (No electric refrigerators and certainly no freezers) About every other day the 'milkman' would stop by her house, pick up the empty glass milk bottles at the back door and replace these bottles with fresh milk. The bottles were conformed in such a way that cream (for their coffee) covered the top three inches of the bottle. If you broke any of these glass milk bottles you seriously thought about running away from home. As a young boy, I remember both the 'ice man' and 'milk man' coming to my grandma's house in horse drawn carriages. That's the way to travel…no stopping off at a Holiday station for gas every day.

I still can picture that old gentleman with a long beard riding up and down Edmund Street in his horse drawn cart hollering the phrase, "Aaaaaaaaaaa". My mother later told me that what he was really saying was "Ragsssss". That's right, he was looking for old rags and anything else you were willing to give up that he could then sell. We called him the 'ragman'. Years later, I learned that the descendents of this ragman became some of St. Paul's richest and most prosperous citizens. They were the ones who ended up owning many of the large salvage yards along the Mississippi River. Remember that old saying, 'One man's junk is another man's treasure!'

It was not an unusual occurrence to hear a knock on the door and be confronted with one or two hoboes's asking for the opportunity to do any household or yard tasks in exchange for a free home cooked meal.

My mother and many of the other neighborhood ladies could usually find something for these men to do and then reward them with a good meal. These weren't bums or free loaders. These men were victims of the depression during a time when jobs were hard to find and survival was the name of the game. These were men who rode the rails from town to town and with the Great Northern railroad tracks just a few blocks to the North, we were good pickings. Once the War began in 1941, jobs became plentiful and we never saw another hobo.

The Opitz family decided to build a house on Thomas Avenue two doors down from Oxford St. It was an exciting experience for us kids to watch this construction. I still remember that work crew excavating the full basement using picks and shovels. This would be an unheard of task today where bobcats and excavation machines are so plentiful. Digging anything by hand seems unthinkable in today's world and anyway it's probably against Minnesota labor union rules!

Most men in our neighborhood, the lucky ones who had a job, worked six days a week including my Dad. I still remember the day he came home from work and announced that he would no longer have to work on Saturday afternoon and would still get the same pay. My mother was ecstatic! This occurred in the late 1930s when so many of our neighbors and many of my dad's friends were still unemployed. These men would have gladly worked all day Saturday and even Sundays if they were given the chance. The Second World War, which began for America in 1941, really ended the depression. All the young men, and even a number of women, enlisted in the armed services with every other able bodied man and a good share of women entering the work force. It was an amazing period of time, from massive unemployment to an over abundance of jobs. Who would have expected that the devastation created by World War II would actually cause America's economy to again flourish, ending the mighty depression? It all happened before my eyes and I honestly didn't have a clue what was happening!

Speaking of WWII, I belonged to the St. Columba Boy Scout Troop in the early 1940s. One of our tasks was to serve as 'Blackout Watchers.' My assignment was to monitor those homes on Edmund and Charles Street, between Chatsworth and Mackubin Streets. I had the responsibility to make sure each house in this square block area had all of their lights out and/or windows covered on practice blackout nights. There was fear that either the Japanese or Germans would bomb St. Paul. The 'blackout' would make key targets in the city difficult to locate. Fortunately, no bombing ever occurred. I'm not sure what I was supposed to do or where to hide if the Kraut or Jap planes did reach St. Paul. I'd probably just run like hell for home!

The War changed our lives in many ways. Ice cream, for example, was rationed and Sherbet was right there to take its place. Can you imagine a growing kid like me without ice cream? The horrors of war! Gas was rationed with different classifications assigned to individuals. My Dad's fire department shop car had a sticker on the windshield with an 'A' rating because it was considered important for national security. Our family car had a far lower rating. Certain foods were also rationed. We quickly learned that anything affecting the War effort was given Top priority... but life without ice cream, WOW! Looking back, I don't know how I managed to survive.

As a kid, I remember stores being closed tighter than a drum on Sundays. Sunday was considered a day of rest and not a day to shop. It was only in my later teens (late 1940s) that some stores were allowed to be open, but only to sell a limited selection of products. These open stores would cover all of the products that were not approved with a white sheet. I believe it was in the early 1950's when all restrictions were thrown by the wayside and you could buy just about anything on Sunday except liquor and automobiles. I don't know how the Detroit Automobile lobby ever let that slip by.

My mother had me all decked out in a fancy pair of knickers for my first day of school. That apparently was the dress of the day for kids. The knickers were kind of baggy and ended right below the knees; usually pulled together by elastic. I also wore those knee-high socks that were held up by the elastic band of the knickers. Most of the time that elastic did a lousy job of holding my socks up. I also wore short pants on many occasions but still wore those knee-high socks. I remember first wearing long pants on a regular basis about the time I entered the third or fourth grade of school. The only time you see knickers today is when one of those traditional English golfers plays in an American golf tournament. Knickers may not be popular today but they were the 'cats meow" in the 1930s.

I don't know the origin of the baseball uniform but call them what you may, from the 1930's through the 1960's, baseball players wore knickers. Let me describe the baseball uniforms we wore in that time period. First, I put on my white socks and covered them with colored knitted knee high socks. The only difference from the high socks I wore as a kid and my baseball socks was I used tape to hold the baseball socks up. The bottom of my baseball socks had high stirrups so you could see the white of the under socks. Seeing those white socks was really important…the more white the better. My baseball pants were baggy and ended right below the knee just like the knickers I wore as a kid. I figured these pants were baggy to add to a player's mobility. My deduction must have been wrong because most baseball players today wear their pants long ending at shoe level. There are a few players however, who have bucked the trend and still wear their baseball pants like knickers so everyone can see those colorful long socks. Unfortunately the stirrups showing the exposed white under-socks have gone by the wayside. These players just don't understand that those exposed white socks is what added class to the uniform!

Wearing Rose Colored Glasses

During the time I lived on Edmund Street I thought that life in our extended family was kind of problem free with one exception. I had a personal problem that I tried real hard to keep a secret. I was a <u>bed-wetter</u> ...so now you know but don't tell anybody! My mother was very understanding and tried every trick of the trade to rid me of this problem but to no avail. The rubber bed sheet was the best solution but certainly didn't stop the problem. This is a very anti-social problem to have. You never go on overnight outings, never stay overnight at a friend's home, and never have friends over. They just might discover your problem and that wasn't going to happen. Believe me, bed-wetting is very socially limiting. Interesting enough, when I started getting pimples at about age fifteen this problem suddenly disappeared. Thank God for the pimples, but it sure would have been nice to get them 10 years earlier!

I alway thought my parents had the perfect marriage. I never saw them argue or get upset with each other. I asked my mother about this after she moved into the North Ridge Retirement Center. She laughed and said, "Oh yes, we had our share of arguments and disagreements but we avoided sharing them with you kids." With a smile, I asked who won the arguments. She said," I don't know if either of us ever won. We would go two or three days without talking. You know Vernon, sometime it takes a few days to forget and forgive." I wish I had the opportunity to ask my dad this same question. His answer might have been just a little different, because as I remember he seldom considered himself wrong.

My Grandma and Grandpa Wahlberg always seemed to get along quite well. I knew my dad was not always pleased with his step-dad. He didn't like his periodic drinking and the fact that he retired at an early age right after his marriage. I think 'freeloader' might be an appropriate term my dad would use to describe his stepfather. Well, after my Grandma had her stroke later in life she really let off a full head of steam against my Grandpa. She apparently told my dad, in no uncertain words, to make sure, "He doesn't get any of the estate and to kick him out of the house." Believe me, my grandpa really began to worry about his future. Fortunately or unfortunately, depending on the way you see it, he arrived at a solution to this problem… he died first! I must have really been naïve. I didn't think they had a problem in the world.

We visited my Uncle Mike and Aunt Laura and their family on a regular basis. We spent every Christmas at their home and they would spend many holidays at our home. They seemed to be a wonderful family free of any problems. My uncle Mike seemed to be a jovial Irishman and my Aunt Laura seemed happy and was always cooking up a storm. My mother in her later years said that we saw the best side of my Uncle Mike. She said that when we were not around he could be grouchy, bossy, opinionated, and hard on the kids and his relationship with my Aunt was strained. Sometimes the cover doesn't tell the true story of the book.

There were other relative problems hidden away in the closet that my mother shared with me as well. My Uncle Bernard, a favorite of mine, apparently went to work on the Alaskan Pipe Line to make big money during the depression period. Unfortunately he gambled and drank it all away and came home broke. I guess he had a really great time though! To his credit, when he returned home he became a model citizen. He was one of my favorite Uncles probably because he was a terrific trumpet player. He could play without music and was a true musician. I couldn't figure why my folks were so upset with him, after all he could really play that trumpet. They just didn't see the big picture.

My wife Toodie and I attended the wedding of one of my cousin's children in Washington State. While at the wedding a lady came up and introduced herself as Patricia LaRose, my first cousin. Here I was in my mid 60's learning for the first time that I have a first cousin I never even knew existed. When I returned home I confronted my mother, "What gives? How could I have a first cousin I didn't even know existed?" She said, "Well, her brother Albert's wife never got along with my Grandma LaRose so they sort of just exited the family." I didn't have the courage to ask her if any of her other brothers or sisters had exited the family!

Let me throw another one at you. After 28 years of marriage Toodie received a phone call from her dad asking to come to our home for a visit so she could meet her sister. This was a little confusing because Toodie had four brothers and no sister…at least that's what she thought. During this traumatic visit, Toodie learned for the first time that her dad had previously been married and this lady in her 60's who she just met was the product of this marriage…her sister! Needless to say Toodie in her state of shock didn't throw her arms around this gal, give her a big kiss and say… hi Sis! If I remember correctly, I think she said, "… What?"

Years earlier when Toodie's older brother was killed in the Second World War her mom also let the cat out of the bag and informed Toodie she had been married before and that Earl, her older brother, was a product of her first marriage. In the years that followed Toodie repeatedly asked her mother for more family information and why she wasn't told earlier in her life that both her mom and dad had previously been married. Her mother would just throw up her hands and say she just didn't want to talk anymore about it and to just leave well enough alone. Now that her mother has passed away Toodie knows absolutely nothing about her mom or dad's past. I guess the moral being; keep it all a secret and it will just go away. Unfortunately for Toodie, she has been left with a gaping hole in her personal family history. I suggested to her that it might pay to dig further into her family history…Who knows, she may have a rich uncle!

Maybe life wasn't as perfect for our parents, grandparents and some of our relatives as I naively thought. It appears those folks I thought were 'perfect' had some of the same personal and family problems that we face with family and friends today and maybe even more. There is a difference however; they hid their problems far better than we do. They made the decision to put blinders on and just hung in there. For whatever reason there were few if any divorces or even separations that I am aware of. As far as I know no one in our family went to jail or into treatment. These folks just dug their heels in and made the best of things. There is a saying. "Problems are really just Opportunities." I have the feeling that our grandparents, relatives and parents tended to see their difficulties more as 'opportunities' rather than 'problems'.

SECTION II
THOSE CAREFREE YEARS
1944 - 1948

The Hockey Neighborhood

Our family lived on Edmund Street until I was almost 15 years old. When my younger brother Ronny came along in 1939, this home became a little tight for space. In 1944 we all packed our bags and moved to the classier Como Park neighborhood. Our new home at 1420 E. Como Boulevard was larger in size but ironically contained only two bedrooms; actually one less than we had on Edmund Street. Would you believe this new home also had just one bathroom? It must have been the beautiful view of Como Lake or maybe my folk's majestic master bedroom that covered nearly the entire second floor that brought about this move. Bunk beds and a small single bed made the second bedroom adequate but slightly tight for the three of us. I still can't believe that Loren, Ron and I actually managed to contain our clothes in one tiny closet…and it was tiny. This lack of closet space prevented any of us from being fashion plates. Loren, being a really nice brother, resolved this space problem when he entered the Navy in 1947. Thanks a million Loren! Ron and I really want to thank the Navy for getting you out of the house and giving us more bedroom and closet space.

I wasn't all that excited about leaving my neighborhood on Edmund Street to embark on this move to Como Park. How could my parents expect me to be happy away from all my friends, my favorite White Castle Restaurant and Lexington baseball Park? It wasn't that I didn't like our new house, the view of Como Lake, and the close proximity to Como Park, but this move required making new friends, attending a strange high school and leaving what I considered the best neighborhood in St. Paul. To be honest making new friends turned out to be the least problem of all. In a few weeks I ended up with as many, if not more, friends than I had on Edmund Street. All of these new friends however were outstanding hockey players and I was a real klutz on the ice. I kept looking but couldn't find one basketball hoop on anyone's garage. No wonder the high schools (Washington and Murray) that served the Como area had such lousy basketball teams.

The big challenge facing me with this move was deciding which high school to attend. Most all of my grade school friends were heading to Cretin Catholic High School or to Wilson High School in the Midway District; just a block away from St.Columba grade school. Loren had already introduced me to Wilson by inviting me to play my horn with his music group at a Wilson Assembly while I was still in eighth grade. I had my heart set on being a Wilson Redman (and Cretin was just too far away). My problem was that Wilson was a long five miles away from my new home. Everyone in my new neighborhood either went to Murray or Washington High School. I planned to be a pioneer and change this pattern.

It took time, but I convinced my folks that the school for me to attend was Wilson High School. Apparently in the 1940's the St. Paul School District really didn't care which school I attended just as long as I attended somewhere. The major problem facing me was figuring out how I was going to get to a school five miles away. There was no school bussing in those days so I came up with a very simple transportation solution. I would hitchhike back and forth to school each day. Once in a while I walked or ran those five miles and occasionally got a ride from my folks or a friend. By the time I reached my junior year I secured my drivers license and was able to drive once in a while. Fortunately I had friends with cars as well and that eased my burden. Thank God school bussing didn't control my destiny …as it does today. Hitchhiking was kind of exciting and certainly not boring because I could ride in a different model car every day.

In those days, hitchhiking was a valid and safe means of transportation. I thought nothing of hitchhiking to ball games, swimming, downtown or anywhere. I was just a long block away from Lexington Ave., which was a main north-south thoroughfare in St. Paul. It might take three or four rides, depending where I was heading, but I never had a major transportation problem. The Como-Harriet streetcar line was a few blocks away but there was no direct streetcar line to my old neighborhood or to school. To get to these locations on the streetcar meant going down town and then transferring to the Hamline Cherokee or University line. This was just too cumbersome… hitchhiking saved me a ton of streetcar tokens.

I made some great friends in this Como neighborhood. Like I said, they were all outstanding hockey players because they skated and played hockey day and night right out their front door. The City Parks department constructed hockey rinks each winter on Como Lake and built and maintained a professional speed skating oval that was home to the National Speed Skating races. Believe me, Como Lake was a highly popular playground every winter and it was located just a few steps away. To bad I was born with such weak ankles!

My dad and mom loved long blade skating. In their early courting years skating was a very popular date. They skated on Como Lake well into there mid '60's and regularly attended the fairgrounds Hippodrome rink where long blade skating was so popular. I suspect their love for long blade skating had something to do with their decision to move to the Como area. A move to the Hamline University Midway neighborhood where basketball predominated would have been my preference. At that time Hamline University ranked with the top basketball teams in the nation and in the late 1940's was actually named National Champion. If I recall correctly, there wasn't one skating rink within a two-mile radius of the Hamline University field house. My folks loved skating so Como won out. Actually they didn't ask for my opinion anyway.

My dad regularly attended the speed skating races on Como Lake and became acquainted with the speed skating club officials. He offered to rig up a hand operated siren, secured from the Fire Department that would signal the final lap of each race. The Club Officials thought this was a great idea. I can still see my dad dressed in his white fireman's coat winding up that siren which sat on a wooden pedestal to signal that final lap. He loved to be on the ice and participate in those racing events. The Como Lake oval speed skating rink was home for the National Speed Skating Races each year during Winter Carnival week. My dad became an integral part of this racing event. In those days, the names Fitzgerald, Bartholomew and Seaman were Minnesota's leaders in National speed skating. Many years later I met Art Seaman at one of the Richfield VFW Senior dances where our Hi Hats band was playing. He told me he was 84 years old and still skated every morning and danced at least three times a week. I guess that saying, 'Once an athlete…always an athlete' is really true!

.

I spent most of my winters during grade school playing basketball at the St. Columba grade school gym. We played almost every day and in the 7th and 8th grades I played on the school traveling team. I did ice skate once in a while, but basketball was by far my favorite pastime. My ankles always seemed to get tired when I skated and when I fell, which was quite often, it hurt! After moving to Como I found out that my new friends skated every day and for some reason their ankles never seemed to bother them. I also found out they cared even less what a basketball looked like. It became quite apparent to me that a person's sport of preference depended a great deal on what neighborhood you lived in. I did attempt to play hockey with my friends at Como but it was embarrassing. These guys could skate rings around me. It was an easy decision for me to continue with basketball. I didn't belong any where near a hockey rink…anyway my ankles kept hurting!

Many of my Como friends ended up stars on the Murray, Washington and Cretin High School hockey teams and a number ended up all-city players and college stars. Ron, my young brother, being ten years younger than me, really was raised on Como Lake and became an excellent hockey player for St. Agnes High School. Maybe I wasn't the greatest basketball player in the world, but it was blatantly obvious that I wasn't meant to be a hockey player!.

Como Lake was also home to the Winter Carnival Mutt races. Anyone with a dog could register for entry into these races. Each dog would be hooked up to a sled driven by a boy or girl. The races were held on a track that covered a good share of the Lake. My folks entered Ron in this race along with our dog, Ginger. The race began with Ginger running at a steady but not very fast gallop around the track. Most of the dogs racing far ahead of her decided that fighting would be more fun than running. Bedlam broke loose but Ginger just kept up her regular pace with no interest in fighting. It was like she was wearing blinders. Ron and Ginger ended up as champions while the others dogs were still fighting away. The moral being, 'Stick to the task at hand, don't let distractions lead you astray'…or…Own a mellow dog!

Those Great High School Years

Hitchhiking was my most common mode of transportation for my first two years at Wilson High School. By my junior year I secured a drivers license and used every persuasive technique I knew to get the use of our car. Loren had entered the Navy about this time so at least my competition was gone. Getting the car on Monday and Tuesday nights was almost a sure bet because those were the evenings my mother worked at the Northern Pacific Hospital just a few blocks away from Wilson High School. It was my responsibility to get her to the hospital by 7:00 and to pick her up promptly by 11:00. By my junior year the folks were pretty liberal in letting me use the car and fortunately a number of friends had cars so my need to hitch hike did diminish somewhat. If we would have been a two-car family my transportation problem might have been totally resolved. A friend, Bob Knowlen, had this great car with a rumble seat that I would have killed to own. I just don't understand why rumble seats aren't popular today. I remember the thrill of crawling out of the car window and into the rumble seat while the car was going at a good clip. The kids today would just love rumble seats. Gosh, I wonder why they don't make cars with rumble seats today?

I remember vividly my first day in Mr. Carlson's physics class at Wilson. He was checking the class roster when he came to my name. He stopped and asked if I was Loren's brother. I said I was. He went on to tell the class what a wonderful student Loren was, and how we would be using some of Loren's inventive devices and machines he had designed for this class two years ago. I remember sinking a little lower in my seat wishing Loren had gone to Washington or Murray High School like he was supposed to. Maybe Mr. Carlson thought he had another physics wiz in class; but I certainly knew differently. It didn't take long for him to figure that out as well.

I wasn't any better a student in chemistry or mathematics than I was in physics. We were working on some kind of chemistry experiment in the spring of my senior year. Mr. Mike Ettel was our chemistry teacher and very conscious of safety in class. I apparently didn't listen to the lecture on safety very well. I remember mixing one unknown solution with another unknown solution and all I remember was 'pop' and the mixture sort of exploded in the test tube. It splattered into my face and right eye and Mr. Ettel went bonkers. He immediately washed out my face and eye but my eye started to swell and close up. I was sent to the hospital emergency room where the doctor put some solution in my eye along with a bandage. Fortunately, it did clear up in time. There were two things I remember after this incident. 1). Mr. Ettel left his teaching job that spring and went into the Insurance business. It's possible I may have precipitated that move, and, 2). I played a high school baseball game that very afternoon and went 3 for 4 with a patch over my one eye. I should have left the patch on the rest of the season.

My son Tom asked me once if I was a good student in high school. I said, yes, as long as I could pick my subjects. The subjects to avoid would be physics, chemistry, mathematics and spanish. I loved band, physical education and all sports. English, history and social studies were also O.K. I learned early that the secret to making high school fun, and to even help get better grades, was to be active and get involved in school activities. Teachers seemed to love students who participated and were willing to volunteer. It's a secret I never forgot. I found out it isn't always the A+ student who gets the top job, or the best athlete who is selected team captain, or the sports official who scores tops on the test who gets picked to officiate the championship game. More important than being the top scorer or being ranked the 'best' is being identified as the hardest worker and being that person willing to go the extra mile. I learned that there is hope for us 'average' guys.

Keeping this fact in mind, I joined the band, played three sports, joined the student council, was a class officer, and participated in a few dozen other school activities as well. I ended up president of the band, student council president, captain of the baseball team, and class president. These activities certainly made school more fun and I know had a positive effect on my school grades. In my grade school years I really was quite shy with little confidence in myself. These high school experiences played a big part in helping me change that attitude. When I left school I was ready to take on new challenges with considerable more confidence in myself. I quickly learned it's not very smart to be a wallflower!

My favorite teacher was Bill Fitzharris who also was the baseball and football coach. I understand he began his teaching/coaching career at New Prague High School then came to St. Paul and was assigned to Wilson High School. After two years he left Wilson to enter the Navy in the early 1940's. When the war ended he returned to Wilson, that was my freshman year. He made learning fun and also was a dynamic coach. He really was my hero and I am sure had a lot to do with my eventual decision to become a teacher and coach. He looked like a coach, acted like a coach and talked like a coach. I wanted to be just like him. He wore his baseball cap low over his eyes and had a unique way of personally modeling how to avoid being tackled, the technique of blocking and each phase of the game. He would do this modeling in slow motion, over- emphasizing his instruction in a unique theatrical style. I was always impressed with this technique and later tried to emulate his style but never came close.

I also had the thrill of coaching against Bill Fitzharris later during my coaching tenure at St. Agnes High School in the early 1950s. He obviously had far more coaching skills then me because he took us to the cleaners. I also officiated football with him a few times after leaving coaching and was really impressed with his knowledge of the game and his reputation in coaching circles. There is a story told of a game he was officiating at St. Thomas College that involved a measurement for a first down. As head linesman he was carrying the chain to the spot of the measurement when he tripped and lost his marking. He said that it sure looked like a first down to him and in his dramatic style gave the first down signal. No one batted an eyelash or complained. If I were faced with that situation it would probably have resulted in my being tarred and feathered and hung from the goal posts. Bill Fitzharris was truly a unique individual and with his 'oozing with confidence' style could get away with it. I wanted to be just like him, but now I realize that was impossible. He was one of a kind.

Russell Peterson, our High School Principal, ran a pretty tight ship. Anyone who screwed up in school usually got sent to the Principal's office and either received a tongue-lashing or got school detention. Any boys who consistently caused trouble, however, got invited to the men teacher's room for a special orientation on following school rules. The coaches usually handled this bit of counseling. There were times I remember hearing loud voices, and unusual noises coming from this room. For some unknown reason I was never invited to this room so I had little direct knowledge of what occurred behind those close doors. Frankly, if I had been sent to the teacher's room I would have had more consequences to face at home from my parents. I don't know where they sent the girls who regularly caused trouble…but then all the girls were perfect. Frankly, I'm not sure if the women teachers even had a private room. Thinking back, it was only the boys who were bad in those days…the girls were all prim, proper and pretty!

School and It's Kicks

I really looked forward to Band practice which was held third hour. Band was a blast and I mean that literally. Fifty or more of us practiced in a regular sized classroom with no sound acoustics of any kind. We had some excellent musicians, but I firmly believe our primary goal was to be the loudest band in the city…not necessarily the best band. I know that I tried as hard as possible to play my saxophone louder than the trumpet section but never achieved that goal. Loren, Bud Trimmer, Judd Rostrum, and the rest of the trumpet section, saw to that. Doc Raymond, the band instructor must have ended up with a serious hearing disability. I trace my current need for two high powered hearing aids right back to that band room.

I tried the difficult task of participating in three sports and playing in the band during my high school career. This turned out to be a source of many problems and considerable controversy. The bandleader gets upset when a sporting event conflicts with a band activity and the coach gets upset when a band activity interferes with a sporting event. On more than one occasion I found myself in a no-win situation. For example, during the 1940s all St. Paul high school's played their basketball games at the Hamline University field house. Two games would be played on Thursday evening and three games on Friday evening. Wilson was scheduled to play Harding high school the final game on one of those Friday evenings. The German Band I played with was also scheduled to play between the first and second game. Everything would have been fine if our coach, Corlus Huntley, didn't catch me playing the tuba. I thought he was going to have a seizure. Apparently he thought my tuba playing was going to tire me out and I wouldn't be at full speed for our basketball game. He may have been right because we lost badly. Frankly, my tuba playing had little to do with this loss. Harding was just better than we were.

During my senior year, the Wilson marching band was scheduled to participate in the annual police boy parade that went from down town, across the Mississippi River to Harriet Island. I normally played the saxophone in the band, but Doc Raymond was short of tuba players so he asked if I would play the large sousaphone in this parade. I loaded this heavy instrument onto the bus and realized while lining up for the parade that the mouthpiece was missing. I didn't have the courage to tell Doc Raymond so I marched the entire downtown parade route without playing a note. I simply held my hand over where the mouthpiece was supposed to be and pretended I was playing. He never found out. I must admit carrying that heavy sousaphone all afternoon was a tiring experience. Unfortunately, I was scheduled to pitch for the Wilson baseball team later that afternoon against Humboldt high school. I had little steam on my pitches to say the least, and we lost 4 – 3. Coach Fitzharris would have killed me if he knew what I had done. It was a stupid move on my part. I'll bet if I had substituted for the flute player, I would have shut-out Humboldt. Unfortunately Doc Raymond didn't need a flute player!

My Music Gigs

In the middle of my junior year of high school, a few members of the Wilson band decided to form a 'German Band'. This Band didn't need a saxophone player but desperately needed someone to play the tuba. I really wanted to be a member of this German band. There was an old beat up dented Tuba in the instrument closet of our band room that was not being used. Loren had taught me the fingering for his trumpet that was similar fingering for this tuba. I took this ancient instrument out of storage, oiled it up and immediately became the German Band's tuba player. I was a big fan of both Whoopee John and the Six Fat Dutchman Polka Bands and was enamored with their great tuba players. I couldn't read a note of tuba music so I just listened to them on the radio and tried to copy their style. Everybody in this German band followed the notes in that German music book but me. I just 'faked' it! I turned out to be the best' faker' in the band.

This German Band, called the Sauer Krauts, consisted of Boots Johnson on the accordion, Wally Russell on trumpet, Howie Peterson was the trombone player along with two other players (whose names I forget). Our leader was Dick Morrison who had already graduated from Wilson and was attending the University of Minnesota as a theatre major. He would dress in a German outfit, throw in some German words along the way, and led us in a humorous manner. We played for school assemblies, community events and even took first place on two of the 'Stairway to Stardom' radio shows hosted by Cedric Adams, the noted newscaster. I just kept 'faking' my way through each performance. Isn't show business wonderful?

After graduating from high school, the Sauer Krauts were invited by Dick Morrison to participate in the play 'Of Thee I Sing' at the University of Minnesota. We performed as the pep band in this political oriented play. We also acted as sightseers along with playing a few other minor roles. This was my introduction to real 'show biz' and I loved every minute of it. After the play ended our German Band hung it up with the members moving on to College and jobs. Playing in this band taught me an important lesson for the future. I discovered that most people enjoy music, but when you add a little fun and laughs to the performance they like it even better. Every time Dick Morrison pulled those woman's panties out of my tuba it got a laugh…except from Mr. Peterson, the school Principal. It seems principal's didn't have a sense of humor, but everyone else did. By the way, I never returned the tuba to the school and now some 62 years since leaving high school, whenever our Hi Hat band plays a polka, this tuba sees action. I probably should confess this tuba theft to the Priest in confession but I think the statue of limitations has already run out. I bet Doc Raymond would have a smile on his face knowing this old tuba is still cranking out music!

The German Band on stage at Wilson High School.

The 1940s were the hay day of the big Band movement. Stan Kenton, Woody Herman, Benny Goodman, Jimmy Dorsey and, of course, Glen Miller were the top bands of the era. We could hear all of them and more when they played at the great Prom Ballroom located right across the street from Lexington Baseball Park on University Avenue. This ballroom had a huge dance floor that attracted dancers from all over Minnesota, Wisconsin and even Iowa. If you lucked out and had a date you could rent a booth for ten cents. If you were single, there was a large gathering place right off the main lobby ideal for meeting that perfect partner. Many, many marriages resulted from couples meeting at the Prom. Not to brag, but I always had a date when I attended dances at the Prom and being a big spender always got a booth. That doesn't mean I didn't check out the "Singles' gathering area. After all, you just never know…

There were a number of big local bands that operated in the twin cities as well. Johnny Baskerville, a Central high student, started his own big band. With encouragement from my dad, I auditioned and joined the 'Baskerville and the Hounds' band when I was just a junior in high school. We played at many of the Friday night Teen Canteen dances held in the Wilson High School gym. The band branched out playing at other high schools, the Catholic Youth Center (CYC) and for many other events. We continued to play together throughout my college years. Like those famous bands of the 1940s, our band also had four saxophones, three trumpets, a couple of trombones, a piano, a drummer and a stand up bass. John had bought his music arrangements from another band that had disbanded. His music contained all the big hits of the day and the arrangements used by the top bands in the country. The only problem with having a big swing band was to get gigs that paid enough to pay twelve band members. In time, this economic issue led to the ultimate demise of the 'Baskerville and the Hounds' band. I became good friends with a number of the band members and we continued to socialize years after the band folded. Judd Rosten, lead trumpet, Dick Wilson, piano, Leo Kasnick on bass and John Baskerville on drums were all excellent musicians and we became long time friends. Can you imagine… a band with no guitars!

Over the years I played in other bands, but I remember the Baskerville band best. John had purchased a large yellow Chrysler town car that was used to carry his drums and as many instruments that would fit in the back seat or the large rumble seat. Fortunately we carried no microphones, speakers and sound systems that all bands use today. This shocking bright yellow car was a real gas hog getting all of three to five miles to the gallon. John bought it used and obviously abused because it was in the garage getting repaired most of the time. I'm convinced that any band money John made, which wasn't much, went right back into keeping that car running. I sort of forgot all the music we played, but will never forget that ugly, bright yellow, gas hog car that seldom ran.

I remember playing for a Friday night Teen Canteen dance at Wilson High School with Bruce Trimmer as lead trumpet. He was a good looking but kind of a short-tempered guy. When he saw his girl friend dancing and apparently having too good a time with another fellow, he slammed his trumpet in anger over the music stand creating quite a scene and nearly destroying his trumpet. Oh yes, they later got married; but it didn't last very long. She had flaming red hair and he was short tempered... apparently not a good combination

My Romantic Life

I never dated and seldom even talked to a girl until I reached my junior year of high school. Isn't it awful to be shy or was I just too busy? There was this one gal who was really popular. She was a top student, on the cheer leading squad, a reporter with the school paper, and active in a million other things. I thought she was the cutest gal in the school. She also worked as a waitress at Madeline's Ice Cream Parlor on Snelling Avenue. Her name was Beverly Trygeseth. I started frequenting Madeline's on a pretty regular basis, spent lots of money on ice cream and finally got the courage to ask Beverly on a date. I fell for her big time and just when I considered her 'my steady' she dropped me like a cold potato. Looking back, I probably wasn't exciting enough which was probably true… in addition to being cheap!

After the emotional trauma of being dumped, I really had very few dates. I did ask another gal to the prom my senior year but this wasn't a serious date. In fact I can't even remember her name. To be perfectly truthful I didn't want to miss all the fun and excitement of going to the Prom. Anyway, how would it have looked for the class president not to attend? I should mention that there was this really cute gal, Toodie Jeanson in our class. I would have asked her for a date but she was already dating the football quarterback who was a very popular guy in our class. It wasn't until the summer after I graduated that she came into my life. If only that quarterback would have gone to another school. Unfortunately the quarterback was one of my best friends and he wasn't going anywhere.

During those Wilson high school years the clothing style for us guys was pretty simple. You just couldn't go wrong if you wore khaki pants rolled up right above the ankle, topped off with white socks and wore either saddle shoes or loafers. You were really 'In' if you stuck a penny in the front slot of the loafers. I recall owning a dark maroon lightweight basketball warm-up jacket that was the pride of my life. Nobody else owned one just like it and I wore it everywhere but to bed. Eventually the elbows wore out but I continued to wear it anyway. One day it just disappeared. I found it in my mother's ragbag…she just didn't understand.

The trend of the late 1940's was for us fellows with thick hair to comb it in a large wave and if done with enough hair grease gave you another inch or two of height. I honestly believe that my wave reached record heights and uniquely flowed with a slight curl over my right eye. I thought it sort of set me off from the other fellows. I'm referring especially to those guys with heinie haircuts. Those were the guys who couldn't get their hair to stand up even with car grease. I felt sorry for them. My hair was really in style, but it was those darn pimples that kept me from having more dates.

Sports Made The Day

Baseball was probably the sport that I enjoyed most in high school. When I arrived at Wilson I was listed as a pitcher, although I had played a lot at first base. A good friend, Dick Deibel, was a very capable first baseman so I concentrated on being the team's southpaw pitcher. We always had a creditable team but in my four year career at Wilson never won the championship. As a matter of fact, it wasn't until my late twenties playing in the St. Paul AAA League for Lawrence Recreation, that we won the State Baseball championship. Better late than never!

We had successful baseball seasons during my four years at Wilson High School but our major nemesis was Washington High School. Their teams were always outstanding and no matter how hard we played we were putty in their hands. Most of our games were close but Washington always managed to come out on top. Those Washington 'Rice Streeters' were known for producing some of St. Paul's finest baseball players. During those four years I especially remember the names of Red Fisher, Johnny Hislop, and Billy Hafner as standout ballplayers. I could name others, but these three always gave Lefty Schultz (that's me) lots of trouble. They all excelled in the field in addition to being outstanding hitters. If Washington could have been expelled from the league we might have won it all…but no such luck!

Red Fisher was considered one of the best catchers to come out of St. Paul. He was outstanding and had all the tools to make it to the majors. He could hit anything I threw near the plate. I remember pitching against Washington in a tournament at Carlton College in Northfield, Minnesota. Red Fisher showed up late, because according to his teammates, he was out having fun all night. Those late hours didn't seem to affect his batting ability. I don't think that homerun he hit off of me has landed yet. Unfortunately crazy living habits and running into fences eventually ended his career. Red had all the tools to make it to the big time but ran into trouble putting it together.

In the late 1960s I was contacted by my good friend Jim Griffin to join his college football officiating team. What a surprise to learn that Billy Hafner along with Johnny Mauer were the other members of this team. I found it much more enjoyable to have Billy as a team partner than as a competitor during those years he played for that infamous Washington High School baseball team. Billy was an absolutely outstanding football official and a great partner. I should point out that he was equally capable as a basketball official and baseball umpire. I retired from officiating in 1987 but Billy continued officiating well beyond the year 2000. Many consider him the Dean of baseball, basketball and football officials in the State of Minnesota. When you officiated with Billy you were with the best. Like the saying goes, "If you can't beat um then join um!"

John Hislop left Washington high school to excel in football, basketball and baseball at St. Thomas College. He was named 'Mr. Tommy' his senior college year and actually went on to have a tryout with the Minnesota Twins when arm trouble ended his baseball career. John joined the St. Paul school system as a teacher and coach at Mechanic Arts High School. When an opening arose in our School Vocational Rehabilitation Program in 1964, John was my undisputed selection. I figured if he was as good an educator as he was an athlete then we wanted him on our School Vocational Rehabilitation team. He turned out to be an outstanding, innovative vocational counselor for students with special needs. He and I also officiated football and basketball together. Actually, John could have been successful in any field of work he chose. He was a winner at Washington, in our School Vocational Rehabilitation Program and in everything he touched. Boy, can I pick um!

Both Billy Hafner and John Hislop gave me fits on the baseball field during our high school days. I found out that the drive and intensity they exhibited on the athletic field proved to be just as successful in work and officiating settings as well. I didn't feel quite so bad about being a perennial loser in baseball to Washington High School because in time the three of us all ended up on the same winning team. Remember the saying, "You learn more associating with winners than losers!"

Although I enjoyed basketball a great deal I was never of star caliber. I did play for three years on the Wilson team as a guard. I always felt I could 'fake my opponent out' with the best of them, but getting the ball to go in the basket was my main difficulty. With this kind of problem you don't win many games. In my senior year we had just a fair record because all five of us had trouble putting the ball in the basket. The fact that not one of our starters was over 6 feet tall didn't help either. Do I have to say more? At least I knew I was better at basketball than at hockey.

I held off on playing football until my junior year. There were two reasons for this delay. 1.) I was pretty small compared to the other players, and 2.) My mother didn't want me to play because she was scared stiff I would get hurt. Finally, in my junior year I went out for the team over her objections. Wouldn't you know, I broke my finger during the very first practice. When she learned that her prediction about getting hurt came true, she threw up her hands and said, "Go ahead, play and get killed, I don't care." Thank god for the broken finger…it opened the door to my football career!

I played left end and, in all modesty, was a pretty good pass receiver. The coach said I had good hands, but said nothing about my feet. I would have been a lot better player if my feet would have moved faster. Someone accused me of running to long in one spot. I'm pleased to say we were just a hair away from winning the St. Paul conference championship in 1948. We lost our final game 13 - 7 on an unusual 'tackle eligible' play that caught our team completely off guard. The Monroe high school coach, Frank Zucco, pulled the end off of the line, making the tackle eligible to catch the pass. Nobody covered him and he easily caught the pass without a defender near him and easily strolled into the end zone. Bill Fitzharris, Our coach, almost went into depression over that play. To make it worse, Frank Zucco was our coach's football teammate in college. I'm not sure coach Fitzharris ever forgave his college buddy for pulling that trick on him. Actually, the win meant nothing to Monroe with just a so-so record but to us it meant losing the championship. See what friendship will get you!

I have a vivid personal memory of this game. On the final play of my high school career, I missed making a key tackle right in front of the coach. I must have closed my eyes going for the tackle and the runner stepped right over me. Coach Fitzharris benched me on the spot and read me the riot act. Two plays later the game was over along with my budding football career. When I think back to my high school football career, it's that play I remember. I just have to learn to keep my eyes open.

Our gym lockers at Wilson were located in the basement with stairs located right off of the gym area. As you walked down these steps the smell of stale clothes began to permeate the hallway until you entered the locker room where this smell hit you with full force. There may have been ventilation in this cramped room with no windows but I seriously doubt it. I recall no school requirement for taking gym or athletic clothes home to be washed. As such, some lockers contained clothes and equipment that never left this room from September to June. Because of this aroma most of us fellows spent as little time in this locker room as possible. I also remember that deodorant was not that popular in those days. Don't ask how I know.

Toodie informed me that the smell of stale clothes never occurred in the girls' locker room. The gym teacher didn't allow showering after class because it made such a mess. Now I know why the girls were always sweaty and disruffled after gym class. There were very few sporting activities for girls back in the 1940s. One sport they did play was girl's basketball. As I recall, the rules were completely different than boy's basketball. It was purposely less strenuous because the girls in those days were considered more delicate than boys. The rules allowed the girls to take just a couple of steps with the ball and it became sort of a half court game. I don't think they let the girls' shower after basketball games either because, you know, it's very important to keep the locker room clean. Fortunately girls today play the full range of school sports because they are obviously less delicate than in the 1940s. I understand they even let them shower!

We played very few basketball games in the Wilson gym. All conference games were played on either Thursday or Friday nights at the Hamline University Field house located just a few blocks away. There were a few scrimmages and practice games played at Wilson but there were two problems: 1.) The Wilson gym was extremely small with just a few feet between the sidelines and gym wall. There was a large mat hung behind each basket so you wouldn't run into the wall after attempting a lay-up. It was tight! 2.) There was a dead spot on the gym floor right in front of the south basket. Knowing the location of this dead spot gave our team a distinct advantage. When you dribbled and hit this dead spot the ball died. It took visiting teams quite a while to figure out why they kept losing the ball at this one spot on the floor. It would have been the right thing to warn them of this problem, but it was our little secret. Anyway, we considered it as 'leveling the playing field'!

My Introduction To Work

I continued to work at Lexington Baseball Park during my first few years of high school. Playing three sports really didn't allow me to work during the school year so my employment was pretty well limited to the summer vacation period. I do remember one Christmas vacation when my dad got me a temporary job working on a City Public Works sanding truck. I was called to work whenever there was a large snowstorm. I worked with two other fellows on a dump truck loaded with sand. They issued each of us a shovel with instructions to spread sand where the streets were particularly icy. Outside of my hands getting cold it was a good job. Actually the cold weather wasn't that bad because the truck driver managed to stop at almost every bar along our route to let us warm up. Apparently the cold seemed to make the older fellows I worked with very thirsty. Believe me it wasn't Coca Cola they were drinking!

The summer after graduation I got a job, again through my dad, making asphalt alleys for the City of St. Paul. I arrived at the job site promptly each morning at 7:00 A.M. with the responsibility of boiling up buckets of tar. When the crew showed up at 8:00 my job was to spread this hot tar on the alley using an old broom. This would serve like glue holding the asphalt to the ground. I remember wearing wooden shoes and having burn marks up my arms and even on my face from the spray of this hot tar. This had to be the worst job possible especially on those hot summer days. The job itself was bad enough but I always had the feeling the boss had his eyes on me all the time. I don't know if he was waiting for me to goof up or was so impressed with my work that he couldn't take his eyes off me. To be perfectly honest I think I know the answer!

I had a chance to transfer to another City job working on the High

Bridge in St. Paul. Let me tell you, I jumped at the chance to get away from the hot tar, and that crazy boss. It didn't take me long to find out that this job was even worse; it was life threatening! My assignment was to tear out the bridge sidewalk. This was nerve wracking because I was scared of heights and the High Bridge was the tallest bridge in the entire northwest. I remember almost panicking when our crew was assigned to tear out the actual street floorboards. I went home that evening and told my mother how scared I was and she advised me to quit. Actually I had no intention of staying. I still remember tearing out that first floorboard and seeing what looked like miles of sky under me. One of the workers told me that a few airplanes had actually flown under this bridge. Let me tell you, that was a bad summer. The pay was really good; but not that good. It was either quit that job or go into therapy.

In retrospect, working at those two jobs was probably the best thing that ever happened to me. It made me realize that these laboring jobs might pay pretty well, but it wasn't what I wanted to do the rest of my life. My dad was instrumental in helping me get these two jobs. I think he knew what he was doing.

I had no firm plans after graduating from Wilson High School. Making money sounded like a good idea and I wasn't sure I was equipped to go on to college. These two jobs made me realize that going to college wasn't such a bad idea after all. The very next week I went to check out Hamline University. Hamline was a small college just a few blocks west of Wilson high school. This was one of the top basketball schools in the country. I knew all the coaches and had played ball with the basketball coach's son Joe Hutton Jr. (who later played with the Minneapolis Lakers National Basketball Champions.) I was interested in playing college baseball and was aware that Hamline's baseball teams were just so-so. Hamline would have been a pretty comfortable school for me to attend because it was right in the Wilson High School neighborhood. Staying in that friendly neighborhood sounded pretty nice to me. At that point in my life I may have been more concerned about my comfort zone than my education.

I also had given some thought to attending the University of Minnesota. Dick Seibert was the new baseball coach at the University and I knew him from working at Lexington Park, where he was the announcer for the St. Paul Saints. I guess, deep down, I thought it would really be something to play baseball at the University, and especially if Dick Seibert was the coach. To make a long story short, I took a deep breath and decided to register at this mammoth University of Minnesota. I guess my interest in baseball was the force that drew me out of my conservative comfort zone.

To register at the University of Minnesota was a challenge and frankly more complicated than some of the courses I later took. I was being shuffled from one building to another and became very discouraged and maybe a bit scared. The size, scope and complexity of the U of M setting was really making me wonder if this is where I belonged. I recall, at one point, making the decision that if I'm sent to one more building with another long line of students I'm heading to Hamline. Fortunately that didn't happen. Looking back, I have to admit that hanging in there and attending the University was one of the best decisions of my life!

SECTION III
MY UNIVERSITY YEARS
(1948– 52)

Taking That Giant Step

During that first quarter at the University, a few of us Wilson graduates would meet for lunch in the lower level of Shevlen Hall on campus. We all agreed that the University was nothing like high school. There was no one telling us what to do and no special rules to follow. We were really on our own to make it or to fail. I fully realized that my success in school was going to be purely up to me. Some of my friends talked so confidently about their future plans, making it sound like school was just a simple hurdle to future big money. Their concern didn't seem to be directed at passing tomorrow's English comprehension test or next week's psychology exam. Frankly, I was worried about every upcoming test and just hoping to make it through the quarter; and with some luck just completing my freshman year. I studied like I had never studied before. After all, the University was for smart kids and I had never considered myself in that category. I knew when I came face to face with those mathematics courses, the truth would be out of the bag.

To my surprise, I fooled each of my professors that first quarter. In fact, I fooled them that entire freshman year. That's when the realization came to me that if I continued to study hard, and with a little luck just might make it to graduation, Wow! By the way, I noticed that a few of those luncheon friends that had set their sights on a 'big money' future, and not on school, had dropped out along the way. I guess they figured four years was too long to wait to find the 'big money' tree. Confidence in one's ability is fine and having a long-range plan is good, but let's face the facts, anything worthwhile really takes hard work and rarely does it come easy. I seem to remember hearing that statement once or twice along the way. I suppose if you have a 'good daddy' or an Uncle George who can set you up in the family business, that tidbit of philosophy may not be true. Unfortunately, I had no family benefactor offering me a free ride in my future. It was going to be me against the world, and that $65 tuition I was paying every quarter wasn't going to be wasted.

I set my education sights on being a teacher and coach so enrolled in the College of Education. This narrowed down my peer group considerably from the 40,000+ attending the university. Being a member of the baseball team also narrowed my friendship base even more. I rubbed elbows with that 40,000 mass of students each day, but my close circle of friends in education and on the baseball team made my university stay a very friendly and personalized experience. After I got accustomed to life at the University I started to relax and began to enjoy my friends and life on campus. Gosh, all that worrying about being swallowed up in that monster school was for naught.

I've talked with a number of young people over the years who thought nothing of extending their college stay to five or six years or even more, and seemed to care less. It's not uncommon at all for students today to change their major two or three times. That's not the way I looked at college at all. My plan was very concrete. I would attend school for four years and move right into employment. I honestly feel most of my friends felt the same way back in 1948. I remember during my junior year becoming quite interested in being an Athletic Trainer. This would require changing my major from Physical Education to Physical Therapy. Making this change in my career pattern would have required an additional (fifth) year of school. Once I found this out, I reconsidered and stayed on course to be a teacher/coach. Four years of college was going to be it and not one day more. Anyway, I was in love and planned to be married. I needed a job and not more schooling. Wow, was I old fashioned or maybe a better term would be 'goal oriented'. That sounds more professional.

Being a member of the University baseball team offered one huge educational benefit. The athletic department employed tutors for student athletes who might have trouble with selected courses. I took full advantage of this wonderful amenity when faced with a challenging chemistry or science course. The department justified the use of these tutors because most athletes were often absent from classes due to travel required for sports. I might have passed these challenging courses without a tutor but why take a chance and the tutors were free anyway. By the way, I didn't need a tutor for mathematics because I avoided taking any mathematics courses. There is an old saying; "You can't get into a barroom fight if you don't go to bars." Vern's logic says, "I can't flunk any mathematics courses if I don't take any." Who says I wasn't smart enough to attend the University!

A dream Fulfilled

I enrolled at the University in hopes of playing on their baseball team. Although I had been a pitcher most of my career I also played first base as well. In the middle of my freshman year Dick Seibert, the coach, decided that I had a better future as a first baseman rather than as a pitcher. The real truth being that the team had few first base prospects and lots of candidates for pitchers. I had built my reputation as a pitcher on a pretty fair curve ball and not on my fastball. No matter how hard I tried to throw that baseball, it just took to long to reach the catcher. The other pitching candidates did not have this problem so I became an instant first baseman. I learned quickly that it was far more relaxing and enjoyable to play first base versus the anxiety and nervousness that goes along with pitching. I discovered I could actually sleep the night before a game.

Dick Seibert, the University baseball coach, had been a left-handed first baseman for the Philadelphia Athletics during his professional baseball career. When he retired he was hired as broadcaster for the St. Paul Saints baseball team. I got to know him while working as a groundskeeper at Lexington Park. He was really a personable guy and after a year or two of announcing Saints games, took the job as baseball coach at the University. A year later Frank Freislaben, the head St. Paul Saints groundskeeper (my boss at Lexington Park) followed Dick Seibert to the University and became their groundskeeper. It was just like old home week when I joined the University baseball team. Heck, I could call the coach by his first name and Frank gave me that special treatment. Now the shoe was on the other foot. With tongue in cheek I told Frank to be sure and keep that dirt especially nice and soft for me around first base.

I always felt I learned the techniques of playing first base from the master. Dick Seibert was an absolute outstanding coach and in time was considered the dean of all college coaches. He was the first college coach to take his team south for a spring training experience. What a thrill to board the train in Minneapolis on a snowy March day and 24 hours later arrive in sunny Texas. If I recall correctly we began our spring training with games against Baylor University, then to Texas A & M, then the University of Texas, closing out our spring trip playing Oklahoma University. This spring training trip became a wonderful recruiting incentive for many top-flight high school baseball players interested in attending the University. By 1952, the year I graduated, the quality of baseball players' entering the University was improving each year. By the mid 1950s Dick Seibert's Golden Gopher Baseball Team was becoming a perennial big 10 champion. It's the story of my life…things get better after I leave!

Dick Seibert created an atmosphere of fun and competitiveness at those Texas spring training games by mingling with the fans, teasing them and indirectly encouraging their attendance to the next game. His personality and reputation actually helped increase the popularity of these games and as a result increased revenue for the home team. Dick Seibert can take credit for being a pioneer in setting the stage for the many colleges and high schools today that followed his lead in heading south for spring training. It's become the 'thing to do' for northern schools wanting to prepare for their season. He did it all with a smile and some 'schmoozing' with the fans.

I realize now that Dick Seibert was much more than a coach; he was an outstanding teacher. He was the first to record the techniques of hitting, pitching, fielding and other baseball fundamentals into filmstrips for instructional purposes. He gave talks all over the country on the attributes of college baseball. I recall that he had talk's number one, number two and number three; he was prepared for anything. He played a major role in raising the level of college baseball to the point where it has become the major training ground for professional baseball players. This was not the case prior to the 1950's. In my senior year the players nicknamed him "Chief", a name that stuck with him for the remainder of his career. His advice and mentoring during my years at the University made him one of my real-life heroes. After having an undefeated football season at St. Agnes High School in 1953, I invited 'Chief' to be speaker at our victory banquet. What a thrill it was to have him present at this high point in my career. He had a profound influence on my life by making me understand that coaching is truly a teaching experience. Gosh, and I thought it was all about winning!

It was a toss-up if I was to be the 20th or 21st player on a baseball team that suited only 20 players in my sophomore year. The 21st player ends up strictly a bystander. I'd hold my breath each Thursday to see if I made the 20 player roster or not. Let me tell you that was a pretty anxiety producing experience. My big break came during the spring baseball trip to Texas in my junior year. The starting first baseman, Wayne Robinson, had gone 0 for 2 and had made two errors in a game against the University of Texas. 'Chief' called me into action and I fortunately made a couple of good fielding plays and went 2 for 2. I quickly became the starting first baseman for the remainder of the year. I had a better than average year and batted in the mid 300's. Our conference record that year was 6 wins and 6 losses. Those train trips to all the Big Ten schools was something new for me and almost as exciting as the games. I learned that all trains going north end up in Chicago. Apparently, from there you can transfer to anywhere in the world. I also learned that there are a lot of sleazy bars right around the railroad station. In case you don't know, baseball offers many learning opportunities.

In 1952, my senior year, I had the honor of being named Captain of the baseball team. We won more games than we lost that year but still remained in the middle of the big ten-baseball race. Paul Geil was our top pitcher that year and after graduation went on to a professional career with the New York Giants and later with the Minnesota Twins. He was equally a star halfback on the Gopher football team and probably could have played professional football if he wished. He was an outstanding athlete, a wonderful individual and after completing his baseball career was appointed Athletic Director at the University. I remember a young sportswriter for the Minneapolis paper who attended nearly all of our practices and games with his eye especially on Paul Geil. There was little question that Sid Hartman could see a rising star who would make great news copy. It's hard to believe, but some 60 years later Sid Hartman is still writing a sports column for the Minneapolis paper. I'm an avid reader of his column and make a point to listen to all of his morning radio interviews. He has outlasted all of us!

Ken McGonagle was the other starting pitcher on that 1952 baseball team. Ken was not only an outstanding pitcher but was one of the few athletes who was also a member of the University Basketball team. If specialty kickers were in vogue in the 1950s I predict that Ken would have had a good shot at that position as well. He could kick the football a mile. In those days kicking duties was usually assigned to one of the regular team players. A few years later when kicking became a specialty position in Football he would have been a prime prospect for that position. He was a natural athlete who could do everything well. Ken and I were good friends and have maintained our friendship over the years. He became a successful coach and teacher at Evanston High School in the Chicago area. I've always enjoyed our get-togethers over the years rehashing all those games we really should have won.

A Faster Game

The day I graduated from Wilson High School, Bill Fitzharris my baseball coach, had arranged for me to become the paid pitcher for the New Prague Robins baseball team that upcoming summer. I was really excited! New Prague was about 45 miles south of St. Paul and played in the Minnesota River Valley Baseball league. This meant that my Sundays and Wednesday's would be tied up for the entire summer. I could hardly wait to throw that first pitch. I was going to be paid $85 for pitching on Sunday afternoon and $50 to play in the outfield on Wednesday evening. That $130 a week combined with pay from my City of St. Paul job meant I was making really big money. My folks were happy to hear of my good fortune because it certainly was going to take a big financial burden off them. Not only wouldn't I need normal gas and spending money from them, but I also would be able to pay my $65 per quarter University tuition expenses. They didn't get away Scot-free however, because I planned to live at home while attending school. I thought it was only fair that they share some of my burden.

I well remember that very first game I pitched for the New Prague Robins. I sat down the first two Belle Plaine hitters with little trouble. Big Bob O'Brien then came to bat. He had been an all-city catcher at Wilson High School…my old high school in St. Paul. I remembered him as a power hitter. Apparently, their family had moved to Belle Plaine after he graduated. On the third pitch he nailed my fast ball over the distant right field fence. It was my awakening call that this was not high school baseball. Apparently I no longer could just be a thrower. If I was going to collect my $85 a game I'd better start being a pitcher. I seem to remember my high school coach saying something about the importance of pitching to the corners. After this wakeup call things did get better and if I remember correctly we did win that game. This was my rude awakening to the world of 'real' baseball.

That first year I traveled back and forth from St. Paul to New Prague for each game. The drive to New Prague in those days was more than a two-hour ride. Today that drive takes about 40 minutes. The second year, of my four-year stint, I lived right in New Prague staying in a second floor apartment over Reebock's Café. This was Dick Morrison's apartment during the school year. Dick had been the leader of our high school German band (the Sour Krauts). He was teaching English and Drama at New Prague high school so his apartment was vacant for me to use during the summer. I was given a job at the local golf course doing odd jobs and maintaining their 'sand' greens in addition to playing baseball. Can you imagine playing golf and putting on sand greens today?

I was really fascinated with the life style of this small Bohemian town of New Prague compared to the big city of St. Paul. I couldn't believe how friendly the local town people were and how everyone in town knew everyone else. Kids would come into the local pub and get a pitcher of beer to bring home. They would have been arrested if they did this in St. Paul. I ate my first uncooked hamburger called tarter steak in New Prague, and to my surprise I didn't get sick; and it was good! I made many friends and it was exciting to socialize not only with the locals but with neighboring town people as well. It was a way of life that I learned to love and really never experienced in the City. I remember thinking that after graduation from the University my goal would be to locate a teaching job in this type of small town community atmosphere. I never attained that teaching goal, but at least I did experience living in a small town.

The Minnesota River League was comprised of teams representing the communities of Jordan, Montgomery, Belle Plaine, St. Peter, LeCenter, LeSeuer and Prior Lake. Each team had at least one or two outstanding ball players that were paid. The remaining local players just played for the fun and enjoyment of the game. The first couple of years New Prague lacked a capable catcher. Our manager, Dick Vanasek, asked if I knew of any good catchers from St. Paul. I'll bet in those two years I brought at least five different catchers to fill the gap. When one didn't get a hit they would fire him and ask for another. Although I picked the best I knew, none of them really fit the bill. Finally they gave up and Jeff Jelenik a local kid got the job and he didn't cost them a nickel. Thank God for Jeff...it took the pressure off me. I had exhausted my supply of St. Paul catchers.

During my third season in New Prague I was excited to learn that Eddie Patrow another St. Paul resident was hired to play shortstop on the team. Eddie had been a star baseball player in high school and had turned professional and actually played a few years in the big leagues. He was quite a local sports hero in St. Paul. By that time I had access to a car and was driving to our games. Dick Vanesek, the manager, asked if I would mind picking up Eddie in St. Paul and transport him to the games. This was a real thrill for me! I remember picking him up and along the way he would ask me to stop at a number of bars. He said he was selling matches and that I should just wait in the car because it would only take a few minutes. Heck, I didn't mind because he was such an interesting guy and had such great stories to tell. By the time we arrived to the game I did notice a hint of alcohol in the car but didn't pay much attention to it. At his age he was still a good ball player and hit 1 for 3 that afternoon …a liner to left center field for a double. We also stopped after the game at a few bars so he could sell more matches. Let me tell you, Eddie was really industrious.

I remember getting a call from Eddie Patrow about a New York Yankee try-out camp to be held in Hastings, a town just south of St. Paul. He mentioned that I was a really good prospect and should attend this camp. This was quite a complement because nobody else seemed to consider me a professional prospect. He also asked if he could go along because he knew some of the Yankee scouts. I stopped at the Quonset hut where he lived on the east side of St. Paul and out came Eddie, his wife and three kids with a picnic basket. I dropped them off at a park in Hastings where they picnicked all afternoon until I picked them up after attending the tryout camp. Eddie never came near the camp. He said they had a wonderful time and thanked me for the ride. He then asked what time I would pick him up for our upcoming Sunday game in New Prague. Good guy Vern told him, "9:00 Sunday morning." He said to make it 8:30 because he had more matches to sell on the way. It looked to me like he was trying to corner the match concession for the entire southern twin cities area.

After about his fourth game, Dick Vanesek asked if Eddie was drinking on the way to the game. I said absolutely not, but that we did stop a number of times at local bars for him to sell his matches. I remember Dick putting his hand on my shoulder, smiling and in a fatherly way informing me that there were no matches being sold…that Eddie was simply getting his beer fix for the day. He was an alcoholic and, as he put it, was half juiced up before each game. Dick said, "Vern, take him home after the game, with no stops on the way. He's played his last game here!" Boy was I naive…

at that time of my life I would have been a perfect prospect to buy that swampland in Florida.

A year of so later I was working in the Police Department Records Division when a report came across my desk regarding the arrest of Edward Patrow for 'paper hanging'. This is the slang expression for writing bad checks. I learned that he had done this on more than two occasions resulting in a stint in the local City Workhouse for six months. Like so many other frustrated athletes, Eddy was a guy living on his past exploits. I could just picture him buying a round of beer in a local bar talking about those good old baseball days when he was just a step away from making that really big money in the majors. Let's face it, we all know frustrated ex- jocks whose main enjoyment is re-living their past exploits on the ball field. Knowing my athletic limitations, I really never had that problem.

Jim Griffin, Deputy Chief of Police in St. Paul and my officiating partner, shared a story with me about an ex-athlete he knew that never quite made it. A Minneapolis bar owner, who also officiated, asked Jim if he knew a certain ex-jock. Jim acknowledged that he knew this fellow. The bar owner told Jim that If he came across this fellow, to inform him he was not welcome in his bar any more. He went on to tell Jim that this fellow came into his bar, bought everyone a drink and proceeded to spend a few hours sharing 'jock talk.' His check for this round of drinks was returned from the bank stamped 'insufficient funds'. A few weeks later this fellow returned to the bar and was confronted by the owner regarding his bad check. The fellow apologized profusely, tore up the bad check, wrote a new check and proceeded to again buy everyone a drink. You guessed it, this second check bounced as well. Jim said he never did see this fellow. I guess if you plan to live in the past, you should at least be willing to pay for the trip.

When a group of ex-jocks congregate together you can pretty well bet that the topic will evidentially turn to sports. I don't care where you are; the local VFW, your favorite health club, the local bar, church, ball games, you name it, these guys love to talk sports. Rehashing last night's Twins game, the Vikings trades, how bad the Timberwolves are, or if the Wild hockey team will make the playoffs are all common topics. There are those fellows however, who over a beer, tend to focus more on their own personal sports exploits. I've known guys who were so good in baseball they never hit under 350, were the fastest running back on their high school football team, or threw four touchdown passes in the big game. It would be fun to check old newspaper clippings to see just how much of this was true or just wishful thinking. I also have friends who claim they could have made the team but the coach didn't like them or they were better than the other guys but just weren't given a chance. I guess some guys just don't get a break.

I've noticed over the years that those fellows who were really outstanding athletes also love to talk sports but seldom focus on their personal abilities or accomplishments. You never hear of Harmon Killebrew, Tony Oliva or Yogie Berra broadcasting how great they were. On the local level, Ralph Keiger, Billy Hafner, John Hislop, and many other outstanding athletes let their accomplishments speak for themselves. I'm always suspect of those fellows who just love to share their personal exploits on the field, their mastery of a sport, with perhaps the tendency to exaggerate their skills just a bit. These are the fellows who tell the best stories. Remember the saying, "If you have to tell someone how good you were…you probably weren't!"

In the summers from 1948 through 1951 I would join the New Prague town baseball team immediately after the University Big Ten season was over. Conference rules prohibited us from playing any town ball until then. After graduating in 1952 I permanently hung up my pitchers glove and played first base for the remainder of my baseball career. By the mid 1950s small town baseball was declining and fewer and fewer players were being paid. It was a good time for me to return to St. Paul and participate in their Summer AAA baseball league. I found playing first base was pure fun and devoid of any of the anxieties associated with pitching. It was also a lot less work!

Those four years of playing baseball for New Prague were enjoyable years with many fond memories. We had just an average baseball team and generally ended up in the middle of the pack. As their pitcher, I won more games then I lost and had about a 300 + batting average. I wasn't 'great' but managed to satisfy the town folks and manager for those four years. (1948–1951) I made enough money to pay for my University tuition, my dates with Toodie and enough left over for my regular Pepsi and White Castle hamburger fix. I felt my priorities were right in order.

My grandson, Casey Jr., asked me a few years back if I was a good enough ball player to have made it to the big leagues. I explained to him that a major league player had to do four things really well. First off, he had to be a fast runner, second, he had to be an excellent hitter, third, he had to be able to throw really hard, and fourth, he had to have a very positive attitude. I told Casey that I had a very positive attitude! I think he got the message. Actually, I had a pretty good roundhouse curve ball but lacked the blazing fastball that was an absolute requirement as a pitcher. I followed my dad's advice and kept kicking my leg as high as possible, but that ball still wouldn't go any faster. Maybe I should have been raising my arm up higher...who knows?

One phase of the game that I did excel at was my ability as a lefty to pick runners off first base. I averaged at least one pick off a game and sometimes two or three. In fact, the St. Paul Dispatch paper did a write-up about this skill that was apparently kind of unique. Unfortunately having that blazing fastball was more important than having a good pick-off move. It was my one claim to fame that got me absolutely nowhere.

Traveling to New Prague on Hwy 13 required that I pass right through the town of Prior Lake. Toodie and I would often stop for lunch in Prior Lake and, in so doing, found two great swimming beaches that we frequented; Sunset beach on Spring Lake and Pockner's beach on Prior Lake. These beautiful sandy beaches were free to the public and considerably better than beaches the St. Paul area had to offer. I remember thinking how nice it would be some day to live in a small community, right on a lake, with all it's fishing, boating and swimming amenities. Little did I realize that this would actually happen some 18 years later. I can honestly say that my baseball career in New Prague turned out to be the door opener that led to our move to Prior Lake in 1968...the smartest move we could have ever made. The population of Prior Lake in 1968 was a little over 600 residents and today the population exceeds 20,000. It appears a few other folks had the same dream that Toodie and I had.

In the early 1950's some of the out-state baseball teams began to get carried away with hiring more and more paid out of town ball players. Apparently there were a few town teams that wanted to win at all costs. I knew a couple of teams that actually flew in ex–professional players for their games. Paying more and more players and increasing salaries began to put an undue burden on local businesses footing the baseball payroll. This practice forced many teams to reduce their number of paid players and others to return strictly to local talent. I was fortunate to have played in the hay-day of small town baseball when paying just one or two selected players was popular. When I left New Prague in 1952 it was just about the time the hiring of paid players was declining. I left town just at the right time with money in my pocket. I'll say it again, "timing is everything"!

In 1953 I resumed my baseball career by joining the Lawrence Recreation baseball team in St. Paul as their first baseman. I had decided to hang up my pitching glove for good. I was married and found it so much more convenient and family friendly to play ball right in my home community. I felt that the quality level of baseball in this AAA league in St. Paul was actually superior to what I had observed in the Minnesota River League. The players who normally would have been paid to play out state were now playing in their home community, so each of the teams in our AAA league had nine quality players. We had an excellent team and for the next few years Lawrence Recreation was the perennial league champion. It was certainly more convenient to travel a few blocks from home to play a game rather than that two-hour trek to New Prague twice a week. My salary for playing in St. Paul was a big zero – but it sure was a big savings on Gas.

Harry Bealke, the Lawrence Recreation Manager, pulled together some of St. Paul's finest players including Ralph Kieger, the oldest member of the team who held down center field and was our 'clean up' hitter. He was an outstanding player and nobody I ever knew loved baseball more than Ralph. Our other players either had played for the University, other local colleges or were stars from high school. Our starting pitcher had actually played for the Minneapolis Millers American Association team. If you play along side of good players you end up playing better yourself. I was fortunate to be named to the league All Star Team each of the years I played for Lawrence Recreation. Having played on a few losing teams over the years, I found it much more fun and enjoyable to be associated with a winner! By the way, when you win the beer tastes lots better after the game!

I moved to West St. Paul in 1957 and decided to leave the Lawrence Recreation team and immediately joined the West St. Paul Baseball Team. They also had an outstanding team that won their league championship the two years I played. With a growing family, and a number of work and officiating responsibilities, I closed out my baseball career in 1959. I figured it was time to start playing more catch and 'pepper' with my two growing boys.

Vern and son Thomas preparing for a West St. Paul game.

Coaching Independent teams like Lawrence Recreation, New Prague and West St. Paul was a lot different than coaching a high school or college team. When you play on an Independent team a manager is generally less demanding of players, has fewer rules and even less 'signs'. These players are participating for the enjoyment of playing and generally don't expect to be bossed around and certainly not hollered at. Both Harry Bealke (Lawrence Recreation) and Dick Vanasek (New Prague) played their manager role beautifully. They made the game fun, listened to the player's views, and ended up being predominantly 'organizers', and yet did everything possible to win ball games. They believed in the philosophy that, "Baseball should be fun… but lets do everything possible to win"! Harry's favorite saying was, "Remember fellows, the beer always tastes better after a win." My hat is off to all the Harry Bealke's and Dick Vanasek's who give their time, patience and skill in coaching town ball and Independent teams throughout our State. Baseball owes these dedicated coaches a real debt of gratitude…and their wives a gold medal!

You probably know that beer and baseball go hand-in-hand. Drinking beer after a game is a well-known tradition. Many a keg has been emptied after a win, and yes, even after a loss. I well remember two distinct episodes that convinced me to become a Pepsi drinker rather than a beer or booze drinker. I have kept these episodes to myself over these many years but seeing my folks have passed away, the time has come for true confession.

In my junior year, our University baseball team was scheduled to play a two game series at Iowa State. We played awful that first game and lost badly. That evening after the game I happened to pair up with some of the players who were ex-service men attending school on the GI Bill. These guys had seen the world and were out looking for a little fun in a 'dry' city; meaning no booze anywhere. Well, at least that's what I thought. Somehow these guys managed to find a drinking parlor on the second floor of an office building. It didn't make much difference to me because I didn't drink anyway. Well, before I knew it there was a glass of whiskey sour sitting in front of me. I decided to be one of the boys and in one gulp it was gone. Then there was another…than another…and another. When I returned to my hotel room I was feeling no pain but my stomach was rumbling. My roommate, Dick Mikelbust was sound asleep. Before I knew what was happening I 'heaved' all over the blanket covering him. In total desperation, I slowly and silently removed his blanket from the bed, folded it nicely and stuck it into one of the dresser drawers…then slowly and silently placed another blanket over Dick. Fortunately he never woke up or he would have killed me. I often wondered how long it took for the maids to discover that stinky blanket in that dresser drawer. By the way we went on to win the second game and I went two for three. Who knows, maybe a drink or two before each game might have improved my batting average!

My second drinking episode occurred in the lower level party room of the Lawrence Recreation Bar after we won the league championship. It was a night of free drinks to be followed by an all you could eat spaghetti dinner. A very pregnant Toodie was with me and we were having a great time downing a few beers and sharing baseball stories. Then it happened! They brought the spaghetti out and the smell got to me. Toodie told me later that she thought I actually turned green. I told her in no uncertain words that we were going home and she should drive. She had two comments. I'm hungry and I don't have a driver's license. I said we would have spaghetti another day and drivers license or not, she was driving home. Things were quite cool around the house for quite a while after that experience. I must have some genetic or hereditary defect that acts up when alcohol gets in my system. Some day I'll have to ask my Doctor if there isn't a pill......

After these two embarrassing episodes, I decided my stomach just wasn't geared to alcoholic drinks and if I wanted to maintain my marriage I better turn to Pepsi as my drink of choice. My decision must have been a good one because we're still married after 58 years and I have at least one Pepsi each night. To be perfectly honest, I never really liked the taste of beer anyway!

Living It Up After High School

When I arrived in New Prague the summer of 1948 I learned quickly that this town had a great dance hall called the Park Ballroom. Some of the great old time bands, the likes of Whoopee John, the Six Fat Dutchman, Babe Wagner and other well known music groups regularly played there. One day I called Boots Johnson, a good friend and the accordion player in our German band, and told him about the Park Ballroom. I told him to get a date and come on down that next Sunday afternoon. He could watch me pitch the afternoon game and that evening we would dance the night away at the Park Ballroom. He asked who my date was and I told him not to worry I'd find someone. Well it wasn't that easy. I was totally devoid of any feminine attachments when I ended my career at Wilson High School in the spring of 1948. I called every gal I knew and they all had plans for Sunday…at least that's what they said!

I had exhausted my supply of possible dates when Boots suggested I call this gal Toodie Jeanson who was in our class at Wilson High School. She was really cute, very popular but always seemed to have a boy friend. I took a wild chance and called her on the phone from New Prague. Toodie did remember me, but was a little hesitant when I asked for a date. She asked her older brother if she should accept and he apparently gave the O.K. There was a pause, then sort of reluctantly she said 'yes'. I then added a postscript by telling her I couldn't pick her up, but Boots would do the honors. I held my breath when I added this tidbit. Fortunately she had already committed herself to the date so could hardly say 'no'. I did take a sigh of relief however when she agreed.

We played the game that Sunday afternoon and won handily. Being the winning pitcher, I figured Toodie would be impressed. I'm not sure if she was or not. It was a real scorcher that afternoon and I must have lost at least 10 pounds. That evening we danced the night away and had a ball. She was an absolutely terrific dancer! That's when I learned she had taken tap dancing lessons while in grade school. Boy, did I luck out having her for a dance partner. The ballroom that evening was an absolute oven. I probably perspired more dancing then during the afternoon ballgame. Air conditioning would have been nice, but frankly it didn't matter because I was dancing on a cloud that evening!

I had my dad's car so I was able to drive Toodie back to St. Paul that evening. I remember the trip home very well. Driving through the town of Jordan I got an awful leg cramp, slammed on the brakes and jumped out of the car. I can still see Toodie crouching in the far corner of the car wondering why she had dated this nut, and where she could locate the nearest cop. She did relax after I explained the problem. I told her that muscle spasms often occur after a full afternoon of kicking my leg up so high with each pitch plus all that heat. Well, fortunately she bought my explanation and agreed to continue our ride back to St. Paul. I didn't know if she would even want to see me after that frightening experience. I held my breath when I called her for a second date the very next day. This time she said 'yes' right away. It was the beginning of many, many dates that have continued on for over 62 years and hopefully for many more to come. I wonder what would have happened if a cop had been nearby? Maybe I don't want to know!

For the next four years Toodie was my steady date. We went dancing, to the movies, and out to dinner when I could afford it. I'd hate to count the hours I spent at her home. Her brothers loved to play cards with me because I was a perennial loser. Her mother's cooking was wonderful and I never refused a meal. Her mother loved having company and on a moment's notice could prepare a meal for from two to fifty people. The number really didn't matter. The holidays were wild at her home when the brothers and relatives arrived with their rapidly growing families. By the way, I was considerably taller and larger than any member of the Jeanson family. Size, however, apparently had nothing to do with winning at cards. Instead of playing hearts or poker, they should have renamed the games we played, "Beat the big guy!"

One of our favorite dates was having dinner at the Roman Café in downtown St. Paul. This turned out to be an unforgettable experience. For a total of $4.00 I could purchase two bacon wrapped Tenderloin steaks with full trimmings. We would go there often and I could pretend to be 'the big spender'. Can you imagine what that meal would cost today? Another restaurant we frequented after attending a dance or show was a quaint French restaurant on the corner of Selby and Dale Street. Our meal would consist of cinnamon toast and fruit cocktail. Sounds kind of strange but it was good and also very 'cheap'. In the 1950's a barbeque rib restaurant called Roadbuddy's opened near Rondo and Dale Street. This was in the Black neighborhood but frequented by everyone in St. Paul because the ribs were outstanding. Barbeque ribs were something really new to many of us in St. Paul at that time. They used a special southern sauce and cooked the ribs over an open pit. Roadbuddy's became so popular that it soon outgrew its location and moved to a larger building on highly traveled University Avenue. We loved those ribs and had them often. After a late date we often stopped for a dozen Dixie Cream donuts that, when hot, literally melted in your mouth. Dixie Cream was located on the corner of Chatsworth and University Ave. It took a full dozen of these frosted donuts to fill you up because they were filled mostly with air. When I say they melted in your mouth I'm not kidding. You can see that I wasn't a big spender on our dates. Let's just say I was frugal with a buck!

After being acquainted with Toodie in high school for four years and then dating her for another four years, I announced to my parents one evening that we were planning to get married. I still remember my dad saying, "Don't you think you'd better wait a while!" That's when I realized he really was a slightly conservative individual. Actually, my parents loved Toodie and were pleased with this announcement. By this time the Schultz's and Jeanson's had become just one big happy family.

This courtship with the daughter of a good Swedish family taught me a few things worth sharing with the reader. I suggest you take this advice seriously:

a. <u>Avoid dating gals that come from money</u>. Toodie's family wasn't poor but they certainly were not wealthy. She wasn't accustomed to receiving extravagant gifts, fancy dinner dates or expensive nights on the town. This meant I never had to take a loan from the bank or borrow money from my dad to go out on a date. With limited funds in my pocket, Toodie and I enjoyed those free events and inexpensive dates to the hilt. That's right, if you can read between the lines…I'm frugal!

b. <u>Eat everything your girl friend's mother puts on the table</u>. Toodie's mom cooked up lots of food that I had never eaten before. I figured that anything my mother didn't make was not fit to eat. I quickly found out how wrong I was. One example really stands out in my mind. I ate spinach for the very first time at Toodie's home. I loved it! I asked my mother why she never made spinach and her response was, "Because I don't like it! Remember this fact, 'What the cook doesn't like …you're never going to get.' Also remember to eat everything your future mother-in-law puts on the table, even if you never heard of it before, because that's what you'll probably be eating after you get married. Thank God, I liked everything Toodie's mom cooked!

c. <u>Send greeting cards to people on special occasions, especially prospective in-laws.</u> My mother was perfect in almost every way but she wasn't big on celebrating key events or sending cards on special occasions. Well, let me tell you, that is big time stuff for many families. My in-laws loved celebrations, holding dinners on special occasions, sending cards for all key events and making a big thing out of any personal accomplishment. It took me a while to catch-on with help from Toodie. By the way, I'm still learning… and I am finding that those cards are getting expensive!

d. <u>Shaking hands is no substitute for hugging</u>. Being raised German style means that a good handshake is an acceptable greeting for friends, relatives and family. I think the old German saying translated to English goes something like, "Don't touch me unless you love me!" That's fine for us Germans but not totally acceptable to the Swedes, Italians and some Irish. I learned quickly that my Jeanson in-laws, from good Swedish heritage, prefer a good hug to the mundane handshake. It took a while to learn this important fact and many years to loosen up to the 'hug'. For the good of my marriage, I think I've finally caught on. Some might consider me a slow learner.

e. <u>Don't play cards with relatives for money</u>. All of the Jeanson's loved playing cards. I don't know if it was because of all the cards Toodie's brothers played in the service, but they loved poker and were good at it. Whenever I was with their family, her brothers would entice me to 'get in the game.' Frankly, I didn't care much for cards and never could remember the winning order for playing poker. What do you do however, when your future brother-in-law's almost force you to play. They became like my best friends…why not, I was providing them with daily pocket money. But I won out at the end. After Toodie and I were married I turned down all their invitations. Why waste my time and money when I didn't need their support any more.

f. Buying fancy clothes isn't necessary. Just about the time I was leaving high school and in my early University years, the 'Zoot Suit' became really popular. The zoot suit consisted of pants with the belt line wore high above the hips, wide pants at thigh level and narrowing at shoe top level. A long key chain hanging from the belt to the pocket was a popular addition. The Suit coat was extra wide and padded at the shoulders with the coat tapering down to just above the knees. The Zoot Suit was kind of a fad that lasted through the early 50's then just died off. I kind of liked this new clothing style but felt it was a little too far out for Toodie's taste. Actually I think if I showed up in a zoot suit for a date that may have been our last date. I have little recollection of what Toodie and her girl friends wore in high school except I do remember the dresses were long, and slacks were verboten. Apparently in those days the men wore the pants in the family…I wonder when that rule went out of style?

I never owned a zoot suit but did buy the very finest suit money could buy in 1952 just before I graduated from the University of Minnesota. I figured this suit would really impress Toodie. It was dark tan in color, had extra wide shoulders and fit me to a 'T'. Check my U of M graduation picture and you will see me wearing this suit. I paid the enormous sum of $50.00 for that suit which was a fortune in those days. I still remember my mother warning me not to tell my Dad what I paid. He had kind of a conservative attitude when it came to spending; do you suppose that's where I inherited my frugality? If he found out what that suit cost, his comment would probably have been, "You could have bought that same suit at Jake Juhl's and bargained it down to half price." I just wasn't into haggling over the price at Jake's Clothing Store at that point of my life. The time comes when you just have to step up to the plate and do your thing. But why take a chance, so I never did tell my dad.

This suit was so special I figured it should only be worn for special occasions. After my graduation there really were few special occasions. I didn't have money to go on fancy dates or to take Toodie to those high priced restaurants. I kept this suit hung neatly in the closet, covered with plastic, all ready to be worn for the perfect occasion. Two years later I was invited to a wedding and figured this was one of those special occasions. That's when I discovered the suit didn't fit any more. Apparently it was that 25 pounds of extra weight I had put on since graduating that was my downfall. I only hope the St. Paul Goodwill found just the right 160 pound fellow who would love that suit as much as I did. Just think, I paid the unbelievable price of $50.00 for a suit I wore just twice. At $25 a wearing, I was really glad I didn't tell my dad the price!

    g. Don't spend cash on something that's free. During our four-year courtship Toodie attended many of my baseball games and became quite knowledgeable about the science of the game. She learned to overcome her hostility for those fans shouting profanities and heckling me while I was pitching. She finally caught on that if the fans paid to attend the game they had license to say or do anything they wanted; including hollering at me. By the way, I got her free passes for these games. She also attended most of the Minneapolis Lakers Professional Basketball games at the Minneapolis Auditorium where I officiated all the preliminary games. We actually sat courtside to watch the World Champion Lakers games; and it was free. The Lakers Management also gave us free tickets to watch those wild and rugged Roller Derby contests also held at the Minneapolis Auditorium. I fooled all my friends who didn't know I got free tickets. They thought I was a big spender!

    h. Buy only quality goods. In the winter of my senior year at the University I decided it was time to pop the marriage question and to purchase an engagement ring. I checked out some of the local jewelry stores for their best deals and also decided to visit 'Bochstrocks'the classiest jewelry store in St. Paul. The Bochstrock clerk showed me their ring selection which was really pricey. There was one ring in their selection for $150.00 that appealed to me and the price was right. It was true that the diamond was a little small and a bit difficult to see with the naked eye, but this ring had a delicate touch and of course Toodie was a delicate lady. The rings I was shown in the other stores were larger and may have had more flair but these were garden variety jewelry stores that didn't have the reputation of Bochstrocks. After considerable thought, I figured Toodie would be much more impressed if she knew that her ring was purchased from the classiest jewelry store in St. Paul. I figured she would buy into the concept of 'quality'. She did seem pleased when I presented her with the ring but it might have been wise to have also provided her with a magnifying glass. Years later she was gifted with both my mother and her mother's diamond rings after they passed away. She wears all three rings together and it looks just like one beautiful setting. It may have taken a few years but now, wearing all three rings, her diamond setting is equal in size to all her girlfriends. It should be clearly understood that I purchased this ring because it came from a quality store, not because it was the cheapest. I may be frugal but I don't want the word passed around that I'm cheap!

Police and Baseball…A Nice Fit

During my junior year at the University, my dad asked if I would be interested in a job pitching for the St. Paul Police Baseball team during the summer. They had some excellent players but apparently had no pitcher. My Dad explained that they played only two games a year against the Minneapolis Police team. One game was played at Lexington Park, home of the St. Paul Saints, and the other game at Nicollet Park, home of the Minneapolis Millers. These were money-raising games with the profits going, I believe, to the police pension fund. He said that if I was interested in being their pitcher, to call Police Chief Charlie Tierney for an interview. It sounded like an interesting challenge so I made the call. Officer Schultz had an interesting ring to it!

Chief Tierney was very gracious and was pleased to learn I was interested in joining the team. He did say, however, that I would have to be an employee of the police department to make it legal. I explained that I was still in school. He said that I could work during the summer and, if I wanted, during the year as a part time employee. He then asked if I could type and I said that I had taken typing in high school. That was good enough for him and I was assigned to work in the Police Records Division when school was out that June. I failed to tell him that I really only had one quarter of typing during my sophomore year of high school and wasn't sure if I remembered where the typewriter keys even were. Actually, he didn't care if I could type or not, he simply wanted a pitcher that could beat their archrival, the Minneapolis Police. I was obviously their man!

I began working in the Police Department Records Division that summer along with four or five other permanent staff. I had responsibility for typing the hundreds of police reports for every type of problem the police department was supposed to solve. We also took all missing persons reports, maintained pawnshop files, typed and distributed the police bulletin and took hundreds of phone calls a day. This office used manual typewriters with the requirement that we make 5 – 7 carbon copies of all reports. This meant you had to really bang the typewriter keys to get legible copies and fortunately for me, typing errors were acceptable. In time I became a fairly proficient typist and learned a few tricks to speed up completion of these reports. I ended up working full time for the next two summers, and on weekends and some midnight shifts from 1951 through 1959. It turned out to be wonderful supplemental income for me while at the University, later during those financially lean years of teaching at St. Agnes, and during the initial years of my State Vocational Rehabilitation job. Unfortunately, I had developed this bad habit of securing low-income jobs, so part time supplemental work was pretty much a requirement to keep the wolf away from the door.

I'll always remember the first time I was assigned to work the midnight shift in the police records division. One of my job duties was to type up the police bulletin, mimeograph 300 copies, distribute them throughout the department and finally mail copies to each police department in the state. After placing a bulletin into each envelope I would lick the glued envelope and seal it ready for delivery. After about ten envelopes my tongue was beginning to get slightly raw and after 100 envelopes my tongue was totally dried and raw and I was in pain. I finished this task with my tongue in absolute agony. The next day I asked another clerk if they had the same trouble I had in mailing out the police bulletins. The clerk said, "You did use that white water wheel to moisten the envelopes didn't you?" I must have missed that bit of information in my five minute training session. Two weeks later my tongue began to heal and I slowly regained my taste for food. This is what you call learning the hard way!

Looking back, I feel this job in the Records Division was really unique, although I didn't realize it at the time. The office Manager, Mike McLaughlin, was something out of the dark ages. He apparently was an ex-alcoholic who was transferred from a patrol job to this position. He was as gruff as they come and I frankly don't believe he knew a thing about office work. He had a spittoon right near his corner desk and there was a distinct ringing sound when he scored a hit. It was obvious to the whole office when he missed! When I was first hired this was an all male office, but later a couple of women joined the staff. Believe me, hiring women to work in this office was not to Mike McLaughlin's liking and he would literally growl at them. He also seemed to enjoy verbally harassing a couple of the more mild male members of the staff as well. He was of the old school…I mean the really old school. I got along fine with him probably because Chief Tierney personally hired me and let 'Mike' know it. They tell me he was a fun loving guy till he quit drinking. Actually, I think he should have kept drinking!

Chief Tierney must have been pleased with my appointment because we managed to beat the Minneapolis police team in all four games played in 1951 and 1952. This certainly helped add to my job security as a Police Department Records Clerk. It was a great job because I could work as many hours and any time of day I wanted. There was always a backlog of work. In the summer and fall of 1952, I worked 7 days a week, 10 hours a day. I was paid a day's wage for each team practice and paid two days wages for each game played. During that period of time I unofficially became the highest paid worker in the St. Paul Police Department, actually making more money then the Chief of Police. Needless to say, when this was discovered, some adjustments were made. Jealousy is a terrible sin. Just think, for those few months in an entry-level clerk job, I made considerably more money than my dad. Wow, I guess I didn't need a College education after all!

The St. Paul–Minneapolis police baseball rivalry actually ended after the 1952 series. Fortunately the Department allowed me to continue my work as a records clerk. This supplemental job turned out to be my financial salvation as Toodie and I began to face some serious financial challenges. I should add that in addition to the financial benefits of this job, I learned invaluable office management skills, techniques in dealing with the public, the intricacies of how the community and it's varied agencies work, and most of all, I made connections in the community that were invaluable to my future employment. None of my University field training experiences even came close to the day-to-day reality based learning that I experienced in this police department job. By the way, I never was issued a badge, carried a gun, wore a police uniform or was called Officer Schultz…darn it!

Blowing The Whistle

There was a notice on the Cook Hall Athletic Department bulletin board at the University advertising for basketball officials to work intramural games. I thought this might be fun and a chance to make a few bucks so I signed up. My good friend Ken McGonagle and I started officiating these games on a regular basis. I later learned that the Catholic Athletic Association (CAA) in St. Paul was in need of officials on weekends. I applied and began officiating three basketball games each Sunday afternoon. If I remember correctly, we earned two dollars a game or a sum total of $6.00 which I considered pretty good pay for a Sunday afternoon. It certainly beat watching golf on TV that could cost me at least two dollars for Pepsi and chips.

I also began officiating some City of St. Paul municipal league basketball games during weekends and on Thursday evenings. At times these games could be considered a 'hazard to your health'. If you could handle these games with all the rowdy behavior, threats and insults, you could handle anything. There were some evenings a police escort would have been nice to have available. I remember one game held at the old Mechanic Arts high school gym where I fouled out three players from one of the teams by the third quarter. The game was called because that team couldn't field the required five players. I didn't bother showering after the game. I just ran as fast as I could for the car in my uniform and took off!

My partner Ken McGonagle and I really lucked out when we were offered the chance to officiate all of the Minneapolis Lakers preliminary games at the Minneapolis auditorium. We were paid only two dollars a game but were given seats right on the sidelines to see some of the greatest basketball players of all time in action. At that time the Minneapolis

Lakers, led by George Miken, were world champions. On two occasions, officials for the Lakers games failed to show up because of inclement weather conditions. We were on site with uniforms and all, so were called on to become instant NBA officials. We hardly had time to get nervous. Our instructions were quite simple but fairly direct, "Only call shooting fouls…the fans aren't here to watch you blow your whistle." I remember one of these games had the Minneapolis Lakers facing the College All-stars and the other game was the Lakers facing the Harlem Globetrotters. We followed the management's directions and never had a problem. By the way, we got a check for four dollars for each of these Lakers games. Wow, we were in the big time and it certainly had to impress our girl friends. I remember our biggest challenge was throwing the ball high enough for jump balls. Those professional players are really tall!

During winter break of our senior year at the University I was hired to referee a Brainard High School basketball game. I honestly don't remember how we got selected to officiate a high school game while still in college. My referee partner and I were really excited about this opportunity and jumped at the chance to enter the high school referee circuit. It turned out to be an unforgettable experience. Believe it or not, our car had four flat tires while traveling the 200 miles to Brainerd, Minnesota. I can still remember hitchhiking the last ten miles and being dropped off at the Brainerd gym. I walked into the school with my duffle bag and rolling a flat tire that hopefully someone would get fixed while we were officiating the game. Actually the game went well and one of the Brainerd teachers gave us a ride back to our car with the repaired tire. I often think back to this auspicious debut to my high school officiating career. Nothing like it ever occurred again in my 37 years of officiating!

I joined the St. Paul Officials Association just prior to graduating from the University of Minnesota and continued to officiate CAA and Municipal League games until the door was finally opened to begin officiating high school games. Apparently working that one Brainerd high school game my senior year at the University didn't impress Jerry Flathman, the St. Paul Officials Association secretary. I had to climb the ladder just like all the other Association members. Being assigned that first football game at Zumbrota High School in the early 1950's, some 75 miles south of the twin cities, was a real thrill. Wouldn't you know, I forgot to pack my whistle and had to borrow one from my partner. What a way to begin!

SECTION IV
THE BEST OF TIMES –
THE WORST OF TIMES
1952– 1964

A Beginning Together

Although Toodie and I were very much in love, there was one potential obstacle to our marriage that had to be faced. Toodie was raised in the Lutheran faith and I was raised in the Catholic faith. In the 1950's this was a very touchy issue, particularly with the Catholic Church taking a pretty conservative stance on mixed marriages. Toodie and I had agreed that we would continue to attend our respective churches after we were married but that our marriage ceremony would take place at my family church; the Maternity of Mary Catholic Church in St. Paul. As a preparatory step, we met with Pastor O'Donnell to discuss our arrangements and to plan the service. Unfortunately this did not turn out to be a friendly comfortable meeting. I can still smell that pungent odor of garlic on Father's breath from his dinner meal. The idea of a mixed marriage was not to his liking at all and he let us know this in no uncertain terms. I was hoping for a more pleasant meeting that might have better set the stage for Toodie's feelings about the Catholic Church. I suppose the meeting could have been worse. He didn't threaten to excommunicate me or perform an exorcism to remove the Lutheran demons from Toodie, although I felt he came close. As I left that uncomfortable meeting I thought elopement would be an excellent alternative. Whenever I smell the strong odor of garlic in the air I am reminded of that unfortunate meeting!

I graduated from the University of Minnesota on June 13th of 1952 and a week later, on June 21st, Toodie and I were married. In case you're wondering, I gave up on the idea of eloping when we realized there would be no gifts; which we really needed. Our marriage did take place as scheduled in the Maternity of Mary Catholic Church followed by a family luncheon at Toodie's folk's home. There was a wonderful reception that evening at the East Side Hall on East 7th St. with dancing music provided free of charge by the John Baskerville band; minus the saxophone of Vern Schultz. This was their wedding present to us. I was working at the police department at the time and, wouldn't you know, a squad car showed up and stole the bride away. They were nice enough however, to return her in short order. It wouldn't have done much good to call the police department to get her back!

We honeymooned in a quaint little cabin on Lake Osakis. A college friend, Bob Gelle, had suggested that a perfect honeymoon location would be in one of those quaint little cabins on Lake Osakis in western Minnesota near his home town. It sure sounded romantic to me and I proceeded to make the reservation. I failed to remember that we didn't really fish, and he failed to tell us that we would be sharing this cabin with a local mouse. Toodie found that mouse to be unnerving to say the least. Life isn't always perfect and we were together, so what else mattered. Heck, the fish weren't biting anyway!

About eight years later we were at a party with a number of friends and the conversation got around to honeymoons. There were some very romantic stories told, until it got to Toodie. She responded with, "We had a terrible honeymoon, fishing and mice - yach!" Actually, if it wasn't for the $100 we collected from the dollar dance there may not have even been a honeymoon. Apparently we should have gone to some exotic place to honeymoon – like Chicago! What did I know? I had never been on a honeymoon before!

A few years later my mother shared a discussion she had with Father O'Donnell that took place the Monday right after the wedding ceremony. She said that he was very upset because someone in our wedding party had been smoking in the church and left a cigarette stub and ashes on the altar. My mother told him that couldn't be true because no one in the wedding party smoked, which was absolutely true. Apparently he was very indignant about this. My mother was still upset when she told me this story. The only thing we can figure out is that the photographer might have been the culprit while he was taking the formal wedding pictures on the altar. You know, I don't think Father O'Donnell would have made a good missionary. He probably would have required all his converts to wear shoes to church!

My brother Loren had a similar unfortunate experience with Father O'Donnell the year prior to our wedding. His fiancée, Arlene Hagen, also was Lutheran and they were trying to make a decision as a married couple whether they would both join the Catholic or Lutheran faith. Their plan was to have a visit with Arlene's Lutheran minister and with Father O'Donnell before they made this decision. Loren told me that the meeting was very cordial, relaxing and informative with the Lutheran Minister and diametrically opposite with Father O'Donnell. He was negative, very curt and one sided in his approach. Loren said after that upsetting meeting there was no question which direction he was heading. He has been a faithful member of the Lutheran church for the past 60 years. On a positive note, there apparently was no pungent odor of garlic at Loren's session with Father O'Donnell!

Moving- A Part Of Life

I learned from a co-worker at the police department that a reporter from the St. Paul Dispatch Newspaper had a nice fully furnished apartment available to be sub-leased for six months in that fancy 'silk stocking' Grand Avenue neighborhood. This apartment had everything including a music room with a piano. In fact, after we moved in, I enrolled in the Charlie Johnson Quick Style Piano course to add to my music background. What I learned is that Charlie Johnson was lying. There is no quick way to learn the piano; at least in six months. I'll bet it took Charlie a lot longer than six months for him to learn.

After living for six months in this lap of luxury, the reporter returned to town and we were forced to find another residence. We really humbled ourselves by moving into a second floor share the bath apartment on Hague Ave. The owner had converted the second floor of his home into two small apartments. I remember our front door opening directly into the bedroom that led to the living room then to the kitchen. It was quite an interesting layout. We shared a bathroom at the far end of the entry hall with the elderly lady who lived in the other apartment. What a change from that Grand Ave luxury suite of rooms. The rent was cheap, the elderly lady was nice, the apartment was close to everything, and we were together so who cares? Love always wins out over a few inconveniences.

I believe it was the spring of 1953 when we decided to make the big financial plunge and buy our first home. After all, by this time we were old married folks. We came across this bungalow at 2030 Reaney Street on the East side of St. Paul. It had an attached garage in front of the home with a deck on top, a nice back yard and future expansion potential in the attic area. The price was $10,500 which was a lot of money at that time.

If I remember correctly we put about $4000 down, was approved for a $5000 loan and our realtor, Mr. Hathaway, agreed to carry us for a $1500 contract for deed. We could afford the monthly loan payment but it was that $15 a month Contract for Deed payment that was tough to come by. Money was really tight that last week of the month before payday. Toodie would take the streetcar downtown the first of each month before we paid any other bills to hand carry that $15 contract payment to Mr. Hathaway. Today we would have written him a check for $1500 and walked away, but not in 1953 when I was making just $300 a month.

We lived in that house on Reaney St. approximately four years and under Toodie's management made it a very warm, comfortable home. I remember three things, however, that made us anxious to leave and make a new start.

1. We purchased this house from the Reiger family who were in the process of building a new home on the lot they owned right next door. They immediately began construction of their home and decided to move into the unfinished basement. It was pretty rough living for them and it showed by a growing negative attitude within their family and to all us neighbors as well. To put it bluntly, there was lots of shouting and hollering going on in that basement. They turned out to be grumpy unpleasant neighbors. Living next door to them became almost unbearable. I learned in those very early years of our marriage that grumpy neighbors can make life miserable. In the years that followed we learned what a treasure it was to have good neighbors. From that point on we really lucked out!

2. Our three children, Michael Timothy and Patrick, were born during the time we lived in this home. Due to a rare genetic illness all three children unfortunately passed away while we were living there. These were not good memories and a change of scenery would offer a fresh beginning for us.

3. We purchased a lot in West St. Paul and began construction of a new home before selling our home on Reaney St. Don't ever do that! We felt selling this home was a sure deal. Unfortunately, we guessed wrong and went weeks without a buyer. This became a financial crisis for us because the money for the new home was to come totally from this sale. Finally a buyer showed up with a meager $500 down payment. At one point the buyer threatened to back out but we pleaded

with our realtor to sweeten the deal if necessary. After a few sleepless weeks we finally did close on the sale of our home. A huge weight was lifted from our shoulders and we were absolutely ecstatic. We immediately canceled our reservation at the Poor House!

Talk about hard luck, the fellow who bought our home on Reaney Street couldn't find a buyer for his own home. Finally, in desperation, he had to resell our house. Just thinking about what could have happened if we hadn't sold this home gives me goose bumps. There's a moral here somewhere, "Never ever buy another home when you already own one; especially when you are cash poor!"

Our new home built by Howard Runge Construction in West St. Paul, was the first home that we played a major role in designing. It had a couple of features that I really loved. The living room had a seventeen-foot long white brick fireplace wall that faced three large picture windows with a nice view. The back of the fireplace was fire red brick that enclosed a built in refrigerator, oven and stove. I loved this design with one exception. I was enamored with those new homes having cove beamed ceilings. We had failed to include this in our plan. We lived in this house from about 1958 to 1962. It was a wonderful home to begin our new life with Tom, Casey and Patty; our brand spanking new adopted family!

That 'beam ceiling' issue never really left my mind. One day I came across a home for sale in the Mendota Heights area of town that had a beautiful beam ceiling plus many other amenities, plus it was in an upscale neighborhood. They were asking $26,000 for this home and I offered them $22,000. They immediately accepted my offer. That should have made me just a little suspicious. I put our home on Edith Drive up for sale and it sold quickly. My lawyer said everything looked legally OK with this new home however there were a couple of plumbing liens that would have to be cleared up before the purchase. To make a long story short, we closed on the sale of our West St. Paul home on a Friday morning and attended the closing of the new home that same Friday afternoon. I had already made arrangements for new flooring to be laid that next week and some brick work to be installed on the fireplace. (The bricks were already delivered). I may have been just a little too anxious!

At the closing table my lawyer informed me that the plumbing liens had not been cleared up because the owner was in California and couldn't be reached. At this point I thought the very worst. I deducted that these plumbing problems were the reason the price was reduced so dramatically.

I broke out in a cold sweat and asked my lawyer to leave the closing table and to meet privately with Toodie and me. I remember vividly saying to him, "Can I walk away from this deal?" He said, "Yes, but I should be able to work this out." I told him to cancel the deal and get me my $500 down payment back. Toodie and I walked out of the office to the dismay of the closer and headed directly to a pay phone on the corner. I immediately called Wards to cancel the new carpet and the stone mason to cancel his stonework. I offered to pay both parties but they indicated that would not be necessary. I could hardly wait to get home to tell my folks who were babysitting what I had just done. Let me set the scene for you. We had three little kids, it was the middle of winter, we had to get out of our home the next week and we had absolutely no place to go. Needless to say my folks were absolutely speechless or maybe dumbfounded is a better term. They probably wondered if I had suddenly lost my mind or if I needed to go away for treatment. Someday in the distant future I plan to ask Toodie, when she's in a good mood, how she really felt about my abrupt turn-about decision that afternoon.

To add to this crazy scenario, my lawyer was killed two days later in an auto accident. By the way, I never did get my $500 down payment back. On Monday morning we located a brand new twin home that was just constructed in South St. Paul. By Tuesday we were packing up and on the move. This rented twin home was simple but adequate under the circumstances. Six months later we finally exchanged a muddy yard for sod and got sidewalks installed. Who says that life isn't exciting? By the way, this was just the beginning of our nomad existence…there are more moves to follow.

This move to South St. Paul was sort of a hasty, emergency move. I immediately began scouting for another lot to build that new house with beam ceilings. I found a great lot in South St. Paul within a stone's throw of St. Paul and West St. Paul. I designed a split entry home that seemed to fit this lot quite well with a wonderful view of the airport, the Mississippi river and lots of RR tracks. The lot was on a hill with a view forever. I couldn't afford a full garage so I built a carport and, of course, had those beam ceilings I always wanted. Life would have been lots simpler if I had just tore off the roof of the home in West St. Paul and replaced the ceiling with Beams. At the time it just never crossed my mind.

This new home in South St. Paul was located in a wonderful neighborhood with lots of people our age and young kids. Tom had to walk a few blocks up a hill to attend St. Michael Catholic School in West St. Paul and Casey walked down the hill to attend the Wilson Elementary school in South St. Paul. This is what happens when you live on the side of a hill. We would have gladly remained in this home for a long time until we learned in 1965 that plans were being laid for construction of the new Lafayette Freeway that would front right up to our back yard. That was not to our liking, so we were ripe for another move. We were becoming very nomadic!

Toodie and I agreed that this might be the perfect time to consider a move from city to lake living. We remembered the enjoyment and fun of swimming in both Spring Lake and Prior Lake during my ball playing days in New Prague, and the dream we had of some day actually living on a lake. We checked out lots on both White Bear and Bald Eagle Lakes but the cost of lots on these lakes exceeded our price range. We headed toward Prior Lake on two occasions but turned back each time after deciding this distance was simply to far for me to travel back and forth to St. Paul for work. We made it all the way to Prior Lake on our third try however, and that did the trick. We found a wonderful lot on Martinson Island that was perfect and the $8000 price tag was within our price range. Toodie and I both agreed that Martinson Island was the ideal location to permanently settle down and raise our family. I decided to deal with that long commute to St. Paul at another time.

I designed a type of 'A' frame house and had a local contractor give me a bid. His construction bid of $23,000 was within our budget so we began preparations to sell our home in South St. Paul. A few weeks later I stopped to see the contractor on the way home from an out of state training session. He informed me of a mistake in his estimate and that the price should have been $25,000. This amount exceeded our price range and we unfortunately had to walk away from this deal. Six months later we decided to take the plunge and begin building no matter what the cost. To our dismay the price of the lot had skyrocketed from $8000 to $18000 in that six month period. We were committed to living on Martinson Island and fortunately came across a lot right across the street that faced the Prior Lake bay with an asking price of $6000. We purchased it on the spot, paid $27,000 for construction of our new house and became official Prior Lake residents the summer of 1968. We made a vow...no more moving for a while. At least I know Toodie made that vow.

Our new home on Prior Lake wasn't ready for occupancy before we had to vacate our home in South St. Paul. This required a temporary move into a rented home in Inver Grove Heights for a few months until our home in Prior Lake was completed. Another move...another change of schools... will it ever end?

An Amazing Beginning

I continued to work part time at the St. Paul Police Department after our marriage in June of 1952. I also had the good fortune of being offered an opportunity to assist Charlie Schuman as assistant football coach at St. Agnes High School that fall. I jumped at the chance and, because this was not a full time job, decided to also enroll in graduate school at the University. In the spring of 1953 I was offered the baseball-coaching job at Concordia Academy in St. Paul. We survived financially that first year of our marriage life with income from these coaching jobs, plus my wages at the police department and Toodie's income from her Brown and Bigelow job. It was a busy but very enjoyable first year as a couple. I thought that the first year of our marriage was just a breeze, so let's see if year two can go as well.

I recall the St. Agnes football team had a 5 – 5 season record that year. I learned a lot about coaching from Charlie Schuman. When I took over the baseball coaching job at Concordia that spring, I was told that nearly all of the previous year's team had graduated...along with the coach. I fielded a team comprised of nearly all sophomores. In mid-season the administration learned that four members of the team were caught drinking requiring that they be cut from the team. Just my luck! We were fortunate to win at least a couple of games. I am pleased to report that two years later Concordia ended up champion of their baseball league. Most likely this was due to the instruction I had given them in their sophomore year. I can dream anyway!

My major employment break came in the summer of 1953 when I was hired as teacher and head coach at St. Agnes High School. Charlie Schuman had taken a job at Annandale High School and recommended me as his replacement. I would be coaching football, basketball and baseball plus teaching five subjects each day. I was offered the opportunity to live in the apartment located right in the high school as well. Charlie Schuman had advised me to stay away from the apartment. This had been his residence. He said people would knock on the door at all hours of the day and night to get into the school. "It was like being on call...Vern, live any place else!" I accepted the teaching/coach job but wisely turned down the apartment. A guy has to have some privacy.

When you teach or coach in large city public schools you encounter various unions which protect the jobs of the people in those unions. You're not allowed to do anything but teach. Teachers couldn't clean their classroom, paint the walls, etc. I found out quickly that there are no unions in the parochial school system. Once I took the job at St. Agnes, I soon found myself painting the locker room, putting lines on the gym floor, sweeping my office along with various other sundry projects. Being a first year teacher I could have been asked to paint the church steeple and probably would have done it. I also remember selecting and ordering new football uniforms, new helmets, purchasing equipment, preparing football strategies and working like a fool even before football or school began that fall. This was all volunteer work because my pay began the day school officially opened. This was going to be my career, so I loved every minute of it!

Football practice began in mid-August just a few weeks before students reported for their first day of school. I remember spending most of that summer designing a practice schedule, formulating the offensive system we would use and making contact with both the veteran players and new freshman recruits. Never having played football at the University level I had to rely on my past football experience at Wilson High School, the football methods courses I took at the university and my previous year helping Charlie Schuman. I was very impressed with Wes Fesler who was the University of Minnesota Football Coach and Football Methods Course instructor. He taught us his football play system and told us something I have never forgotten. He said, "You have to convince your players that they have the finest football system in the country. They have to believe that your system is so effective it has to be kept a secret from other coaches and players, and if they master it effectively will win them the championship." I really bought into Wes Fesler's system and shared this 'secret 'with the players every day we practiced. Maybe Wes Fesler didn't win a whole lot of games at the University but we sure did. Gosh, maybe I was a better salesman then Wes Fesler!

I could fill this book with stories about that first football season but modesty prevents me from patting myself on the back. Let me simply and humbly say that our 1953 St. Agnes football team finished the season undefeated, handily winning all 8-conference games and losing 0. There were articles and pictures every week about the team (and coach). I think Sister Mary Alphonse, the principal, thought all this winning might have a negative affect on me. She called me into her office right after the final game and said, "Mr. Schultz, it isn't always going to be this way!" I said, "I know Sister, but I'm sure going to enjoy it while I can." Of course she was right. My second year we won 4 games and lost 4 games. Gosh, maybe I wasn't on my way to being the Notre Dame Football coach after all!

This team was made up of some really outstanding football players. Harvey Perusse at quarterback, Larry Mazenek at tailback, Jack Schmidt at left end, Ron Concelius at left guard, and I could go on. Mike Kelly, however, was the real powerhouse of the team. He was a hard charging fullback on offense and the middle linebacker on defense. He averaged at least five yards on running plays and was involved in 90% of the tackles on defense. He was a unanimous selection to the all conference team. I vividly remember in the game against Rochester Lourdes, Mike made a tackle and got temporarily knocked out in the third quarter. His absence from the lineup was notable. This is a quandary every coach faces at one time or other in their career. Do you play an injured player when he might be the difference in winning or losing, or do you put the health of the player first and be willing to accept a loss? I remember saying to Mike in the fourth quarter, "You're OK to play aren't you, Mike?" What else could he say but "Yes" and so I put him back in the game; injury and all. We went on to win that game but my decision to win at all costs, and to put Mike's health in jeopardy has bothered me over the years. That decision was the only negative ingredient in an otherwise unforgettable season. I'm afraid at 23 years old I thought winning was everything. Being just a bit less competitive today, I think I would keep Mike on the bench and implement a touch of psychology in my approach. I'd call a time out and challenge the team to give it all they've got for Mike (just like Knute Rockne did with the Gipper in that Notre Dame movie). I would then return to the bench and do lots of praying. At least that's what I think I'd do!

Coach Schultz with St. Agnes High School football co-captains
Mike Kelly and Jack Schmidt.

My first year basketball season was a little less than average. As I recall we didn't have a player over 6 ft. tall and a few of them still thought they were playing football. We had fun however, and surprised a few teams. The baseball team did really well that spring of 1954. We held our own against those giant Cretin, St. Thomas and DeLaSalle teams and ended up with a winning season. I specifically remember playing the Concordia team that I had coached the previous year. They were leading their conference and were expecting to run us into the ground. We beat them handily. They left the field that afternoon a much more humble team. I figured they forgot everything I taught them.

There were some experiences at St. Agnes during my first year of teaching that I remember so very well. Outside of the shop teacher, I was the only man on a faculty with all nuns. The nuns treated me great and fed me hot dish lunches that overflowed the plate. They didn't pay me very well but fed me like a king. In the fall I weighed about 160 lbs. and by spring I reached 190 lbs. I outgrew all my clothes so this weight increase ended up costing me money. My contract should have included a clothing allowance.

The scare of my life came in mid-year when one of the nuns teaching Religion became ill. I was asked to temporarily take her place. A Religion teacher I am not. With so many nuns available and qualified to teach Religion classes, I concluded that this was obviously a test of my knowledge, or lack of knowledge, of the Catholic faith. Fortunately the nun returned a few weeks later and solved my dilemma. Toodie say's that when I try to make a point, I talk extremely loud. While teaching that class, I was shouting most of the time.

My pay that first year was a huge $3000 for my ten month contract. This was a pretty meager salary for coaching three sports, teaching five classes a day, running a Saturday sports program, being in charge of discipline for the boys and being required to wear a tie every day. I worked the weekend midnight shift at the police department for much needed supplemental income and to keep from being bored. I'll always remember meeting with Monsignor Gruden at completion of my first year. He was Parish Pastor and School Superintendent. I asked for a raise based on what I considered a pretty successful first year of teaching and coaching. He got very serious and said that any increase in salary was impossible as the parish had many financial problems. That's when I realized my tenure at St. Agnes would be limited to two years. I remembered that unwritten rule in Education, "Its good politics to stay at a school at least two years before leaving." I had no trouble staying for another year because I absolutely loved my job. It was just that I couldn't make enough money to feed a budding family and put gas into my 1950 Desoto.

I resigned my position at St. Agnes at completion of my second year but continued to work on a full time basis at the police department. My goal was to find a teaching /coaching job out state in a smaller town beginning that fall. I was always impressed with the friendly atmosphere and apparent enjoyment people seemed to have living in a smaller community. Who knows, maybe I could even afford to live on one of those 10,000 Minnesota lakes. There was a problem however in achieving that goal. It was the period of time when we had our sick children and leaving town and our doctors in St. Paul just wasn't in the cards. Fall was just around the corner and I had no teaching job. Those medical bills were slowly eating up the little savings we had accumulated. About September First, with no teaching job in sight, I was starting to climb the walls!

As Athletic Director and Coach at St. Agnes, I hired all the sports officials for our games and when time permitted was doing some officiating myself. Many of the officials I hired became good friends and officiating partners. Ray Dolan, Principal of the brand new Hazel Park Junior High School in St. Paul, was one of the officials I regularly hired and he found out I was available for a teaching job. Just a few days before school was to open that fall of 1955, he called and offered me a teaching job in his new school. One of his teachers had resigned at the last moment. I jumped at the chance and showed up at the school the next day. That's when I learned that the job was to teach 8th and 9th grade Science and Mathematics. Actually I wasn't licensed or trained to teach either of these subjects, and in fact, they were my two worst subjects in high school. I really needed that job but to teach Science and Math, wow!

I talked to Ray Dolan about this dilemma and he said, "Vern, just keep a page ahead of the kids and you will do fine." I left Hazel Park school that afternoon in sort of a daze. I needed the job desperately but how could I teach something I was absolutely unqualified to teach. It literally wasn't fair to the kids. I remember talking to my dad about the situation. I just knew he would tell me to take the job anyway. He really shocked me when he said, "If you don't think you should do it then don't take the job." It was great advice! I turned the job down that next morning. Ray Dolan thought I was crazy but I felt it was the decision I had to make. It's interesting to note that almost 10 years later, almost to the day, I did join the St. Paul School District, not as a teacher, but as Supervisor of their new Special Vocational Services Program. Sometimes life takes some crazy twists!

Fortunately, I was able to work full time at the police department that fall, but this position offered only a limited salary and didn't fit my career plans at all. I found myself between a rock and hard place. I continued looking and applying for teaching jobs all that fall. I remember spending hours at the library checking out the various Federal and State Civil Service jobs in the field of education that might be available to me. One of the State Civil Service jobs I discovered was that of Vocational Rehabilitation Counselor. I read the brochure for this position, got pretty excited and immediately applied for the job. As I understood it, the purpose of this position was to help in the training and placement of individuals with disabilities so they would be better prepared to enter the working world. I saw that word 'training' and got excited!

A Surprise Career Switch

I scheduled an interview with a gentleman named Jules Kerlan at the State Vocational Rehabilitation Central Office, located in the Commerce Building in St. Paul. He was a very energetic enthusiastic man, with one amputated arm. He had been both a teacher and coach before joining the Vocational Rehabilitation program. We seemed to get along great and he strongly encouraged me to take the State test for this job. He mentioned that Vocational Rehabilitation was recently funded by Congress to expand services to the disabled in all 50 states. He said, "Join this program and you will be on the ground floor of an exciting new future." This sounded great to me but first I better learn how to spell 'Rehabilitation'!

I took the test at the State Civil Service Office and unfortunately didn't pass. It was a test with primarily a counseling and psychology focus; not exactly my background. There were a number of questions about theories held by Dean Williamson and Carl Rogers, two prominent psychologists. I didn't even know their batting averages! It was a real disappointed that I didn't pass until I got a call from Mr. Kerlan asking if I was interested in joining their program as a trainee. He said I would make $20 a month less than the other counselors, and would have to agree to return to the University and take certain required courses. He figured that I would become a full-fledged employee within the year. I jumped at the chance, signed up, and became a State Civil Service employee. I actually didn't leave 'Education' because this Agency functioned as an arm of the State Department of Education. In a million years I never believed I would be heading back to the University to learn all about Carl Rogers and Dean Williamson and their theories on Psychology. This was going to be a far cry from my original goal of being a history/social studies teacher and Coach.

It looked like my coaching career was a thing of the past so I figured officiating would just have to take its place. Who knows, maybe those Psychology and counseling courses I would be taking might provide tips on dealing with a few of those wild basketball and football coaches!

Mr. Kerlan informed me that I was being assigned to their Crookston Vocational Rehabilitation regional office. I talked it over with Toodie and she agreed to make this move to the far northwest corner of the state; almost to Canada. We really wanted to remain in St. Paul because of our sick children and their need for medical care, but I needed a job and this position sounded exciting. My goal had always been to live in a smaller town and Crookston was certainly a smaller town. We began to make moving plans, checking on doctors in the Crookston area, and reading up on what the Crookston community had to offer. Two weeks before our move I received a call from Mr. Kerlan informing me that a gentleman who lived in Crookston was hired to fill that vacancy. I thought my job had just been terminated when to my surprise he asked if I would be willing to fill an opening they had in St. Paul. I said that we would be happy to remain in St. Paul. Little did he know that Toodie and I were absolutely ecstatic! Who says prayers don't get answered?

The St. Paul District Vocational Rehabilitation office was located on the 4th floor of the Commerce building in downtown St. Paul. This is where I met my new supervisor Ezra Engelbart, a past school superintendent, Don Allert, a previous YMCA worker, and Mary Sweeney, a wonderful lady who taught school for years in St. Paul. Mary was given the assignment of teaching me the ropes of being an effective Rehabilitation Counselor. She was a very nice lady but pretty aggressive, pushy and very direct in her approach to counseling. She was willing to twist the rules to help a client and maybe even be willing to fib a little to achieve her goals. What a great lady to train me in! I didn't care much for her style but I really appreciated the way she went about achieving her goals. She was tough, but in a socially acceptable way. No rules, regulations or administrators were going to stand in her way to provide the best service to her clients. She taught me how to get around corners, to circumvent the system, to verbalize and document reports that would guarantee service to my clients. Mary was a true advocate for her clients. She despised bureaucracy and the formal government system. By the way she was 100% Irish, a strong catholic lady, and had the same birthday as my son Casey. She was the perfect person to train me in. Even though she was in her mid 60's... I loved her! Her philosophy might best be described as, "Beat the system… service the client." I wish I could be Irish just like Mary Sweeney!

Before counselors were allowed to work with a client it was necessary to first determine the existence of a disability. Dr. William Lick, a local Internist, was hired to review the medical files of all referred clients to officially verify the existence of a physical disability. Dr. Louis Flynn, a local Psychiatrist, was responsible for verifying the existence of a mental or psychiatric disability. When Mary Sweeney had a referral where the existence of a disability might be under question she would wait till the very end of the consultation time when Dr. Lick or Dr. Flynn was preparing to leave the office. She would then rush in with the questionable case hoping that the consultant would just sign off without a careful review. You know, this technique really worked! She was committed to serve every client that entered her office. I filed this technique away in my book of tricks and resorted to its use a few times …and it worked!

Back in the 1950's, I soon realized that Mary Sweeney was typical of the type of women who attained management responsibilities in this field of Vocational Rehabilitation. In those days, management positions in this profession were predominantly male. There were relatively few women counselors and I could count on one hand the number of women with any management responsibilities. In addition to Mary Sweeney, Petra Howard was the Vocational Coordinator responsible for the Deaf and Hard of Hearing. She, like Mary Sweeney, didn't hold to any eight hour work schedule. She worked off of her dining room table in the evening just as much as she worked in her office and in the community. She was a widow whose social life as well as her work life revolved around her deaf and hearing impaired clients and the deaf community in general. Grace Polski, who managed the home crafters program, fit this same exact mold. Her life was her work. I had the distinct honor of meeting Mary Switzer, a top Washington figure in Human Services, in my early career. She was almost a legend as a humanitarian at the National level and had devoted her entire life to the needs of others. She must have been something special because they named the Mary Switzer building in Washington in her honor. These women were all strong, highly dedicated and tough enough to fight their way into this male dominated field of work. They had to be strong and willing to outwork any male to obtain these positions of responsibility. These ladies were true role models when it came to defining the word 'dedication', and in opening the door wider for the women following in their footsteps.

When I joined the St. Paul Schools a few years later, one of my assigned schools was the Crowley School for mentally retarded young adults. The Principal of Crowley was a lady named Tish Henderson. Like Mary Sweeney, she was a take charge gal that ran the school with an iron hand. There was no question that she was in charge of the Crowley School. On the other hand, when it came to her students, she had a heart of gold and was willing to spend a considerable amount of her own money and spend whatever time was necessary to meet their needs; and believe me many of these students had a number of needs. She was a single lady who took on the role of 'Mother' Henderson in addition to her role as Principal. She presented a tough image but was a soft touch when it came to her students. I remember Crowley School being one of St. Paul's oldest schools and an absolute fire trap. When you entered the Principal's office of this ancient school you were greeted with the pungent odor of cigarette smoke, and could actually see smoke rising out of the lower right hand drawer of her desk. Being a chain smoker she used this drawer as her ash tray. I really don't know if the District Administration or the Fire Marshall was aware of her dangerous smoking habit in this fire trap of a building, but if they did I'm not sure any of them had the courage to tell her to stop. By the way, the building never did burn down, but if I was a betting man I would have put my money on a fire. Tish Henderson later applied for the Director of Special Education position in the early 1960's. She never had a chance. I figured the Superintendent didn't want her burning the Court House down!

It was in the 1970s and 1980s when concern for Equal Opportunity legislation came to the forefront and women began to move into leadership positions in many areas of work. When the Superintendent of Schools position opened in St. Paul in the 1960's there was never a question that a male would be hired to fill this position. I figured Dr. Irma McGuire, who was the Director of Elementary Education and an absolutely outstanding leader, would have been the perfect prospect for this position. Unfortunately, in the 1960's she wouldn't have been given a second glance. Compare that with the changing times of the 1990s to the present, where the last three Superintendents in St. Paul have all been women. My, how times have changed. Irma, you were born 20 years too soon!

Getting My Feet Wet

My first assignment as a Rehabilitation Counselor was twofold; to serve the vocational needs of handicapped clients residing in Chisago County, just north of the twin cities, plus those Tuberculosis patients confined to a restricted area in the old Ancker (General) Hospital in St. Paul. My job was to get these disabled folks trained and back to work, and I had a checkbook to help make this happen. It was a challenging assignment but also very exciting. I remember wearing a white gown and mask when I interviewed my TB clients on the fourth floor contagious ward at Ancker Hospital. By the way, this was at the same time that Patrick, our third son, lay dying in the children's ward on the first floor of this same hospital.

I later was assigned to serve clients with mental illness leaving the Hastings State Mental Hospital. This turned out to be an even more challenging assignment. It was very difficult to predict the emotional stability of these folks. Many of my clients appeared perfectly normal in the hospital setting but when confronted with reality in the community, could result in significant personality changes. I had to be willing to accept failure but also willing to offer a second and third opportunity at job training/placement if necessary. I learned a great deal about working with both staff and patients in this assignment. A favorite saying at the Hastings Hospital was, "The only way you could tell the difference between the patients and the staff was who carried the keys"!

I was given an additional assignment to serve clients with disabilities living in Washington County, just East of St. Paul. I'll always remember an experience I had on this assignment while training in a new counselor. I was in the process of interviewing a client right after lunch in a rural school building that was hot and stuffy. Believe it or not, I sort of dozed off during the interview. If it wasn't for this trainee who bumped my arm to wake me up, I might still be there sleeping. Ironically, that trainee, Charles Hagen, later became Director of Special Education for the St. Paul Schools; my boss for some 25 years. In retirement, he and I still have a chuckle over that experience.

Vern Schultz with Charlie VanHeuvlin manager of A.T.S.
(Accounting & Tax Service).

Frankly, this problem did not go away but seemed to get worse. I had that uncanny ability to fall asleep in my office, in staff meetings, in training sessions and just about any time I was in a relaxed setting. This problem came to a head the day I was standing in the hall talking to a co-worker and proceeded to fall asleep in the middle of our conversation. I can still hear her say, "Vern, you're sleeping! That's when I saw my doctor who referred me to the sleep apnea clinic at Fairview Hospital. Apparently

I had a significant sleep disorder and was fitted out with one of those fancy sleep masks that I use each night. The mask has pretty well solved my sleep problem, but mask or not, some of those staff meetings would put anybody to sleep.

Our District Rehabilitation office was located in the Commerce Building pretty much in the heart of downtown St. Paul. Parking was always a problem. I couldn't afford parking ramps and to use parking meters was a real gamble because of the itinerant nature of our job. My best solution was to walk across the Wabasha Bridge and park on Harriet Island. This was a long walk and a bitterly cold walk in the winter. I was still working weekends at the police department and one day shared my parking dilemma with Boots Michael the downtown traffic officer. He said I can solve your problem. "Put one of the police bulletins on your dashboard and park your car on the tunnel ramp going from Wabasha St. down to Lambert Landing. When I come by and see the bulletin on the dashboard you'll be safe." This worked absolutely perfect and totally resolved my parking delimma. No one in the office could figure out why I wasn't ticketed. Unfortunately, six months later, Boots took a couple of day's vacation and his replacement didn't understand the game we were playing. I ended up with two parking tickets. Have you noticed that every great idea has a catch?

Being located downtown does have some advantages. Shopping is at your finger tips, there are loads of available restaurants, you're located in the heart of the job market and in the very center of where all the action takes place. Just two blocks away from our office was the historic Ryan Hotel that offered a fabulous all you can eat lunch buffet for the unbelievable price of one dollar. Now that dollar wasn't easy to come by at our meager salary but we couldn't resist that lunch at least twice a week. Unfortunately that bargain lunch went south when the Ryan Hotel was tore down in the late 1950's to make way for a brand spanking new office building. Our one dollar value meal was gone forever. With the loss of this dollar meal it was a perfect time for our office to move as well. We packed up and moved to the Griggs Midway Building in St. Paul's Midway District. The big advantage of this location was the available parking right in front of the office door. We had no more dollar lunches…but we did have free convenient parking. By the way, that's when I started carrying my lunch from home.

In the course of my Vocational Rehabilitation job I began to send a selected few clients to the Elizabeth Kenny Institute in Minneapolis for vocational evaluation services. Douglas Fenderson was in charge of this Kenny Vocational Program. When he decided to change jobs, he recommended me to replace him as Program Director. I had only been a rehabilitation counselor for about a year and a half and just recently had completed my University coursework and became a full-fledged counselor. It was really a complement to be offered this job when there were so many individuals far more qualified than me to take this position. I remember saying, "Wow, I just learned to spell Vocational Rehabilitation, now I'm being offered the job of Director." It seemed like things were going awfully fast. I guess Jules Kerlan was right when he said, "Vern, join this program and you will be on the ground floor of an exciting new future!"

A Fast Promotion

The fear of failure and loss of the State security blanket and its many benefits really made me question whether I should consider the Kenny Institute job. I was absolutely distressed over what I should do but finally took a deep breath and made the decision to take the leap. It was one of the best decisions of my life. In spite of my fears and lack of confidence, the Kenny Institute Vocational Program flourished and grew in size and scope during my tenure. This is when I realized that it might not take an M.D. or a Ph.D., like all the other staff at Kenny Institute, to be successful. Within the first year we had developed a Work Evaluation Center that was being used not only by the Polio inpatients at Kenny Institute but by a growing number of handicapped individuals in the community referred through State Vocational Rehabilitation Counselors. The increased fees received for this service along with additional Federal funding allowed us to expand this program to its maximum size. It was decided that a new facility to house this expanded Vocational Evaluation Service should be relocated into a new building to be constructed right next door to the Kenny Institute. It would be called the Minneapolis Rehabilitation Center. I designed the work evaluation portion of this new Center and was appointed Assistant Director. This facility is still in operation today serving the vocational needs of many disabled and disadvantaged in the community. I learned from this move to Kenny that some times in life you've got to be willing to take a chance and forget about the security that a civil service position offers. Believe me, it's not easy for some of us conservative Germans to venture away from the comfort of the Civil Service safety net!

Kenny Institute was known world wide for its success in dealing with polio patients. At the time I joined this Institute, Polio was on the decline and Kenny was in the process of expanding services to stroke victims and other disability groups. Their fund raising program was phenomenal because of Kenny Institute's success with polio cases. It's interesting however, how things can change so quickly. A few weeks after I joined the Kenny staff I was asked to develop a Vocational Services display to be exhibited at the American Medical Association Convention in Atlantic City. Kenny sent three displays to this Convention. I fronted my display while a couple of beautiful female models fronted the other two displays. I never did figure out why my display didn't warrant a beautiful model. Maybe they figured I was pretty enough! I had an unlimited expense account, stayed in the finest hotel in Atlantic City and even went to New York with priority seating to see the play, 'My Fair Lady'. It was my first experience of living first class and I loved every minute of it. Let me tell you, I didn't have to eat any cheap 'White Castle's' at this convention… it was steak and lobster all the way!

Two weeks after I returned home, The Minnesota Attorney General, Walter Mondale, indicted Marvin Kline, President of the Kenny Foundation and Fred Fedell, head fund raiser, for inappropriate use of donated funds. If I recall correctly, a majority of funds raised ended up as administrative expenses with far less funds allocated to medical services. Both administrators ended up in jail for an extended period of time. This court case did much to raise the political ambitions of Walter Mondale who later became Senator Mondale and eventual candidate for the President of the United States. The medical and Institute staff were totally innocent of any wrongdoing but everyone, including me, suffered from this negative publicity. The Kenny Institute lost some of its luster and support after that expose. At just about this same time, I had bought a new car and purchased my new home in West St. Paul. You can imagine the kidding and jibbing I took from my friends after all the publicity broke in the local papers. Frankly, if I was on the take, I would have purchased a Cadillac rather than a VW Beetle and built an attached garage to my new home. I guess I just wasn't thinking!

During my tenure at Kenny Institute I was invited to speak at a local Rehabilitation Association meeting to describe our Kenny Vocational Evaluation Center and review plans for the future. I spent my twenty minutes extolling our program successes, describing future plans and giving credit to staff and the fine support that the Kenny Administrators were giving us. When I finished my talk Gus Gehrke, the State Vocational Rehabilitation Director who was in the audience approached me. I figured he was going to complement me on my wonderful presentation. I vividly remember his statement to me. "Vern, who has been providing the major funding for your wonderful program and sending you referrals?" I said that his Agency, the State Division of Vocational Rehabilitation, had been really generous and that we couldn't operate without their support and funds. He then said, "When you make a presentation to the public like you did today, don't you think an acknowledgement of this fact might be in order?" His comment hit me like a lightning bolt! I had spent my twenty minutes talking only about the success of our program and the Kenny staff. I had totally neglected any comments about the vital support and contributions his Agency had been giving us. In truth we were dead in the water without their financial and referral support. I realized what I had done and vowed I would never make that mistake again. Give credit where credit is due… or you may find yourself out of business.

Moving Up The Ladder

I had just completed designing the layout of the Vocational Evaluation Unit to be located at the new Minneapolis Rehabilitation Center when I learned that the Vocational Rehabilitation District Supervisor position in St. Paul was open. I was strongly encouraged to apply for this position. So, in 1960 I returned to St. Paul as District Supervisor for about 9 months then was promoted to the State office as Consultant for Medical Services, Rehabilitation Facilities and Staff Training. Promotions come fast when you join a brand new program and you are one of the first employed. Good timing and a little luck sometimes overcomes experience...anyway changing jobs keeps you on the ball.

Becoming a Consultant at the State Office of this Vocational Rehabilitation organization was a completely new experience for me. I had no quotas to fulfill, no program down the hall to manage, or a set schedule to follow. I spent lots of time in a State car traveling to the various District Offices located all throughout the State. For example, I would go to Rochester once every week to check on a fledging workshop in need of guidance. I would also accompany our State Medical Directors on visits to the various offices. Another job duty required me to write various Federal Grants to develop new services. Being a State Consultant was an OK job but you had limited accountability and not much to put your finger on in terms of accomplishments by the end of the day. Don't quote me, but I viewed this position as not too exciting and a pretty good pre-retirement job. There is something to be said about the excitement associated with facing client challenges and meeting agency goals. A Rehabilitation Counselor in the Minneapolis Office developed a quaint label for us three Rehabilitation Consultants (Chuck Hagen, Ed Schoppert and me). He called us the three 'millstones.' This was a term we did not particularly appreciate even though it may have been true. I enjoyed the job as a Consultant but felt I was too young to be out of the daily action of directly serving clients. To put it bluntly, I saw this job as heavy on bureaucracy and light on "action". Maybe being labeled a 'millstone' wasn't too far off the mark.

Both Gus Gehrke, the agency director, and I felt that far too many young people with disabilities were graduating from high school ill prepared for the world of work or dropping out without graduating. To magnify the problem was the fact that Minnesota high schools turned out to be our primary referral source. Gus Gehrke came up with a unique idea for a new service program that would introduce Vocational Rehabilitation Services directly within the high school setting and wouldn't cost school districts a cent. Funding for this service would come totally from State/federal matching funds. He labeled it the VAC (Vocational Adjustment Coordinator) program. Gus Gehrke was a leader with unusual vision and enthusiasm to improve services to individuals with disabilities. He prodded us to 'think outside the box'. Gus would say, "There's always a way... you just have to search for it!"

Settling In

I was assigned the task of writing up this VAC proposal in Grant form so needed funding would be secured from both the Federal and State Governments. This proposal also had to have the approval of local school districts to implement this service. Once the proposal was written with funding and necessary approval received, I received a call from Jim Geary, the St. Paul Director of Special Education. He asked me to leave my State Consultant position and come to St. Paul and implement this new pilot service in the Capitol city. I saw this as a great opportunity to get back in the trenches. On July 1st, 1964 I joined the St. Paul School District to put this new VAC program into action. Our pilot program in St. Paul was extremely successful and over 40 school districts throughout Minnesota eventually adopted this model. This VAC service revolutionized the secondary curriculum for students with disabilities. It introduced a strong component of work preparation, job training and work experience directly into the secondary school curriculum. This program resulted in a dramatic reduction of special education school dropouts and helped students become better prepared to enter the working world after graduation. These students really didn't need another course in English or mathematics; they needed to develop work adjustment, vocational skills training and actual experience on the job. It was exciting to watch so many students with special needs, who had been dying in the traditional classroom setting, come to life when exposed to a hands-on reality based learning environment!

How ironic, Ten years after turning down that Mathematics/ Science teaching job in St. Paul, I find myself an employee of the St. Paul School System not as a teacher or coach but in a Special Education Supervisory capacity. Who knows where life will lead us? In 1954 I couldn't spell Vocational Rehabilitation and in 1964 I could spell it backwards. I would remain with the St. Paul Schools for the next 29 years until I retired in 1993.

Officiating – An Alternative To Coaching

After graduating from the University, I continued to officiate both football and basketball games for the CAA (Catholic Athletic Association) and for the St. Paul Parks and Playgrounds Department. I also joined the St. Paul Officials Association in hopes of breaking into the local high school officiating ranks. Jerry Flathman was Secretary of this Association and also was in charge of all St. Paul Municipal Athletics. He was instrumental in helping me officiate as many Parks and Playgrounds football and basketball games as I wanted to work. If he liked your work in the St. Paul Municipal league he would assign you to games in one of the various high school leagues around the State. I must have passed his test because he scheduled me to work my first high school football game at Zumbrota high school in the fall of 1952. It was the beginning of 35 years of officiating high school and college games. It turned out to be as much fun as coaching…with a few less headaches!

While at St. Agnes, I was limited by time and school schedule as to how much officiating I could handle. After leaving St. Agnes in 1955 I was free to work a full officiating schedule. In the 1950's I remember earning $15 for a high school football game and $12 for a high school basketball game. If you worked the B game you received another $5. By the time you paid your share of the gas and had refreshments after the game, you probably took home $10.00. In those years this was pretty good money, but the enjoyment of socializing with your officiating partners and the excitement of the game itself made that $10 seem like $100. I made many life long friends through officiating. It also provided me the opportunity to keep my hand in 'sports' now that my coaching career was over. I think Toodie secretly liked the idea of me leaving coaching. Now we could talk at dinner instead of her eating in silence while I would be totally engrossed in planning my football strategy for the next game. She welcomed me back to the family with open arms. I never knew I was away…but she did!

I'm not sure how Toodie felt about me being away from home so often during football and basketball season, but she never complained. That officiating money helped buy those little extras and a steak in front of the fireplace on those Saturday nights I was home. I recently asked my daughter, Patty, if she minded me being gone so much on the weekends. She said, "Absolutely not, especially when you brought those Bridgman malted milks home for us each Friday evening after you officiated." I would put the malt's in the freezer when I arrived home and they were frozen solid by morning. I can still see Tom, Casey and Patricia eating those malt's in front of the TV on Saturday morning engrossed in their programs. Bribery really pays off!

As a rookie official in the 1950's, most of the high school games I officiated were some distance away. When you worked in the Northern Rum River League, the Wisconsin Border League or the leagues south of the Cities it meant meeting your partners as early as 4:00PM or maybe 4:30PM to get to a game that started at 7:00. After the game I would arrive home anywhere from 11:00 to 12:00 midnight. From a time standpoint, I probably averaged a wage rate of $2 an hour. Sometimes it's best to look at work from a job satisfaction standpoint rather than from a monetary viewpoint.

With more experience and improved skills, I began to obtain assignments in the more prestigious Suburban and Lake Conferences and also in the St. Paul and Minneapolis Leagues. This was nice because it meant less traveling, slightly more pay and a little more status. It was kind of a thrill to be assigned a game at Central Stadium in St. Paul where I had both played and coached football. By the mid 1950s I still hadn't broke into the College officiating circuit but with the help of my good friend, Jim Griffin, I was getting close.

Family Life-The Worst Of Times

We were living on Reaney Street in St. Paul when Michael, our first son, was born in the fall of 1953. It was an exciting moment in my life. I had a wonderful wife, a nice home, a great job at St. Agnes High School, was the coach of an undefeated football team and now I had a son. I was sitting on top of the world! To make things even better I didn't have to pay the doctors a nickel for the medical costs of Michael's birth. We actually received a check back from the Insurance Company. I had medical Insurance through my job at St. Agnes and Toodie had insurance from her job at Brown and Bigelow. They both paid for the birth and we received the 'left-over' monies. This is how it worked in the 'good-old-days', but not the way it works today. In any event it was the period of my life when I had the world by the tail. Everything was coming up roses!

As great as I felt at the time of Michael's birth, six months later my life went into the pits. Michael was a happy smiling perfect baby for that first six months of his life. At that point a change began to occur. He began to cry more than usual, he was hard to hold because he would arch his back and scream in apparent pain, and began showing some signs of being disoriented. We became concerned and decided to make an appointment with our physician, Dr. Flanagan. This medical clinic we attended had a real Irish ring to it; Dr. Flanagan, Dr. Galligan, Dr. Walsh and Dr. O'Brien. I often wonder if they would have allowed a Dr. Schultz to join their practice.

Dr. Flanagan did a whole series of tests on Michael and said that something appeared to be wrong but couldn't put his finger on the problem. After more diagnostic studies he still was unsure of a specific diagnosis but thought that Michael might have Cerebral Palsy, whatever that was.

Michael's condition continued to deteriorate rapidly and in time total paralysis set in. Dr. Flanagan secured an emergency consultation with Dr. Ritchie, a well-known Neurologist. Dr. Ritchie indicated that perhaps the only hope for improvement might be through brain surgery. The surgery turned out to be unsuccessful and Michael died a short time later. Having him progress so well for six months and then see him deteriorate so quickly was absolutely devastating. The doctors could give us no definitive answer as to the reason for this dramatic and abrupt turnaround. The question I kept asking myself after Michael's death was, "Could this happen again?" I justified in my mind that this was just a once in a lifetime fluke of nature so, let's move on!

Timothy, our second son, was born some months later. Our whole world became positive again. I remember his birth very well. It occurred at the same time I was playing baseball with the Lawrence Recreation Baseball Team. We had a very successful season and ended up playing for the State Baseball Championship in St. Cloud. Toodie had her children by Caesarian Section so could pick the date of birth. Wouldn't you know, the day she selected was the same day as our State Championship game. Right or wrong (I'll let the reader decide) I kissed my wife, wished her the best and headed for St. Cloud. I'm pleased to say that we won the game and became State Champions. When Toodie's nurse asked her if I was in the waiting room, and learned I was playing baseball, my name became mud. When I did show up after the birth, I was definitely not 'Mr. Popular' with the medical staff. All right, before you attack me…what would you have done? Maybe I really don't want to know!

For the first six months after his birth, Timothy progressed wonderfully and we were all so pleased and relieved. Then, at that fateful six-month period we again noticed some of the symptoms that Michael had shown when he reached this same age. I remember taking him to see Dr. Flanagan again, holding my breath that nothing was seriously wrong. Dr. Flanagan examined Timothy then shook his head in frustration and stated the same problem had again raised its ugly head. He said that Timothy had similar symptoms to those present in Michael and sadly to say, there was no known cure. He was now able to hang a label on this problem. He said it was a genetic anomaly called Schilders Disease; not Cerebral Palsy. This was a rare incurable neurological problem involving young children that was progressive and eventually fatal. In time Timothy, like Michael, became totally paralyzed. When we could no longer care for him he was placed in Childrens' Hospital and within two years passed away. Let me tell you, things weren't going well for us at all and suddenly life wasn't 'coming up roses' anymore. We were beginning to learn that life has its downs as well as its ups.

I believe Dr. Flanagan was as frustrated as us and recommended we make an appointment with the Dight Genetic Institute at the University of Minnesota for an evaluation of this rare genetic problem. The Dight Institute's evaluation verified that this was a genetic problem but that it most likely would never occur again. They encouraged us to feel free to have another child if it was our desire. We desperately wanted a family so were relieved to learn that this devastating problem would be something in our past. We decided to take an optimistic approach rather than living with the fear, worry and anxiety that this killer disease would rear its ugly head again. We wanted a family more than anything in the world and trusted in the Dight Institute's judgment…after all they were the experts. At least we thought they were!

We were so pleased and excited when Toodie announced she was again pregnant. It appeared that finally a healthy baby was on its way. Believe me, life was looking a lot better for Toodie and me after this announcement. Then an unusual event took place. A letter arrived in our mail box mixed in with all the usual junk variety mail. As I was getting ready to throw most of it in the wastebasket, I noticed a letter postmarked from the Montreal Neurological Institute in Canada. I figured it was just another request for money, but my curiosity got the best of me and I decided to open it. The letter began, "I believe there is a definite chance that Mrs. Schultz's third child might be afflicted in a similar manner as her two previous children who are now deceased." The final paragraph of the letter literally took our breath away. It read, "I believe that if you were our patient we would recommend termination of pregnancy with sterilization." Who in the world was this 'Institute' who felt they had the right to tell Toodie, who was about five months pregnant with her third child, to have an abortion and surgery that would prevent any further pregnancies? I should have thrown this letter out with the other junk mail!

After receiving this letter I immediately contacting our family physician and learned that the doctors from the Dight Institute had sent our medical history to the Montreal Neurological Institute for a second opinion. Apparently this Institute was one of the leading genetic research centers in the world. According to their letter this third pregnancy was doomed to failure. We apparently had jumped the gun!

Toodie and I were now faced with a really tough decision. What do we do about this pregnancy? Should we follow the recommendations made by these Canadian genetic specialists? If their findings were correct, having an abortion would avoid putting us once again through the emotional anguish, stress and depression of bearing a third child that was predestined to a slow, painful and agonizing death. On the other hand, the doctors at the Dight Institute offered us hope and were much more optimistic. It certainly was a possibility that the physicians from the Montreal Institute were wrong. Who knows, with a little luck and a whole lot of prayer maybe the odds of finally having a normal healthy child were in our favor. Talk about being between a rock and a hard place.

Prior to the birth of this child, Toodie had made the decision to join the Catholic Church. Both of us now were strong supporters of the Church's stand against abortion. We felt however, that with the medical profession actually recommending an abortion, maybe we were an exception to these church rules. Our dilemma was shared with a couple of Catholic priests and found them to be sympathetic and understanding, but not one of them ever mentioned, "Making us an exception to church rule." On the other hand, if we had taken a poll of our friends and relatives, I believe most would have said, "Your situation simply doesn't fit the Catholic rule book on abortion. Listen to those Doctors and have the abortion." Think about it for a moment…what would you have done?

Well, we were optimists and made the decision to follow the 'Catholic Rule Book.' There would be no abortion! We were convinced this was the right decision, that is, until we met with our physician right after Patrick, our third son, was born. I remember meeting with him in the lobby right outside the operating room. He kind of looked down at the floor and said in sort of an apologetic tone, "I'm not absolutely sure, but it doesn't look good, there appear to be some mild negative symptoms." He later met with Toodie and me advising us not to take Patrick home. He recommended that we place him in a special residence in the city of White Bear for infants with serious health problems. He said that if there were no new symptoms in six months, to then take him home. He explained that the emotional pressures and stress would be immense if we took Patrick home and built a strong parental attachment. He said, "Let's see what happens…we will know for sure in six months." We reluctantly followed his advice.

It was a particularly tough six months. Patrick, like our other two children, prospered in every way during that six-month period with no apparent signs of having Schilders Disease. Our guilt for not taking him home grew with each visit to this residence. It was an agonizing time for us. I well remember some of the questioning comments made by the director of the residence. I'm sure she couldn't figure out why a perfectly normal child like Patrick would be at this residence when his parents should be caring for him at home. She had every right to be thinking this way because all the other infants in her care were obviously ill and Patrick appeared perfectly normal in every way. I fully understood why she would be perplexed with this strange situation. Like I said, our guilt grew stronger with each visit!

When Patrick reached six months of age, almost to the day, those full-blown symptoms of Schilders Disease showed up again to our total distress. Patrick began the slow agonizing illness that evidentially led to total paralysis and finally his death two years later in Ancker Hospital. To add to our ill fortune, the stress of three Caesarian Sections resulted in the rupturing of Toodie's uterus. This is what you call getting double-teamed. Not only did we lose our third child, but at 26 years of age, our hopes of ever having a family appeared wiped out. That term, 'three strikes and you're out' goes beyond baseball!

It would be a lie to say that the devastation of losing our three children didn't play havoc with our lives. I had resigned my position as teacher and coach at St. Agnes with plans to take a position away from the twin cities. It was necessary for me to set these career plans aside temporarily and settle for working at the police department so I could remain close to home and our doctors. Excessive medical expenses put us deep in the hole financially and we were actually forced to seek State medical assistance. Our physical and mental well-being was in question and our religious convictions up for grabs. This just wasn't the way life was supposed to be. We started out so well…what happened?

My mother's good Catholic advice at the time was, "Vernon, get on with your life, have faith in God, and *time* will eventually heal these wounds." I remember thinking, where was God these past few years and could you be a little more specific about the '*time*'. It was without question the very loneliest and depressing period of our lives. We felt we had hit rock bottom. This was truly the pits. It appeared that our hope of having a family was gone forever.

I will always remember one specific moment while working the midnight shift at the police department. It was about 2:00 A.M. and I was alone, standing at the Records Division Counter. As I stood there I thought, "Vern, nothing in your future life can or will ever be as bad or depressing as you feel at this very moment." I was really down. I made a promise to myself, that when faced with future problems or challenges, I would make a point of remembering back to how I was feeling at this exact moment standing at that counter. It would be a reminder to me that no problem, of any kind, could be as devastating in my life as the problem I was suffering through right then. Whatever those future problems might be...they would all be insignificant in comparison. Over the years I've been confronted with a number of serious problems and challenges that at times seemed almost unsolvable. Before getting all frustrated and losing sleep I ask myself a simple question, "Is this problem as bad or depressing as the problem I was facing the morning I stood at that Records Division Counter?" The answer has always been, 'absolutely not...not even close!' This approach has made me an eternal optimist and kept me off the Psychiatrist's couch. Thank the lord for that 2:00 A.M. revelation at the Records Division Counter. It has allowed me to approach problems with more optimism, view life using rose colored glasses...and I also sleep better!

After that fateful letter arrived from the Montreal Institute along with its negative contents, our doctor suggested we meet with Father Frances Curtain, head of the Catholic Charities office in St. Paul. If this Institute was correct in their prediction, then adoption might be the only course of action for us to follow if we wanted a family. It would be sort of a 'cover all the angles' meeting. We followed our doctor's advice and arranged a meeting with Father Curtain who turned out to be just a wonderful robust Irish priest who was more than understanding of our dilemma. After he listened to our story I'll never forget his comment, "Don't worry Vern, if your third child is Ill, I guarantee that you will have a family." As it turned out we would have to take him up on that promise.

Father Curtain was true to his word! When it was determined that Patrick was terminally ill Catholic Charities got right on the ball and provided us with our first adopted son, Thomas. Patrick was still living and residing in Ancker Hospital when Thomas arrived. We have just one picture of Thomas and Patrick together that we treasure. Two years later Daniel Casey (we call him Casey) entered our family and in another two years our daughter Patricia joined us. Each of our three adopted children were infants when they arrived in our family. In those days secrecy was the name of the game so we received very sketchy background information on the children. We were provided their given name at birth, some health information and just a 'hint of information' about the mothers. We cared less about any further information. We were the most thankful couple in the world. God, through the Catholic Charities, had made our dream come true...We had a real honest to goodness family. To make it even better, Tom, Casey and Patricia had three Saints in heaven to watch over them!

Toodie holding Patricia, Casey sitting on the roof, Tom ready to drive the VW and Vern leaning on the car door.

At the very time Toodie and I were dealing with our children's illnesses a letter arrived from the Ramsey County draft board requesting that I report for my physical examination. I was in the A-1 category and a top prospect to help end the Korean conflict. My doctor strongly advised me to request an exemption from the service based on the situation with our children. I wasn't anxious to join the service but also was willing to put in my service time like everyone else. I also realized it would be unfair for Toodie to be left alone with the many challenges of our sick children and the uncertainties of their future. Under these circumstances I decided to request an exemption and it was approved. I often wonder the road life would have taken if I would have entered the service and left Toodie to carry the burden of these children by herself. Looking back I realize there was really no other decision I could have made. On this past Memorial day, at completion of the church service, the Priest asked all the Armed Service Veterans in the congregation to stand up for a blessing. I must confess it was difficult for me to sit during this blessing knowing that I was just a spectator at the game while all those folks standing were the players.

Hands-On Awareness

During the time Michael was ill, Dr. Flanagan suggested that we look into joining the Cerebral Palsy Association, which had recently been formed in St. Paul. This was when his initial diagnosis indicated that Michael had the disability of Cerebral Palsy. Both Toodie and I attended a meeting of this association, which was held at the St. Paul Rehabilitation Center. We met many parents and family members whose children had this disability. It was my first experience with any disability group or with a community organization with this type of cause. Frankly, it was an eye opener for me to learn that there were many individuals in our community afflicted with Cerebral Palsy who would be facing significant obstacles in their future. These parents had formed this organization to figure out ways to help their children survive in a very competitive world. I must say this was quite a leveling experience for me at that time, thinking about Michael's unknown future. As crazy as it sounds, I realized that Michael might never have the chance to play baseball…and I couldn't tell him to kick his leg higher.

I was very impressed with the members of this organization. They were deeply committed to developing services in the community to better meet the needs of their children with Cerebral Palsy. One major task they took on was to develop a workshop for the older disabled adults who were currently house-bound or resided in state institutions. Developing a sheltered workshop would be one way for these folks to get out of their home or institutional setting, be productive and feel that life had meaning. Even after Michael passed away I got caught up in this movement and was involved in helping to open that first Cerebral Palsy workshop in the basement of an old storefront on Selby Avenue. This Organization raised enough money, through a telethon, to buy the entire building using the main floor for the Association office and the basement for the workshop. The State Division of Vocational Rehabilitation approved a $10,000 grant to install a hand operated elevator to transport the workers, many who were in wheel chairs, up and down to their worksite. Someone with good use of their arms was needed to operate this elevator. It was truly a deathtrap in case of fire but it was a start. Current industrial regulations would never have allowed this workshop to be located in such a dingy basement area where the only escape route was that hand operated elevator. It was a beginning however, and Henry Ford's first automobile wasn't perfect either!

The first workshop assignment was for the workers to construct wooden toys. This was a beginning but it didn't take long to realize the market for these toys was very limited and the quality of the toys was not always up to standard. In time, it was decided that sub-contracting various work tasks from existing companies in the community was the avenue to follow. The challenge was to find the right kind of work that these folks could handle because of their varied physical limitations, and to convince companies that the workshop could actually produce work in a quality manner. In time, this subcontract work increased, the number of workers grew and new larger quarters were needed. By the 1970s this workshop was relocated to a large industrial building on the east side of St. Paul. At that point they changed the name of the workshop to 'Midwest Services Industries'. From such a meager beginning this workshop is flourishing today offering employment opportunities for over 200 individuals with all types of disabilities.

There were some really interesting people in the Cerebral Palsy Organization. I learned quickly that disability occurs in families of the wealthy, the poor, the middle class, the famous and the unknown. I remember my mother saying that when you retire and move to Texas it didn't make any difference if you were the bank president or the janitor, you were all in the same boat… it was only good health that mattered. This concept certainly was true for the folks in this organization as well. There was this one uniting feature that brought this diverse group together; to develop improved living and work opportunities for their disabled children. Their enthusiasm and efforts really helped influence and motivate me in my future Rehabilitation career. I remained active with this organization for some time and served on the Board of Directors for a number of years. My involvement with this Association served me well with my eventual employment in the Division of Vocational Rehabilitation. In the early

1960's when I served as Rehabilitation Facilities Consultant, I actually served as State Liaison Officer to this workshop plus others throughout the state. It's a small world, isn't it?

F. Hall Roe was one of the first disabled individuals I came in contact with and especially remember after joining United Cerebral Palsy. Hall was in his 40s, the son of a wealthy lawyer from Chicago. He resided in a room at the St. John's Hospital and ran their hospital newspaper. He used an electric wheelchair for mobility and, because he couldn't speak, communicated through a unique talking board that he personally invented. He had severe spasticity requiring him to use the typewriter by striking the keyboard with a wand from his mouth. Although he was profoundly handicapped, he used his intelligence to adapt his life, work and living setting to the point where he could operate almost independently. When he wanted to leave the hospital and have a cocktail, he would have an aide call a cab that would take him to the Capri hotel where a waitress, or friend, would use a shot glass to carefully pour him his drink. This task required a quick wrist and perfect timing was essential. More than anyone else, Hall taught me that anything was possible if you possessed the right motivation. One day he wrote on his talking board, "There is always a way to do a task and the fun is to discover that way." Hall had a profound influence on how I approached my work as a Rehabilitation Counselor.

My involvement with the Cerebral Palsy Organization really opened my eyes to the needs of a hidden segment of our community; those individuals with disabilities. Up to that time my focus had always been with the able bodied, the athlete, the skilled performer. In fact, as a coach, you simply cut from the squad those young adults who weren't skilled performers. With this organization, however, you did just the opposite by focusing attention on the needs of those who weren't skilled performers. As a Board member, this required me to make a 180-degree change in my thinking… helping folks with disabilities become more independent and self-reliant.

It was at this point, in the mid-1950s, after leaving St. Agnes High School and while working at the Police Department, that I began to explore other possible job choices. Looking back now I realize that my involvement in the Cerebral Palsy Association played a key role in helping me explore more seriously occupations in the 'helping professions'. When I saw that job bulletin for the Vocational Rehabilitation Counselor position, I knew this was the direction for me to follow.

SECTION V
SETTLING DOWN
1964 – 1993

I seem to have a much more vivid memory of what occurred in my life before 1964 than after 1964. After all, it's hard to forget those exciting and challenging events of starting from zero, the struggle through College, getting married, starting a family, beginning a new career, buying and building your first homes and surviving all of this. I remember all these events very clearly because everything was exciting and new. This period from 1964 – 1993 seemed to go so quickly, that it has become sort of a blur in my memory. Actually it was a wonderful period of my life with so many events occurring, so many changes and decisions, and a time to mature with age and experience. The difference however, was that up to 1964 I was 'fighting for position' and after 1964 I fought like mad to 'maintain' that position. Some might say that 1964 was my beginning of old age and short term memory loss. Because so much did occur during this 29 year period of my life, I'd like to highlight just a few of the more memorable events.

Changing My Living Style

I should probably have sent a bouquet of flowers to the Minnesota Highway Department for deciding to build the Lafayette Freeway so close to my back yard in South St. Paul. I believe everyone in our family would unanimously agree that the move to Prior Lake was the smartest move of our lifetime. Residing in the large St. Paul metropolitan community presented quite a different style of living compared to the rural community of Prior Lake with its 600 plus residents. We found the small town life experiences in Prior Lake totally different than in the city. Sailing, boating, water skiing, and fishing right in our own back yard were daily occurrences. I'm afraid these were just wishful dreams until we got brave and made this daring move to rural Minnesota. Moving to the small quaint village of Prior Lake brought our family into an entirely new world that I hardly knew existed. My love relationship with this new world began the minute I set foot on Martinson Island. To put it as simply as possible, it was a challenge each morning for me to leave the lake and head for work to that crowded bustling city of St. Paul. No matter how bad a day I had at work, those problems just drifted away as I entered highway 13 on my way home to paradise!

When we first moved to Martinson Island, many of the original Prior Lake town folk figured everyone on the lake, including me, was rich and some of them labeled us the 'gold coast'. Little did they know that educator pay, in that period of time, bordered between lower middle class and the poverty line. It was my officiating pay that kept our financial head above water. In time, and with an increasing number of people moving to the Prior Lake area, that attitude drifted off into oblivion. Actually, I got kind of a kick out of people just thinking we were rich.

We regularly would visit our home on Martinson Island during its construction. Once we arrived in Prior Lake, there were two routes to follow. The easiest route was to go directly through the City of Prior Lake, then circle around the lake to the quaint stone bridge that led to the Island. The other route was to take highway 13 all the way to county road 42, go west two miles, south on county road 21 for one mile then take the gravel road east to the Island. County road 42 in 1967 was a rough and tumble gravel road with limited traffic. Today it is a busy four lane thoroughfare with restaurants, filling stations, shops and businesses of all types lining this thoroughfare all the way to the large Burnsville Shopping Mall. I quickly learned, however, that the shortest route to our new home in the winter was to take county road 42 to highway 13, go south a quarter of a mile, then take a sharp right directly to the lake. Heading due west across the ice you ran directly into Martinson Island. I regularly followed this route all through that winter of 1967 while the house was being built. My folks were accustomed to walking on the ice of Como Lake so they didn't mind taking 'to the ice' when they visited us as well. It wasn't until the winter of 1968 that I learned this might not have been the smartest route to travel. Two cars went through the ice that winter directly along the lake route I followed. In fact the Prior Lake American Newspaper published an article warning the public of the many 'hot spot' areas on the ice that cars were to avoid. Now they tell me! I never did explain to my Dad that the ice on Prior Lake apparently was not quite as safe as on Como Lake. Some things really shouldn't be shared!

One of the challenges when you live this nomadic existence by moving from St. Paul to West St. Paul then to two different locations in South St. Paul and temporarily to Inver Grove, and finally to Prior Lake, was the number of schools our children had to attend. For Tom, it meant that he had to attend five different schools in just a few years. He didn't seem to mind and says he enjoyed making new friends. Patty is the one who faced a real problem when she arrived in Prior Lake. The techniques for learning to read were totally different in Prior Lake than in her previous schools. This created some serious frustrations for her and unfortunately her Prior Lake teacher wasn't very understanding. Patricia announced one day that she didn't like school and was no longer going to attend. Toodie was forced to do some fast fence mending with Patricia's Prior Lake teacher who frankly was quite inflexible in her approach to teaching reading. After that hectic first year, Patricia started fresh in the next grade with a very understanding teacher and did excellent. In a short time she became one of the best readers in her class. It's interesting how some teachers have their focus on teaching to the class as a group, while others focus on teaching to the varied individuals in their class. As a special education Supervisor, I found it a real joy working with those teachers who spent time trying to identify the individual needs of each student and then focusing their instruction to meet these individual needs. I love teachers willing to teach 'out of the box'.

The major challenge facing me with this move to Prior Lake was that 25-mile drive to work each morning and the 25-mile return ride in the evening. I remember buying a new Ford Taurus that could really move on the highway. Three speeding tickets later and a visit to the State Traffic Bureau made me realize I would have to make some adjustments in my driving habits or I would lose my license. I found a great solution. I purchased a Volkswagen Bug that at 50 miles an hour seemed like I was going 110 miles an hour in my Taurus. The result was no more speeding tickets. Actually, purchasing a car with 'cruise control' might have provided a simpler solution… but that would have cost another $350 dollars!

After purchasing our lot on Martinson Island, I showed Tom, our son, where the house would be built and our beach for swimming and fishing. All Tom saw was a weed filled field and a pretty grubby looking beach. Needless to say, he was not impressed and asked why we moved away from his friends and neighborhood in South St. Paul anyway? His attitude changed quickly after the house was built and saw some of the landscaping changes that were made. Those 34 truckloads of sand dumped on the ice that first winter gave us the best beach on the Island and suddenly Tom thought the move was a pretty good idea after all. Can you imagine putting 34 loads of sand on that beach today? The DNR would have me jailed for the rest of my life!

I recall visiting our housing site just after the basement walls were constructed and the floor joists were being installed. A neighbor, Mr. Oldenberg, stopped by and introduced himself. His first comment was, "Mr. Schultz, you're going to have water in your basement!" This statement really threw me for a loop because that's not what I wanted to hear. Each of our previous houses, with exception of one, had a water problem in the basement after a big rain. I had specifically told my contractor that I wanted every precaution taken to make sure this house would absolutely have no water problems. Well, I'm happy to report that Mr. Oldenberg didn't know what he was talking about and I have no idea where he came up with this erroneous information. We never had a drop of water in that basement but his comments really shook me up and led to a couple of sleepless nights. What a nice friendly introduction to my new home by a neighbor who actually turned out to be a really nice guy. It didn't take long for him to develop a reputation in the neighborhood of 'knowing it all'…but being wrong most of the time.

Martinson Island was named after the Martinson family who lived for years on this Island. Jim Martinson was the one family member who still resided on the south end of the island when we moved in. Some folks might classify old Mr. Martinson as a hermit or recluse. His home had no electricity or any of the modern conveniences we take for granted. His refrigerator was simply ice cut from the lake in winter and stored under straw in a small barn. He cooked on a wood stove, used a wood fireplace for heat, had a wonderful garden, trapped beaver and muskrats for their skins, and caught frogs he sold to local restaurants. Get the picture? He was a true pioneer who distanced himself from us interlopers who were slowly but surely stealing away his land and life style. It was interesting that our son Casey became one of his closest friends. Mr. Martinson taught Casey to trap, hunt and enjoy the rugged outdoor life void of any modern conveniences. To this day, Casey considers the time spent with Mr. Martinson as one of the best periods of his life. One thing for sure, he could never have trapped beaver and muskrats at our home in South St. Paul!

At times Toodie would prepare meals on TV plates that Casey would bring to Mr. Martinson. As time went by he became friendly with us but would never enter our home or spend time at our place. We always met on his grounds. He was really a fine person who wanted nothing to do with the modern world that was slowly closing in on him. Local realtors were constantly prodding him to sell his land which was absolutely prime real estate property. Money meant nothing to him and if he did sell the land where would he go? I feel all the pressures put on him hastened his death in the mid-1970s. You guessed it, within a year of his death the realtors gobbled up his land and those monster lake homes began to spring up on his property. I guess that's what you call progress. After Jim Martinson died all the muskrats and beavers left the Island, the fishing wasn't quite as good, and the ducks all flew away. They had lost their best friend.

A few months after we moved to the Island, Casey said that Jim Martinson wanted to know if we had a fishing boat. He said there was a small fishing boat imbedded in sand on our beach area. I checked it out and was not impressed. A few days later Jim had apparently dug it out for us. It wasn't as bad as I thought, and not having any boat, I proceeded to clean it out and painted it with a very heavy, thick green paint. I bought some ores and we used that boat all summer. It was used primarily to take our family and guests for boat rides around Martinson Island. The following year we planned to purchase a motor but figured oars would be just fine that first year. How nice of old Jim Martinson to provide us with a boat as a welcoming gift to his Island. I left this boat just sit on the beach that first winter. In the spring I was shocked to see that the boat had dried out leaving huge gaps between each of the sideboards. I goofed by not planting it back in the muck of the beach to maintain its moisture. The demise of that boat meant I had to open my billfold and buy a real boat with a motor. Let's face it; living on a lake really requires a motorboat. This may not have been true in 1920 but in 1968 it was almost a requirement. My neighbors all had motor boats so what would they think if we didn't follow suit? It doesn't take a Philadelphia lawyer to figure out that Tom, Casey and Patricia unanimously agreed with our neighbors.

Being somewhat limited in cash, that second summer, I bought a very versatile (and inexpensive) boat that had multiple uses. This boat could operate as a row boat, a small motor boat, a sail boat and a diving raft when flipped over. It was made out of a type of corrugated material and was just five feet in length and four feet in width. I paid the whopping sum of $200 for this boat and three hundred dollars for a used three-horse motor. We had more fun with that versatile boat than we did with the three large speed boats purchased in later years. That three horse motor really moved this boat along on the lake because of its light weight and it would sail perfectly just as long as the wind wasn't too strong. There was a time or two when we had to tow it to shore when the wind became too brisk. Who said you needed a fancy speedboat to have fun on the lake? I felt this was the perfect boat for my kids because it did absolutely everything… and it was cheap too!

Actually the best boat we ever owned was an old used pontoon boat that was ready to sink if we didn't have new foam blown into the pontoons for buoyancy. If I remember correctly someone just gave us this boat. It never had to be cleaned, you could roughhouse on it and the upkeep was zero. Those fancy motorboats had to be babied and treated with kid gloves. The motorboats always looked good on the lift and they certainly had their purpose, but they were gas hogs and had to be cleaned all the time. We also spent a fortune on those expensive propellers when the boat came in contact with one of the lakes submerged rocks. The barn swallows also loved to use these motorboats as their toilet stool. The old pontoon boat didn't seem to draw their attention at all. Unfortunately we needed those fast speedboats for waterskiing. When our kids left home so did the speed boats!

Sailing was a really big deal on Prior Lake. Toodie and I joined the sailing club (also called the Yacht Club) that was located in a nifty A frame building right adjacent to Martinson Island. 'C- Boats' and 'Flying Dutchman' were the sailing boats raced on Prior Lake. I didn't own one but did crew on my neighbor's boats and also served as a race judge when needed. I recall one race where the boat I was crewing on was far in the lead until we tipped over. Unfortunately, by the time I got my nose plugs back on and helped to right the sailboat, we finished in last place. That was the last time anyone asked me to be a crewmember. The skipper just didn't understand that I was absolutely dead in the water without those nose plugs firmly in place. I apparently was a failure as a sailboat judge as well. In the middle of one race, the wind went into a complete calm. I decided to cancel the race and took holy hell from the lead racer who was intent on winning that race, even if he had to paddle across the finish line. No one else seemed to complain. Fortunately, I wasn't asked to resign from the Sailing Club because they needed me to play my horn for their dances and parties…free!

Actually, this Sailing Club was much more a social club then anything else. A good number of people that belonged to the club didn't sail and we fell into that group. We loved the parties, socializing with neighbors, cookouts and dances that this Club offered. Jack Andrews, Wally Langhorst and I became sort of the Sailing Club Band. We played for all of their parties. Our reputation spread and we soon began getting invited to play for a variety of other events in the Prior Lake area. Playing at the Sailing Club really was the catalyst for me to eventually get connected with other local bands and my music career was on the rise. Who would have thought that sailing and music had anything in common?

Cleve Mickley, a good friend who lived on the lake for years, offered me a small speedboat that his son had outgrown. It was a one seater with a 19-horse motor and a device on the keel that squirted water high up in the air giving the impression you were going at high speeds. This boat needed lots of repair work before it was useable. My son Casey and I removed literally thousands of screws that held the boat together. We refiberglassed the back end of the boat that was seriously deteriorated and spent weeks replacing old boards, reupholstered the seat and painted the entire boat a bright yellow. Everyone on the lake got to know Casey and his yellow speedboat. It was one of the sharpest looking boats on the lake. After a couple years when time came for its demise we decided to plant it in the back yard making a garden decoration out of it. Every kid on the lake would have died for that boat. Casey really lucked out.

Casey was a real entrepreneur as a young kid. He shined shoes at the local barber shop, helped all the farmers in the area and did all kind of odd jobs. By the time he was a sophomore in high school he had accumulated in excess of $1000 in the bank. He obtained his driver's license and was really hot to get his own car. In my travels I came across an absolutely immaculate English two seater MG convertible (with an attachable hard top) for a sale price of $1000. This car was flaming red in color and Casey fell in love with it at first sight. He purchased it on the spot using all his own money. There were a lot of jealous juniors and seniors in Prior Lake High school when they saw this young sophomore pull up to school in a car they would all die for. He drove the MG to school a few weeks later and when school was out that afternoon his car was nowhere to be seen. He was all shook up and was ready to call the police until he walked into the school swimming pool and there was his MG sitting next to the diving tower. Some of the seniors had picked the car up and relocated it to the pool. He and his friends carried the car back to the parking lot and fortunately there was no damage. At that point he made the wise decision to return to using the school bus for transportation to and from school.

In truth, this MG Midget might have been just a little too nice and too mechanically technical to maintain for a young 16 year old. It quickly began to drain his pocket book (and mine as well) to keep his MG running in good order. He learned quickly that English vintage cars are very touchy and expensive to maintain. A number of months later he reluctantly decided to sell it at a slight profit instead of applying for a bank loan. Deep down I would have loved to own this car myself and it sure looked great sitting in my driveway. The moral of this experience is don't buy a fancy foreign car until you're at least a senior in high school...or a member of your family is a skilled auto mechanic.

Our daughter Patricia loved the water, was an excellent water skier and could swim like a fish. When she entered Prior Lake High School she decided to go out for the swim team. Once she saw the school divers in action she quickly decided diving would be more fun and even more challenging than competitive swimming. When she went for her sports physical examination we were all shocked when the physician diagnosed her as having scoliosis (a curvature of the spine). He said she would still be able to participate on the diving team but serious corrective action would be required. She was given certain corrective exercises and was fitted for a Milwaukee Body Brace that she would need to wear nearly 100% of the time during her growing years. She was excused from wearing this brace only when diving. This diagnosis came as a real shock to all of us and a true challenge for Patricia. The brace extended up to her neck and down to her hips. She wore turtle neck sweaters and loose fitting clothes in an attempt to cover the brace but to little avail. For a teen age girl, wearing this massive brace (she named it 'Hermie') was a very devastating experience. To add to her dilemma, were those few catty girls in school who teased her about her appearance and even accused her of being pregnant. It was not an easy time for Patricia but she understood the purpose of the brace and with unusual maturity for her age, persevered through the pain and discomfort, teasing and obvious change in appearance. Toodie and I were really proud of how she handled this problem, wore that brace every day, followed the doctor's orders and didn't shy away from participating in all the school academic, social and sporting activities. Patricia told her friends that she and 'Hermie' were going steady because they were together all the time!

I vividly remember inviting Patricia to attend a basketball tournament for young people with disabilities at Courage Center in Golden Valley, Minnesota. I was responsible for adaptive athletics in the St. Paul Schools and one of our teams was participating. We entered the gym and when she saw all those young people with their various disabilities she sort of froze on the spot and said she wanted to leave and stay in the car. I realized that she, with her brace, may have thought of herself as being disabled like all the other young people with severe disabilities in that gym and simply 'freaked out'. I obviously made the mistake of not realizing the traumatic effect this brace had on her. Sometimes fathers don't use their head!

During Patricia's final years of high school she was slowly weaned off of this brace and became quite a skilled diver on the school team. She became their number two ranked diver and participated successfully in the full season of diving events. When prom time came around she was given permission to attend without her brace until the magic hour of 10:00 PM. At that point she carried a large pillowcase containing her brace to the women's room and strapped it on for the remainder of the evening. When her doctor announced that the brace would no longer be needed and her spine had been stabilized, I made the suggestion that we hang this brace on the wall and use it as a flower pot. I was harshly and rudely voted down and if I remember correctly that ugly brace quickly found its way to the dump never to be seen again. Another one of my good ideas that bit the dust!

In 1970 I bought a brand new Glastron speedboat with that fancy open bow that slanted down toward the water. This was one sharp looking boat. I picked up a used 75-horse motor because I couldn't afford both a new boat and new motor. I proudly used this boat to give rides to Toodie's family at one of those large Jeanson get-to-gethers at our home. For the last ride that afternoon I took all 12 kids and one adult for a ride. With 14 of us in the boat I simply could not plain off (level the boat to attain speed). I decided to head back to the dock and drop some of the kids off. In so doing, I told them all to get up in the open bow, for more weight, and I gunned the motor. I still couldn't plain off. As I approached the dock I cut the motor from full speed to zero. The next thing I knew the boat became a submarine. The excess weight in front made us dive under water when I cut my speed. What a mess… kids clinging to us two adults and the boat basically hanging under water. Fortunately we were not over our heads and folks came from the beach to drag us in to shore. I should have been put in jail. There were just two life preservers for 14 people in an overloaded boat. I still break out in a sweat when I think of that event! Apparently there are a few of us who know the rules of the lake but are just too dumb to follow them. A good friend told me it happened because I think left-handed…I don't know what he meant by that.

I especially recall one party we held for Tom the evening before he left for school in England. He was offered a once in a lifetime opportunity to attend his junior year of college at Anika Castle in North Umberland, England. Arrangements were made through St. Cloud State College where Tom was attending school. Unfortunately he broke his arm playing in a game of Rugby a week before he was to leave. With his arm still in a cast we decided to host this going away party. It was a great party until his uninvited home town girl friend showed up and added considerable excitement to the evening. Apparently Tom had invited his girl friend from St. Cloud to the party and the word got out. I can still see this local gal storming through the front door, rushing down the stairs to the party and all hell broke loose. She called Tom a few names I hesitate to put in print. After she had her say she stormed up the stairs with tears streaming down her face. Casey was following her up the stairs mad as hell because he felt she had spoiled Tom's going away party. Tom came upstairs shortly after with a smug smile on his face and said, "We're having a great time Dad!"

He left for England the next day and a week later took his cast off, against doctor's orders, and began playing rugby again. Like I said, we had some great parties at our home on Prior Lake!

Our home turned out to be a great location for family gatherings, cookouts and social events. Each year we would celebrate Toodie's father's birthday with the entire Jeanson clan attending. My folks celebrated their 50th Anniversary with the entire Schultz family present. Parties with my work friends, baseball team members and local friends and family were common events. When you live on the lake you seem to have most of the events and parties at your home. Toodie never complained but I know it got to be a chore for her after a while. Many of our friends with lake homes head north most weekends in the summer but for those of us who live on local lakes, you stay home most of the time. With the kids gone and the chores ever present I must admit that lake living was beginning to lose its excitement. My nomadic juices were again beginning to flow.

It was in our Martinson Island home that our children grew up, attended school and graduated, made many friends, played sports, dated, had jobs, learned to drive and made their move into the world. Tom eventually went off to St. Cloud State College, Patty to River Falls and Montana State College and Casey joined the Navy. Both Patty and Casey were married while residing on Martinson Island as well. Lake living offered many wonderful memories and obviously appealed to our family.

Living Rustic Style

In the mid 1980s after 18 years on the lake and with our children out of the nest, both Toodie and I came to the decision that it was time for someone else to take the dock in and out, to clean the beach and to buy swimming suits and boats. We also felt circling the lake in our pontoon boat was beginning to lose its luster and not offering the thrill it once did. One day I was talking to Rollie Haugh, a good friend and local realtor. I told Rollie we were considering a move to the country and if he came across a nice piece of rural land to give me a call. A few weeks later he stopped by and said, "Vern, Get in the car...there's something I want you to see. I got a piece of land right up your alley!"

He drove me to what had been the Wangerin farm just 4 miles south of Prior Lake and just north of Fish Lake. He explained that this was an 80-acre farm that had been divided into 8 ten-acre parcels and was going on the sale market in two days. I was really impressed with this property and right on the spot, without Toodie's approval, picked out two ten-acre parcels to buy. I held my breath when I returned home and shared this information with Toodie. We immediately visited the land and she suggested that we purchase a third ten-acre parcel as well. Wow, we had just purchased 30 acres in the country and were on our way to be farmers. How's that for a couple of city slickers who were cash poor?

The money needed to purchase this land would have to come from the sale of our home so we decided to purchase this land on a Contract for Deed. If I remember right I think we paid one dollar toward the Principal each month. Our tax accountant advised us to claim 12 dependents so we would have enough cash to make our monthly contract payments. I said that was fine but I didn't have 12 dependents...that I knew of. She said this was perfectly legal to do. We struggled making that $600 monthly payment for about a year then took a sigh of relief when our home on Prior Lake was sold. With over $200,000 in our pocket after this sale, I felt like a millionaire. We paid off the land and on a temporary basis moved into the Tower Apartments in Prior Lake (another move).

Sharon Lund, a co-worker with the St. Paul Schools, and I often talked about saving money by building a house without a contractor. The idea kind of scared me but I really wanted to do it. Finally one day while talking about this topic for the umpteenth time, Sharon said, "Vern, do it!" I said, "OK, I'm gonna do it!" I made an appointment with my boss and asked approval for a three month leave of absence. My time had come!

I had always dreamed of building one of those nifty log homes that were featured in the log home magazines and displayed at the local Home Shows. A log home seemed to offer a feeling of warmth and hominess that most houses lacked. While living on Prior Lake, my son Casey had actually built a beautiful log home on a ten acre parcel just a mile north of the land we purchased. He had the huge fireplace, vaulted ceilings and large log front porch. His home looked like a picture right out of the log home magazine. The Hiawatha Log Home Company in Northern Michigan was so impressed with his home they asked if he would like to be their representative in the Minnesota area. Casey asked if I would work with him on this project. I agreed and we immediately decided to set up a display at the St. Paul Home Show. We obtained about thirty log home prospects via the Home Show and followed up with a Log Home Seminar in Prior Lake using Casey's home as our model. I operated as the business manager of this fledging new business with Casey serving as the designer and builder. This business came to an abrupt end however, when Casey was involved in a serious trucking accident that left him with a back injury. This injury made it impossible for him to do the lifting and heavy work involved in construction activities. We had no choice but to dissolve the business. This was unfortunate because a number of prospects contacted us in the months following wanting to build their dream log home. Sometimes our dreams turn out to be nightmares!

When Toodie and I made the decision to build, I spent months working on a home design that would include all the features we considered essential for our dream home. We wanted it to be barrier free with an open floor plan, beamed ceilings, lots of windows and, of course, log construction. We agreed on everything but the 'log construction'. Toodie felt that building with logs would limit the ability to decorate, result in too dark an interior, and frankly logs were just too rustic for her. We faced a real dilemma because I was personally committed to a log home. At the time we were drawing up our dream house plan we traveled to Washington State to vacation at our daughter's home. As we entered Tacoma, on highway 5, I saw a series of model homes advertised as cedar, post and beam vacation homes. It attracted my eye and two days later I visited these models. They turned out to be 'Lindahl Company' homes that contained nearly all the features we wanted to include in our home plan. The difference, of course, was their use of beautiful Cedar wood instead of logs. The light bulb went on. We would simply substitute the Lindahl Cedar wood in place of logs. Wow, we didn't need that divorce after all!

We shared our plan ideas with the Lindahl Company and they proceeded to draw up the final building plan along with 61 pages of construction directions. In early April a large eighteen-wheeler truck arrived at the driveway to our new home site containing the cedar, posts and beams, plus all the other building materials included in our Lindahl building package. At that point we were faced with an unforeseen problem. We had our long eighth of a mile driveway constructed the previous fall and it had hardly been packed down or driven on. The thaw had set in by April and the driveway was soft even to walk on. The truck driver decided to back down the driveway so he could make a quick exit after unloading without turning around. After about 20 feet, the wheels began to sink in and the driver immediately stopped and returned to the hard surface of County Rd. 10. He questioned if he could make it to the pole barn where we would be doing the unloading. We finally agreed that the best solution for him would be to back up farther on County Rd. 10, build up speed and head directly down the driveway going at full speed. It would destroy the driveway but the truck had to be unloaded. Down County Road 10 he came, turning sharply into the driveway, and went to full power. Throwing dirt in all directions he proceeded to make it to solid ground where the driveway ended. He detached the trailer and said he would be back for the trailer next week. He put the gas pedal to the floor and again with dirt flying made it to county road 10 and he was gone. We had accomplished the task but the driveway was in shambles and the loaded truck trailer ended up 60 feet away from the pole barn. It was Easter weekend but we wouldn't be looking for Easter eggs...we had a major task facing us. It would be up to Casey, Tom and me to unload the contents of the trailer into the pole barn. I thought it would be easy but wow, was I wrong!

Tom and Casey hauling Lindahl products from the 18 wheeler to pole barn.

On Monday the driver returned to pick up his trailer. Actually he parked on County Road 10 and walked up the driveway to test if it was solid enough for his truck. He just shook his head and was gone. He was back on Friday and said he just had to get that trailer on the road and using a few unprintable words took off again. When he returned the following Monday he said if that trailer stayed another day he would have to charge us for its use. My response was very simple and to the point. I said, "I want that trailer off of my property right now or I was going to charge the trucking company for illegal storage. Get it out of here!" I figured two can play that game. He gave me a dirty look and was gone. A week later he made it up the driveway, hooked on the trailer without a word and took off never to be seen again. Frankly, I didn't give a hoot if the empty trailer sat there till winter.

When the house was finally completed, there was unanimous agreement that the most difficult task of all over that six month period was unloading those building products from the 18-wheeler and transferring them to the Pole Barn. It was that 60 feet of mud from the Trailer to the barn, trying to keep all the building products clean, that turned out to be the challenge of the century. In desperation, we put straw on the ground to cover the mud and converted a snowmobile trailer to a moving van. Actually, the straw did little good. With the three of us pushing and pulling that trailer over and over again through that muck, we accomplished the task of moving all those heavy building products to the barn. It was a three-day ordeal that I never want to go through again. What a challenging beginning to an exciting building project. Fortunately neither one of my sons quit on the job. They apparently wanted to remain in my will.

Constructing this home was considerably different from my other house building projects. We had no contractor and just 61 pages of complicated building instructions to guide our way. I guess I was the acting contractor with Tom and Casey serving as builders. Bill Miller, a friend of Tom's and a cabinetmaker by trade, was hired to serve as the project manager (master-mind). He was the glue that held this project together and knew all the tricks of building a complicated post and beam house with lots of angles and twists. Thank the Lord, I didn't know before hand what I had gotten myself into. Those 61 pages of instructions were absolute Greek to me. Bill Miller was our savior…he understood every page.

I still remember the very first day we were to go into action. The basement block was laid and Monday morning at 8:00 AM sharp, we were scheduled to put the floor joists down. Everyone showed up bright and early with the exception of our leader, Bill Miller. He was going through a difficult divorce at the time and I was worried that something might have happened. Finally after two hours of total anxiety and depression, here comes Bill down the driveway at 10:00 ready for work. I said nothing to him about his tardiness but learned later that both he and Tom attended a party the evening before and might have had just a wee too much to drink. Tom never mentioned a word to me about the party. Come to think of it, Tom looked a little beady eyed that morning as well.

Bill Miller turned out to be an unusually hard worker and a perfect project manager. He was fussy about the work we did and didn't hesitate to raise a little hell if our work wasn't to his liking. After working on this house for a month and a half, seven days a week, and making excellent progress, Bill failed to show up for two days straight. I got pretty nervous about this and Casey was more upset then me. Tom, on the other hand, asked me how many days Bill had worked without a day off. I told him a month and a half. Tom said, "Dad, don't you think after six weeks, he deserves at least one day away from this job?" Tom was absolutely right of course, but I added that it sure would have been nice if he had said something to us. I figured that maybe a seminar on 'communication' might be in order.

Bill's habit of taking days off without notice occurred every once in a while and I just went along with it. I knew full well that without Bill we were dead in the water. I learned that these infrequent absences from the job always had something to do with Bill's love of hunting. He either was baiting for bear up north, or hunting somewhere. In fact any time a deer showed up in our back pasture, construction came to an abrupt halt. Bill would grab his bow and arrows and go for the kill…unfortunately or fortunately (depending how you look at it) the deer were always too elusive for him. I was pleased that these deer sightings didn't occur often. Bill was a real craftsman and didn't hesitate to 'harass' the owner (that's me) when I screwed up a saw cut or overstuffed insulation into a corner. I loved every bit of guff he gave out because that meant he wanted a quality built house… and you better believe that's what I wanted!

Vern and Bill Miller on lunch break during construction of the home.

Six months after we pounded the first nail, the job was finished. I had lost 30 pounds and was in the best shape of my life. According to the Lindahl construction plan, we built a running header throughout the entire house not just over the windows and doors. Bill called this overkill but said it would take a 200-mile an hour tornado to move this house. I love that kind of comment. I will always be eternally grateful to Bill Miller, Tom and Casey for the work they did. I also called upon my two nephews, Ed and Ray Miller to give us a hand when we were near completion. What a thrill it was for me to be a member of this building crew that constructed the home of my dreams. It had to be one of the real highlights of my life. I can't forget to give credit to Toodie for putting up with six months of widowhood, and also for the work she put into decorating, furnishing and adding those final touches. Of course, I can't neglect Sharon Lund's input when she prodded me with, "Vern, do it" and, we did it!

Two years after our move from Prior Lake to the Tower Apartments, we packed up our belongings again, and moved to 'Cedar Hills Farm.' To borrow a cup of sugar from a neighbor would require driving at least a half a mile to the farms of Willy Brandt or Jerry Roach. There were those who felt Psychiatric help should accompany this move. The word was out that anyone undertaking a task like this had to be crazy and in need of intensive therapy. Actually those 'happy pills' provided by Jack Andrews, the local druggist, worked just fine. Its fun to follow your dreams... everyone should do it.

I'll have to be honest, this decision to build my own home offered more challenges than any previous move we made in the past. Those 10-hour days, 7-day weeks and losing 30 pounds put me in shape to consider renewing my baseball career. I felt that maybe the Twins could use another left handed pitcher. I was in great shape, if they would have only contacted me! There were thousands of rocks and boulders on our land and with Casey's help, along with his bobcat, we used almost every one of them to build a series of landscaping walls that would never end. I asked him if we had used all the rocks and boulders from our land and he said, "Dad, there are twice as many rocks just an inch or two under the ground". Every time I cut the grass I find one or two new rocks popping up. I just ignore them because the bobcat is long gone.

The whole process of planning and constructing this home turned out to be one of the most enjoyable projects of my lifetime. It was even more exciting than our move to Martinson Island 20 years previously. (Toodie will tell you how she feels about this when she writes her memoirs). Maybe when you get older one appreciates the peace and quiet of rural living more than the excitement of the city. At any event, the timing of this move was perfect and has allowed me the opportunity to play farmer and landscaper, something I never dreamed of doing in my early years. I remember Casey as the one in our family who always seemed to have that desire for the rural farming life. His move to the country with his horses and beautiful log home really intrigued me and probably served as the stimulus for my wanting to change my lifestyle as well. I liked the life style he was living which was sort of back to our roots. I do know that participating in the construction of his log home really whet my appetite to build my own log home. To be perfectly honest, I'll credit Casey with stimulating my appetite to go rural and take the plunge. The water was perfect and I found out I loved this swimming hole.

Becoming A Cattle Baron

Now that I find myself living on a 30 acre farm, I certainly want to get that Scott County agriculture tax break. This would require me to either raise some cash crops or have farm animals. With the help of Casey, I decided to buy some young calves and become a part time cattle rancher. I purchased 3 heifers and 2 bull calves that had to be fed a special milk supplement twice a day. This required me to go downstairs to the laundry tub every morning and evening and mix and warm up this special calf formula and head to the barn to personally feed each animal. Believe me, it wasn't a whole lot of fun in the winter. It was fortunate that I already had a pole barn and a corral and was in the process of fencing in my entire 30 acres. I was now fully qualified to start wearing those farmer bib overalls just like my neighbors. One evening I proudly showed off the new cattle to Jerry Roach, our neighbor farmer. He said that the 4 heifers and 1 bull calf looked fine. Whoops, apparently I had made a mistake in my purchase. I would have sworn I had 3 heifers and 2 bull calves. I guess I missed step one; learning the difference between a heifer and a bull calf.

Jerry asked me how I planned to keep the pole barn clean over the winter. I told him I had a new pitchfork and wasn't afraid to use it. He just smiled. You would think that a good neighbor would have told me that manure freezes in the winter and hardens like a rock. In September I could look down at those young cattle standing on the pole barn floor. By March, I had to look up at these same cattle standing on about 2 feet of frozen manure. I worried they might step right over the barn fence. I'm sure Jerry went home that day, doubling over in laughter, knowing the outcome of my folly.

I'll never forget the day Casey said it was time to castrate the bull calves. He had bought a tool with a special rubber band for this operation. My job was to wrestle the bull calf to the ground and he would play doctor. I remember grabbing the calf by its head and attempting to twist its body to the ground just like they do in the rodeos. I ended up rolling over and over in the manure and finally accomplishing this task. Casey had his tool ready and began the process. That's when he said those fateful words, "Dad, let her up!" Apparently heifers don't need to be castrated. Like I said, raising cattle was truly a learning experience. It would have been a lot easier to just call the veterinarian. I bet he'd know the difference between a bull calf and heifer!

Raising cattle required me to fence in my entire 30 acre Cedar Hills Farm property. I ordered wooden posts from Fleetfarm and purchased my 16 ft. wood fencing boards from Walden Lumber in Shakopee. It's impossible to even estimate the number of trips I made to these two facilities. It was a real feat carrying those 16 ft. Boards in the 8 ft. box of my Ford pickup truck. I used hundreds of posts and an unbelievable number of wood boards to complete this task. I not only fenced in the outer perimeter of my property but also fenced in a corral and a middle holding pasture. My neighbors probably thought I was crazy because I did it entirely by myself. If that wasn't enough to do, I had to electrify the fence, put in a permanent Ritchie water system for the cattle, repair some broken drainage tile and buy and install a dozen or so gates. Believe me, it was a never ending task but being of sound German heritage, I did it! Father Rick Banker, Pastor of St. Michael's Church, rented our lower level apartment about the time I began building this fence. Eleven years later when he moved out, I put down my paint brush while painting the fence and waved a farewell. His comment was, "You were building this fence when I moved in and now eleven years later you're still building it… When will it be finished?" My answer unfortunately was," Never…every year there are repairs and more painting." What the heck…it keeps me busy and it beats chasing cows down county road 10!

Building A Program

When I joined the St. Paul School System in 1964 I was employed as Supervisor of this brand new School Vocational Services Program. My first task was to hire staff, prepare a plan of action to identify those Senior High students with disabilities, and to set up a program to prepare these special students for the working world. I immediately selected John Rein as a working partner and in the next three years added John Hislop, Don Jobe, Don McKoskey, Gus Bjorklund and Bernie Daily to our rehabilitation staff. These fellows were excellent teachers, and three of them were also successful coaches. In the mid 1960's there were no tests or screening committees required to select staff. I personally handpicked each individual and, believe me, my judgment was right on target. After some specialized training in Vocational counseling techniques, program guidelines, agency regulations, and varied service options they turned out to be absolutely top performers. The 18 years we worked together were probably the most enjoyable and satisfying years of my working career. I found that hiring top staff is the secret to making the program supervisor look good...an important step in keeping my job!

A few years later everything changed in District personal practices. The hiring process in the schools became much more formal and far less personalized. By 1970 all vacant or new positions had to be posted for a set number of days. A selection committee held interviews with predetermined questions asked of each applicant. This committee would then make the recommendation for employment. It's very questionable whether these five people would have ever made it through this formal process. I knew the kind of person needed to accomplish this task and there was no guarantee that a random committee would have seen it my way. A few years later came 'affirmative action' requiring that a certain percentage of women and minorities be employed. Don't read me wrong, I'm not saying that affirmative action or a more formalized employment system is bad. These changes however, would most likely have resulted in a different selection of staff for our program. I hired the five people I knew would do the job and they did just that. Thank God for the good old days when life was simple. My timing for hiring staff was perfect...was I lucky!

Actually Affirmative Action was very helpful to our Unit in placing a number of qualified young people with disabilities into jobs. Without Affirmative Action legislation this would not have been possible. It did backfire for me personally. In the mid 1970's I had applied for the Assistant Commissioner of Education job vacancy within the State Department of Education. The Commissioner called me into his office after interviewing was completed. He told me that I was the top person on the list and his selection for the job, but the Governor decided it was time for a female to get a management job in the State system. The woman they appointed lasted just one year. I often wonder if I had been selected for the job what my future would have been. Who knows, maybe in a year or two I could have found myself out on the street looking for another job. It was probably to my benefit that I remained in St. Paul because I did like my job and a few years later I retired and preserved my school pension. I must admit however, that I often wonder how I would have performed in that top State Administrative job. I guess it doesn't hurt to wonder!

It was necessary for the School District to find a suitable location to house our program as we began to expand. All available school facilities were filled to capacity so, to our surprise, we were moved into rented space in the classy Commodore Hotel just a few blocks off of historic Summit Avenue. We absolutely loved this location with its distinguished appearance, fancy restaurant and even classier bar just down the hall. Believe me, we were envied by District staff housed in a number of far less romantic settings. All good things come to an end however, and after a few years of luxury we were relocated into the newly constructed school administration building. Although brand new, this building lacked the ambiance and romantic character of the Commodore Hotel. Worst of all, now we were back under the eye of all those school district bosses.

In the mid 1980's a number of changes occurred both within the State Vocational Rehabilitation program and the St. Paul School District that resulted in the eventual phasing out of our School Rehabilitation Program. Initially this program didn't cost the school district a dime with total finances coming from Federal and State sources. In time, as program costs increased, local school districts were being asked to contribute funds from their regular budget for the program. Many local Districts balked at this added financial burden resulting in many of the VAC programs being drastically reduced or dropped. In the 1980's our St. Paul program also bit the dust with staff cut to one Vocational Rehabilitation Counselor and eventually the program was totally discontinued. I guess in time all good things come to an end.

I continued my responsibility of supervising all remaining vocational programs for handicapped students in the St. Paul District even after the School Vocational Services Program was discontinued. In addition to these duties, Charles Hagen Director of Special Education, asked me to take over responsibility for implementing the new Federal legislation titled, 'Education for All Handicapped Children.' This became a major administrative task requiring many changes and adaptations in the service delivery system for children and youth with disabilities. It was the beginning of the "Individualized Education Planning" approach in special education. If I thought implementing the Vocational Rehabilitation Services system within the District was a challenge, then believe me, implementation of this legislation was an even greater challenge. I told Chuck Hagen to," Bring it on!" I was ready for a new battle.

As I look back on those 29 years in St. Paul I find it difficult sorting out all that occurred. I just know they were good years that I wouldn't change for anything. What I do remember about those years are the people, particularly those amazing clients we served who proved over and over again that disability does not have to be a barrier to success. I learned that it's seldom a person's disability that becomes the major challenge, it's the attitude that the individual has toward their disability that determines success or failure. I could write a separate book describing how Dan Fitzpatrick, Charlie VanHuevlin, Joanne Ryan, John Schlatzein, Helen Crawford, Lorraine Zeimer, Dick Ducharme and hundreds of others managed to overcome amazing obstacles to become successful working and productive citizens in our society. Their success has helped me see life from a very positive and optimistic viewpoint. These folks really made what some might term 'a problem' into an 'opportunity! On more than one occasion my children have said to me, "Dad, you're an optimist about everything!" I consider that a compliment. My optimism originates from those people I've known and worked with over the years proving to me that anything is possible…even when deep down, I wasn't sure myself!

Another Shot At Coaching

In the mid-1970's the Prior Lake Legion Baseball Team needed a manager and nobody wanted the job. Tom Mee, who was Public Relations Director for the Minnesota Twins and I both had sons eager to play Legion ball. When no other manager came forward we agreed to serve as co-managers. Both of us had busy schedules so we figured that at least one of us would always be available for practices and games. Our major responsibility was to field a team with nine players, see that the equipment was in the dugout, secure and pay the umpires, determine the lineup, decide who would pitch and when to give the 'take' sign. Frankly there was little time for us to teach the skills and science of the game. A number of the players had jobs so it wasn't always easy to come up with nine players. We fortunately had some excellent core players who never missed a practice or game. Cam Killebrew (Harmon Killebrew's son), Tom Mee's three sons and my boys (Tom and Casey) were always present. They better be!

I remember one game when only eight players showed up. Tom and I hustled over to the softball field looking for a ninth player. One team member had decided to play softball that evening and it took us five minutes to sell him on the idea that baseball was really a much more macho game then softball. We must have been convincing because he ended up playing right field for us filling that required ninth position. Would you believe that he was the player who hit a triple in the ninth inning that scored the winning run? That's when Tom and I realized that every successful coach apparently also has to be a good salesman.

Both Tom Mee and I had a good time and a fairly successful season. We both realized that we did little coaching but lots of managing. It might have been more fun if we would have had more time to coach.

After that season I had far greater respect for all the Harry Bealke's and Dick Vanasek's who gave their time, patience and skills to managing town ball and Independent teams throughout the State. It's not an easy task to manage a team made up of players who are volunteering their time to play on a team, in contrast to coaching a high school, college or semi-professional team where the coach rules the roost. A psychology major should be a requirement for these Independent league coaches!

Getting Serious About Officiating

I looked forward to a career as a coach but what you want isn't always what you get. If my coaching tenure was to be short lived, at least I could enjoy the excitement of the game by officiating football and basketball. It also was a way to make a few extra bucks to supplement my limited income. Someone asked why I didn't become a baseball umpire, after all that was the sport I was most acquainted with. Actually there were two reasons for this, 1). I always figured that summer was the best time to be with my family rather than spending two or three additional nights of the week away from home, and 2.) Baseball games can last an hour and a half to three or four hours. You never know when you're going to get home. Seldom does a football or basketball game go over two hours. Toodie put up with me being gone all those fall and winter weekends but I'm not so sure she would have gone along with my absence during the summer as well. I wasn't going to take a chance to find out and anyway divorces are spendy!

There was a certain excitement about putting on those football and basketball shoes, meeting the coaches, checking the scoring table and flipping the coin. A new world began each time you started game action with a jump ball or blew the whistle signaling the kick-off. From that moment on, any problems or issues in your life or work were erased from your mind and you became totally absorbed in the drama of the contest. The excitement of the crowd, the screaming and booing, and the second-guessing by the coaches all added to the aura of the game. Following the game was that relaxing shower, a beer with your partner(s), a rehash of those tough calls, deciding where you will meet for the next game, and then home with the check. If you had problems in your life, you filed them away for those two hours of action, and those problems never seemed so serious after that shower. Al Pieper, one of my favorite officiating partners once told me, "Vern, by officiating together, I helped get you through your change of life!" He was probably right. We shared a lot of issues driving to and from those ball games and his advice didn't cost me a dime. Who needs a licensed therapist when you've got an understanding referee partner?

I officiated hundred's of games with many different partners over some 37 years. Many of the experiences that stick in my mind were humorous, scary, unnerving and a few games were downright awesome. I'd like to share just a few incidents that seem to stand out in my mind and still leave me with a chuckle today.

Keep the Game Moving -There was a football game we officiated at St. Paul Park with the home team winning by a score of 20 – 0. Everyone commented on how smooth and quick this game went. On the ride home we learned that our Field Judge, the timekeeper, had been keeping 8-minute quarters on the clock rather than the prescribed 12 minutes. We figured the Field Judge either had a date that evening and was running late, or thought he was keeping time for a basketball game. Everyone seemed happy so we just kept that little secret to ourselves.

By the Skin of Our Teeth - Driving non-stop to Houghton, Michigan, to officiate a college football game can be a long tough ride any way you look at it. Houghton is located at the very tip of the upper Michigan peninsula and is home to Michigan Technical College, a member of the Northern Collegiate Athletic Conference. For years, our football officiating schedule required at least one visit to Houghton each fall. This visit was not high on our priority list.

To arrive at Michigan Tech in time for their Saturday 1:00 P.M. football game, required our officiating team to leave Saint Paul around midnight and drive all night and well into the morning. What made this ride especially difficult was that each team member also worked a Friday night football game, which preceded that long ride to Houghton. The opportunity to take a nap or sleep before making this trip was impossible. The ever-present possibility of fog drifting off Lake Superior made this drive an even more treacherous experience. With a little luck, a pit stop or two, and minimal fog, we would generally arrive at Houghton in time for a quick lunch and a change of uniforms; little time for much else. This was not exactly the kind of weekend you look forward to but when you need that 50 dollar paycheck you do it.

When I came up with the unique idea of flying to Houghton, instead of driving, you can well understand why out officiating team all jumped on the bandwagon. I said," Don't worry about the arrangements. "I'll take care of everything." My neighbor across the street, Wayne Konga, had a friend with access to a plane with plenty of room to carry our four-man officiating team plus gear. The pilot, being an avid football fan and anxious to take this trip, offered us an affordable fare – actually less than it would have cost us to drive. We were delighted with this wonderful opportunity and agreed to go ahead under one condition. A call would first be made to the weather bureau late Friday evening to guarantee that weather conditions were totally satisfactory. If good weather wasn't an absolute certainty we would follow our usual plan of driving. Michigan Tech had warned officials that fog was always a possibility in the fall of the year.

After officiating our Friday evening football games, the team members met in Saint Paul and a call was made to the weather bureau at 11:30 P.M. The Saturday morning forecast between Minneapolis and Houghton was for a clear and sunny day. With this guarantee of good weather we all went home for a good night's sleep. At 6:00 A.M. with satchels in hand, we met at the Crystal, Minnesota airport to travel "first class" to Michigan Tech; just like the pros. As we waited to board our plane, the pilot informed us of just one slight change in plans. The plane originally scheduled to carry our entire team was not available. He said, "Don't worry, I've solved the problem." He had borrowed a smaller plane that would hold two members of our team. Another pilot friend with a smaller plane had agreed to fly the remaining two-team members to our Houghton destination at no additional cost. This change sounded good to us. With Billy Hafner (Umpire) and John Mauer (Head Linesman) in one plane and Jim Griffin (Referee) and me (Field Judge) in the other, we headed down the runway ready to fly with the birds. Michigan Tech here we come! As we passed over Saint Paul, both pilots were having a great time talking to each other on the radio and pointing out various sights on the ground. We were all having a ball and I was wondering why we hadn't traveled by air before.

Just about the time we flew over the St. Croix River, the Minnesota/Wisconsin border, we noticed our first cloud in the sky. I remember it looked like a puff of smoke. Within a few minutes there were quite a few larger clouds, and before we knew it, that blue sky had totally disappeared. It might have been clouds we observed, but to be truthful it looked more like fog surrounding the plane. About this time the two happy-go-lucky pilots stopped communicating with each other and, in fact, the other plane seemed to have disappeared. We also noticed that our pilot was no longer in his jovial, happy mood and had little to say. We did observe, however, that he was spending an increasing amount of time peering down at the ground. As we continued to fly over Wisconsin toward out destination, I made two significant observations. Believe me, neither one added to my comfort level. First off, the thickening fog was making visibility very difficult and gave the impression that our plane was being forced toward the ground. It also appeared that the treetops were growing in size and slowly creeping up toward the plane's under-carriage. And second, I realized that the pilot wasn't sightseeing out the window. He was frantically looking for roads, railroad tracks, water towers or any other landmarks that would guide his route. This is when I noticed a few beads of sweat on Jim Griffin's brow.

I remember asking the pilot at this point whether he was trained or experienced in instrument flying and the answer was, "Not really, but I hope to be in a couple of years!" With that answer I knew we were in real trouble, and that long car ride to Houghton was looking better by the second. About this time I also had a few choice thoughts about our weather bureau that, frankly, can't be printed. In fact, at this point in our flight, I would gladly have traded my entire referee check to have both feet planted firmly on the ground. The pilot must have been reading my mind because at that exact moment he suggested we land at the nearest airport and give the fog a chance to blow over. He also mentioned something about an aviation regulation that required aircraft not to fly under 1,000 feet and we were now below 800 feet and dropping. You can believe he didn't get any argument from his two passengers!

Following the railroad tracks must have paid off because a small town water tower showed up on the horizon, along with lights from the local airport. Down we went and the fog came right down with us. I can't tell you what a relief it was to be standing on solid ground. As nice as it was to feel safe again, we were still faced with the serious dilemma of just how we were going to get to Houghton. It was 10:00 A.M. and here we sat fogged in at some godforsaken airport in the middle of Wisconsin. Our contract required us to be flipping the coin on the fifty-yard line in two hours at a football field well over fifty miles away. So close... and yet so far!

Our tension increased with each passing minute the plane was grounded. The Houghton Athletic Director did warn us about "possible fog." Our excuse that the Weather Bureau provided a forecast of great weather simply wasn't good enough. It was our responsibility to be there. After about 45 minutes on the ground with the prospect of staying there indefinitely, Jim Griffin told the pilot in no uncertain terms that we had to be on that football field by 1:00 PM no matter what was in those $#@#$% airline regulations, "So let's take off." I remember saying to the pilot, "But if you don't think we can make it!" I think the pilot really understood how serious our intentions were to leave that fog-infested airport when Jim told him, "If you aren't going to fly this plane then give me the keys!" Jim's little talk with the pilot must have given him renewed confidence. He said OK, and a few minutes later we were back on the runway revving up the engine ready for takeoff – and away we flew. At that moment I wish our plane had a bathroom.

I must say it was exhilarating to be flying at between 600 to 700 feet above the ground able to literally reach out and touch the tops of those beautiful northern evergreens. That final fifty-mile leg of our trip offered us a wonderful view of the forests of Northern Michigan, but sightseeing was the farthest thing from our mind. The pilot decided to use the shoreline of Lake Superior as our guiding route to Houghton, instead of following the more traditional railroad tracks or water towers. His plan must have worked, or we were just lucky, because a little after 12:00 noon we finally spotted Houghton and it's airfield off in the distance. With a major sigh of relief, we placed our feet firmly on the ground at 12:10 PM. Once we had safely landed in Houghton, our attention immediately turned to the whereabouts of the other small plane carrying John Mauer and Billy Hafner. Our concern was short-lived however, as their plane came into sight and landed within five minutes of our arrival. The look in the eyes of these two fellows as they departed their plane clearly expressed the same anxieties and fears that we had experienced in our flight. The big question was whether they would even be willing to fly back to the Twin Cities when the game was over. We would deal with that issue after the game. Actually I wasn't sure I wanted to fly back!

John and Billy later informed us that their plane had remained in the air the entire morning since leaving the Crystal Airport, and yet, they arrived in Houghton only five minutes after our arrival. How our plane could have been grounded by fog for over forty-five minutes and still arrive in Houghton five minutes before they did is a complete mystery to this day. The only plausible explanation is that they went off course, and it took that length of time to get back on target, or who knows, they could have been sightseeing.

Jim Griffin had called the Michigan Tech. Athletic Director during the 45 minutes we were grounded by fog, informing him or our dilemma and asked to have a car waiting for us at the airport. He told him not to worry because we would be there on time. To be honest, I don't think the Athletic Director believed Jim. Fortunately the car was waiting for us at the airport. We changed into our uniforms while on route and walked onto the field at 12:50 P.M. The coin flip took place, and the game began right on schedule at 1:00 P.M. sharp. The game itself turned out to be uneventful, and the fans in attendance were totally unaware of the circumstances that could have canceled that Saturday afternoon football game. I'm not sure how the Athletic Director felt about this fiasco.

By the way, we did agree to return to the Twin Cities in the same planes that brought us to Houghton, but what a contrast. The sky was peaceful, lit up by a full moon and millions of stars that seemed close enough to touch. It was impossible to believe that just a few hours earlier, these skies were so frightening to us and had threatened our very lives. There is a postscript to this story. The following week our officiating team had planned to fly to Bemidji, Minnesota to officiate the Bemidji State College football game. Jim Griffin suggested that maybe it would be more fun to drive. The entire crew agreed and the flight was canceled without further discussion. Driving to games just seemed to be a more relaxing way to travel after that Houghton trip!

The College officiating team. Left to right;
Jim Griffin, VernSchultz, Billy Hafner, John Mauer.

A Fast Get-Away – Jim Griffin and I pulled into Waseca, Minnesota one blustery winter evening to officiate their local high school basketball game. Jim had to be back in St. Paul by 11:30 that evening to work the midnight shift at the police department. He was assigned to a 'plant' detail so he was in his civilian clothes. A 'plant' is where you sit in a store or filling station when you have reason to expect a burglary to occur. The 'B' game went smooth as silk but the "A" game was another story. The lead changed back and forth throughout the game, and in the final second the visiting team made a desperate shot from the corner that (unbelievably) went into the basket to win the game by one point. The Waseca coach, team and fans claimed the shot occurred after the buzzer, but we said, "Absolutely not. That shot was good." We fought our way through an angry crowd and down to the dressing room. Wouldn't you know, our lockers were right next to the home team. Believe me, this was one unhappy team and you could hear and feel their displeasure with us. The room was electric! We finished our shower and got dressed in a hurry. I hope you can understand why.

When Jim, who was one of Minnesota's first black officials, goes on a police 'plant' assignment, he always wears a gun in a shoulder holster. After he put his shirt on, he reached into his locker and grabbed his gun and shoulder holster, threw the holster belt over his shoulder with gusto and then buckled it firmly across his chest. When he did this, the room became absolutely silent and every kid present was open mouthed, staring at Jim in shock. We put our coats on and left. We laughed half way home, trying to guess what they must have thought. This was probably their very first personal encounter with a Black person and then for him to be carrying this gun! You can just imagine what was going through their minds. I just loved to work with Jim Griffin – my protector.

Jim and I worked many games together both in basketball and football. He was an outstanding official and a close personal friend. Later in the 1980's, he was appointed the first black Chief of Police in St. Paul's history. I may not have been the best official in the world but I was really good at picking outstanding partners.

I Don't believe It Happened - I've had some unusual experiences during my years of officiating, but this one tops the list. It was a cold rainy Saturday afternoon at St. Cloud State for their football game with Moorhead State College. A number of the fans present had headed for the warmth of their cars with only a few loyal fans remaining huddled under umbrellas. It was late in the second half, and St. Cloud had a comfortable lead. St. Cloud was in its huddle when John Mauer, the Head Linesman, signaled for a time out. John left his position on the field and proceeded to talk to a fan on the running track next to the playing field. I later learned that this fan had been drinking and had begun to harass the fellow holding the box marking each down. Apparently there was some swearing and derogatory remarks being made so John decided to intercede.

This fan then proceeded to make some dishonorable, nasty remarks to John Mauer that included a remark about John's mother. The next thing we knew, John sent a hard right fist to this fan's jaw and he fell like a sack of flour. John Mauer immediately returned to the field, leaving the fan prostate on the ground, and said simply, "O.K., Let's get the game going!" What this fan didn't know is that it's not wise to offend an official who spent the early years of his life as a Golden Gloves boxing champion!

I've seen and experienced violence toward officials by fans, but I must say I'd never experienced a situation where an official was the aggressor. By the way, I don't condone this type of action and fully expected that our officiating team was in serious danger of being discharged from the League. The newspaper picture of this event in the St. Cloud Sunday paper didn't help us any. Interestingly enough, no negative actions were taken against us and we continued to work on a regular basis in this college league. I must say that this was one of the more memorable experiences of my officiating career, and it was one I certainly will never forget. In the privacy of the car going home, we all congratulated John. The fan deserved it!

Being on time – Our three man officiating team agreed to meet in the White Castle parking lot on south Robert St on Friday evening at 5:00 sharp to drive to Rochester and officiate the Rochester Marshall–Rochester Mayo football game that evening. Both teams were undefeated and this was billed as the 'Game of the Week' in their conference. One of my partners pulled into the White Castle lot at 4:45 but by 5:00 the other partner had yet to arrive. At 5:45 there were still just the two of us. What do we do? If we waited any longer we faced the possibility of arriving late for the game and if just the two of us showed up the athletic director would probably be fighting mad. Facing the ire of the athletic director seemed the better of two evils so the two of us got in my car and raced to Rochester at breakneck speed. Under normal conditions we would have been talking a blue streak on that ride but on this trip silence prevailed. We were in deep trouble and we knew it!

We arrived at the football stadium by 7:30, changed into our uniforms and met the Athletic Director on the field at 7:45 to share the fateful news that our officiating team was one shy. Our feeble explanation of why this happened was not being accepted very well by the Athletic Director when the third official, this lost soul, suddenly jogged onto the field as though nothing had gone wrong. We immediately completed the coin toss and the football was in the air at 8:00 sharp…but unfortunately the Athletic Director was still fuming and trouble was brewing.

The first half went smoothly with Marshall leading 6 to 0. The third quarter was a back and forth struggle by both teams. With three minutes remaining in the game Mayo got possession of the ball on their 35-yard line and began to drive. This drive was aided by three penalties against Marshall that apparently was unsettling to the Marshall Coach. With just 30 seconds remaining Mayo scored, kicked the extra point and went ahead 7-6. As Mayo lined up for the kick-off the Marshall Coach directed his ire at the head linesman who retaliated with a 15-yard unsportsmanlike conduct penalty. This penalty moved the kickoff to the Marshall 45 yard line. As the teams lined up for the second kickoff try, the red flag flew again against the Marshall Coach. I figured a good kick-off from the 30-yard line would probably carry the ball over the goal posts and into the parking lot. Thankfully no more penalty flags were thrown and the game ended with Mayo the winner by one point. When the game was over we made a beeline for the locker room to shower quickly and get on the road. Unfortunately we were using the same dressing room as the Marshall team.

I'm willing to take some guff from coaches and athletic directors after a game but there is a point where enough is enough. I reached that point in this 'shared' locker room. The Coach and Athletic Director's complaints focused on those terrible calls we made near the end of the fourth quarter and those unnecessary unsportsmanlike fouls against the Marshall coach. The major gripe however, was how unprofessional our officiating team was by showing up with just two officials. It didn't help any that the official who arrived late called those two final penalties against the coach. There is no question in my mind that our problems that evening stemmed primarily from our team not showing up in a timely and professional manner. I might have been more forgiving of this absent official if he had shown some remorse. His attitude appeared to be, "I got here on time… what's the problem?"

After taking heat from the coaches and Athletic Director for about 10 minutes, I finally had enough and in a fairly forceful manner told the Athletic Director how unprofessional he was in not providing a private changing facility for his game officials. My comments must have done some good because football officials, from that point on, were provided a private dressing room for all Rochester games. Something good did come out of a bad situation but the non-professional behavior by one officiating team member did set our entire team up for valid criticism. On that matter, the Athletic Director, had every right to complain. I was the Referee so all of the blame was heading in my direction…hell, I was there on time!

In any walk of life, not just officiating, success requires a professional approach to the task. You can be the finest official in the league, the best musician in the band, the greatest athlete or skilled worker on the job. If, however, you don't properly prepare for the task, act professionally, function as a team member, and abide by the rules, you're heading for trouble and unfairly bringing your team or associate members down with you. This experience in Rochester was a prime example of the importance of being a responsible team member and the need for a total commitment to the task at hand when working with others. Frankly, I erased that fellow off of my officiating schedule forever.

Those 37 years of officiating football and basketball games provided a number of valuable learning experiences with carryover value into my personal and work life. Let me share some of these learning experiences with you.

1. **Look the Part** – You may not be the best official in the world, but make sure you look and act like you are. Greet the coach and other game associates like you really know what you are doing…even if you don't. Carry out those preliminary official's duties like you've done it at least once before. Looking and acting like a Professional generally fools most of the coaches and should set the tone for a better contest. Don't do anything that will raise the coaches or fans ire before the game or it may lead to a really long afternoon or evening. For example, it's not a good idea for you and your partners to play catch with the game ball during the national anthem. Get the idea?

The Athletic Director has lots of things to worry about before a game. Show up at least an hour before game time so one item is off his worry checklist. Being late, asking if he has a spare whistle you can use, or wearing a baseball cap because you forgot your stripped officials cap is not something the Athletic Director wants to deal with. He would much rather worry about something important…like why his ticket takers are late. If you cause him any unnecessary problems, you probably won't be back next year. You can't go wrong acting like a professional whether it's in officiating, at work or in social situations. In your personal life, you don't make any points being late for a date or asking your girlfriend to pay the bill because you forgot your billfold.

2. **Keep it Moving** -When you make a tough call that raises the anger of the coach or fans, don't delay action, never try to explain your call to the coach, or look indecisive. Grab the ball and get the game going as quickly as you can. If you feel you have to explain your call to the coach, you most likely blew the call. The faster you can move on with the game that questionable call will diminish in importance. Coaches generally have short memories so those questionable calls you make later in the game will make him forget that earlier questionable call. Why waste time on one tough call when you can lump them all together at the end!

I had helped put together a summer 'Apartment Living' program for a group of severely disabled students in St. Paul. This program was located in a new fully secure apartment building and with adequate staff on hand. In the second week of the program three disabled girls in this program were raped. The culprit was a drunken father of one of the students who asked to be let into the apartment to see his son. He was arrested and sent to prison. The parents were very understanding but the dynamics of this event were shattering to the staff, district administrators and some of the other students. Some staff wanted to terminate the program, others wanted to delay the program till counseling could occur and others wanted to move ahead because this program was so beneficial.

I wasn't against the need for counseling at all, but my reaction was, "It happened, we've resolved the issue, so let's move on." You know, "Get the game going...let's remember the goal of the program." Don't delay and get all hung up on the problem (The questionable call). These kids need to be educated on how to live independently and you can't accomplish this if you stop the program. If counseling is important lets arrange for it but just like in officiating," Move on, don't take time to explain the call!" Get this program back in action!

3. **Face the Challenge** -Jerry Flathman, our Officials Association Secretary, called and asked if I was interested in officiating a Hamline University basketball game. Hamline University was one of the top basketball teams in the entire country at that time. I agreed to take the game but had butterflies all week. I questioned if I was capable of officiating that level

of basketball. As the game date came closer I became more anxious and even considered canceling out. Fortunately I hung in there and showed up at Hamline Field house ready to work the game of my life. The first half went smooth as silk with Hamline taking a substantial lead. The second half however was like a completely different game. Hamline got overly aggressive and I got harassed with every call. Hamline easily won the game and I was elated that I hung in there, called the game as I saw it and ignored the hollering and taunts of the coach and fans. I even got a little cocky and threw in a technical foul against the home bench for good measure...I wasn't going to be pushed around!

I talked with Jerry Flathman after the game and explained to him what had occurred. He laughed and said, "Vern, You made it. In that second half, Joe Hutton the coach, was just testing how you would react under pressure. You hung in there. I guess you're ready for a full College schedule and I'll bet Hamline hires you back!"

Being willing to stand up under pressure and to face life's challenges is not always easy to do, whether it's in sports, work or in one's personal life. There is simply no better way of gaining confidence in one's self then to put our anxieties and fears aside and face each challenge head on. Once you begin that fateful pattern of taking the easy way out and coming up with excuses to avoid trying something new or an activity you just might fail at, you stop growing and mediocrity settles in. Officiating that Hamline basketball game and not taking any guff elevated me to a new level of confidence that carried over into my personal and work life as well. Heck, maybe I should have called two technical fouls against Hamline!

4. **Follow the Rules** – A few days before I was scheduled to officiate a basketball game at Southwest State College I received a phone call from the League Secretary. He said that Southwest State had a player who needed four more points to set a league scoring record, but unfortunately the player had broken his wrist. His wrist was in a cast, and according to league rules, was not allowed to play. The Southwest coach was really anxious for him to achieve this record. He had contacted the visiting coach who, according to him, gave permission for this player to participate until the four points were scored. The League Secretary wanted us to know that both coaches

agreed to this exception to the rules and the league had given the O.K as well.

When my partner and I arrived at the field house, we met briefly with the visiting coach. We wanted to officially verify that he had given permission for the player with the cast to play. He said, "Wait a minute, you're the officials, you make that decision…not the home coach." Wow! Somebody was giving us the snow job. After much discussion and soul searching, right or wrong, we decided to go with the league secretary and allowed the injured player to participate. The player scored his four points, he didn't slug anyone with his cast, and the home team won by over 20 points. Thinking back, we really should have stuck with the rulebook and not tried to be nice guys. It worked out O.K. in this case but has left a bad taste in my mouth even till today. Rules are concrete and specific. There's a reason players having casts aren't supposed to participate. We really allowed ourselves to be talked into making the wrong decision. If someone had gotten hurt because of the cast we wouldn't have had a leg to stand on. What's that famous saying…'nice guys finish last?'

This experience at Southwest State really taught me a lesson. How many times in our personal and work lives are we asked to change the rules, to make exceptions, to tell a white lie or to look the other way? When we decide to change the rules we are asking for trouble. One exception leads to another and pretty soon we find ourselves needing a lawyer to save our skin. It's this kind of situation that makes lawyers rich!

5. **Count to ten** – A difficult question facing all officials is deciding when to call a technical foul in basketball or an unsportsmanship foul in football. I don't know if there is a good answer to that question. I remember calling a technical foul against the home coach in one high school game before two minutes had elapsed. This coach was hollering at us almost before the jump ball to begin the game. I also remember in another instance, driving home after a game wondering if I made a mistake by not calling a technical foul. I've had partners that never called a technical foul and other partners that had a short fuse and seemed to call them at a drop of a hat. In time, I came up with sort of an unwritten guide to follow. See if you agree with me.

There's nothing wrong with a coach letting off some pent up steam. I was a good example of a coach who couldn't sit still or keep my mouth shut during the heat of the game. If the coach's comments aren't negatively affecting the game, and this includes a few shots at you, just let these comments go in one ear and out the other. In the heat of excitement some comments are directed at officials that aren't necessarily meant to be personal, but some officials who have rabbit ears (the bad habit of listening to coaches and fans) may take them personal and the big 'T' follows. I believe, in most instances, that a warning given in a calm but direct manner should almost always precede a Technical foul. I know there are always exceptions that require an 'on the spot' technical foul but they are not all that common. Now if the coach grabs you, puts his face three inches from your face and says you are a !$#%^#$ no good &%$#@^%, or if he trips the opposing player dribbling by the bench, then just forget about the warning.

There was this coach in Red Wing, Minnesota who was a real gentleman and an outstanding coach. When the game started however, he came close to becoming a wild raving maniac. When the game was over he straightened his tie and again became the perfect gentleman. Fortunately most of his wildness was directed at his players and not the officials. My deduction is that these 'wild' coaches probably live longer because they let all their anxieties out for the world to see. I worry about those coaches who smile a lot, don't seem to get excited and hold their anxieties inside. Officials absolutely love to work for these 'nice guy' coaches, but I suspect they all die from heart attacks at a younger age. My advice is count to ten before calling a technical or personal foul and who knows, you may even decide to change your mind.

This same advice holds true when you get in a battle with your wife, your boss at work, or a disgruntled parent or client. Listen to the hostility or anger being directed at you, listen some more, count to ten, and listen some more. If this doesn't calm them down and their hostility persists, then it's time for the technical foul and for you to provide some of your own direct counseling. It's amazing how a good fight can burn out if you patiently listen and allow time for the other party to vent their anger. I know it's more fun to out-shout your opponent to win an argument, but I've never seen anyone win in a shouting contest.

6. **Be Rewarded Early** - You officiate a difficult hard fought game, you shower, and want to make it home at least by midnight but no one shows up to hand you your paycheck. It's no fun to search out the coach or athletic director to get your paycheck after a game. It's especially no fun after a' barn burner' where the home team thinks the officials shafted them.

It's times like these when you wonder if the athletic director is hiding on purpose. Some athletic directors recognize this problem and provide the paycheck before the game; we love these guys. One of my partners always made a point to inform the athletic director prior to the game that he has an emergency at home and would appreciate receiving his check before the game so he can get right on the road following the game. His approach worked to perfection. It's interesting in future years how many of our officiating team members found themselves faced with emergencies at home. There's more than one way to skin a cat…or get your paycheck early.

I found this idea of receiving pay early in the game to be a successful technique in my efforts to place students with disabilities onto jobs or into training settings. Certain students with learning problems tended to lose interest or would see a drop in performance if they had to wait for two weeks or to the end of the month to get their paycheck. I learned that if I could arrange the pay reward at the end of each day or at least weekly their performance and attitude improved. Rewarding these students with pay promptly was no different than receiving our officiating check on time. Who knows, if I could have convinced employers to pay these students prior to working, like some athletic directors did, these students might have performed even better. Isn't it amazing what immediate gratification will do? Just another carryover idea I learned from officiating.

7. **Understand the message** - In the fourth quarter of a football game being played in St. Michael Minnesota, a player from the visiting team approached Jim Griffin, our referee, asking for the time. Jim referred him to me because I was the Umpire and also served as the official timekeeper. I told him there was exactually six minutes and forty seconds left in the game. He said, "I don't care about the game time. I want to know what time it is on your watch because I have to be at work by 10:00." We had a good laugh after the game over this incident. On the other hand it's a good example of how so often we respond to the question asked…but, in fact, it's not the real question being asked.

As a Counselor I was taught that many statements my clients made to me or their responses to my questions did not always reflect their true feelings. It was my job to uncover how they really felt and/or what they really meant. Listening carefully and reflecting back on what he/she was telling me was an excellent approach to uncovering their real issues and feelings. So many times in our lives we deal with people who tell us one thing but really mean another. The coach who is upset and tells you, "You will never work here again" -or- in the heat of an argument, your daughter shouts, "I hate you!" doesn't mean these statements are their true feelings. 90 % of the time it's just their emotions talking.

When emotions are involved, it's not always easy to figure out what the coach, wife, kids or your boss are really trying to say. Much of what they say may not be at all what they really feel. If we understand this fact and listen more thoughtfully rather than react with hostility there would probably be far fewer divorces, family breakups, blackballed officials and fired coaches. I must have had 25 coaches tell me I would never officiate for them again. Six weeks later when I showed up to officiate another of their basketball games, they greeted me with a smile and a welcome handshake and some even handed me a Coke!

8. **Life isn't always fair** - Two of Minnesota's finest sports officials were Jimmy Lee and Jimmy Griffin; both happened to be officials of color. They were regularly hired to work the big games and to handle District and Regional high school and college Tournaments. They must have been special because the Oxford Playground in St. Paul was later named the Jimmy Lee Playground and Central Stadium where most of the cities high school and local college games are played was renamed the Jimmy Griffin Stadium. By the way, the police department station is also named the James Griffin Police Station. These were two of St. Paul's finest! Although they were without question two of the best local officials, they never were invited to work the State basketball or football tournaments or the Big Ten or higher level college games. It unfortunately was not yet the time for 'black' officials to reach this level of their profession. Ironically it was Jim Griffin himself, when appointed to the Minnesota State High School League Board of Directors, who convinced the League to allow the hiring of Jimmy Robinson, the first black official, to officiate in the State basketball Tournament. Jimmy Griffin, with a smile on his face told me, "Vern, My big problem is that I was born 25 years to soon." Like I said before…timing is everything!

Jim Griffin told me one day he received a phone call in mid-April from a high school administrator in southern Minnesota asking if he was interested in officiating their Regional Basketball Tournament the following season. He provided Jim with all the details then informed him that one of the officials was a 'colored' official named Jimmy Lee. He asked Jim if he would have any objection working with a 'colored' official. Jim said that he was perfectly willing to work with anyone they selected. On the opening night of this tournament Jim made a special point to introduce himself to this Administrator. He said, "Vern, you had to be there to observe the expression on his face when he discovered, to his surprise, that he had hired a 'fully integrated' officiating crew!

It's true that life isn't always fair and I'm willing to accept that. My experience of not being appointed to the Assistant Commissioner of Education position because of the Governor's Affirmative Action agenda to hire a woman is a good example. Frankly, I'm not sure that being turned down wasn't a blessing, although I'll never know. I've had all kinds of disappointments in my 80 years. It's really how you react to a disappointment that's important. Jimmy Lee and Jim Griffin didn't quit officiating or become bitter because they were unfairly passed over. They just continued to work at being two of Minnesota's best officials and in due time they were honored for their achievements. Few of us will go through life without disappointments or feel at times that we've been shafted big time! It's just a part of life. My advice is simply to hang in there and, who knows, being shafted once or twice in your life might end up being the best thing that could happen to you!

9.   **Take The Heat And Wait For Better Times** – As a young official I had the thrill of being assigned to officiate with Jimmy Lee, the dean of officials back in the 1950's. He was almost a legend in officiating circles at that time. Jimmy was not only an outstanding official but he was equally a great showman. It also seemed like he knew everyone and everyone knew Jimmy. As far as I knew, he was the first and only black official in Minnesota until Jim Griffin came on the scene. His day job was working at the First National Bank in downtown St. Paul as the 'Elevator Starter'. In this position he would greet the bank employees and customers in the main lobby and then direct them to the next open elevator. He greeted the bank president and everyone else who entered this building by their first name with a big smile, a hearty handshake or a pat on the back. The First National Bank was the largest office building in St. Paul and frequented by just about everyone so

he became one of St. Paul's most notable figures. This position has since disappeared along with the Studebaker automobile and the gas attendant who cleaned your car windshield.

Our assigned basketball game was at Hudson High School just across the St. Croix River in Hudson, Wisconsin. A number of bank employees and customers lived in Hudson. I recall walking onto the gym floor right behind Jimmy when a good share of the fans attending this game started waving and greeting Jimmy like he was their long lost cousin. He actually went into the stands shaking hands, joking with the fans and having a wonderful time. At that moment I realized that if there was going to be any questionable calls that evening the heat would all be directed at me; this 24 year old junior official just ripe for picking. My prediction couldn't have been more accurate. The home team lost but Jimmy was still shaking hands with a big smile on his face as we left the building. After the game the coach shook Jimmy's hand and said," I'll see you in two weeks, Jimmy." He told me, "You'll never work here again!"

In his 50's, Jimmy had a very serious health problem that was life threatening. I was told that as he was being wheeled into the operating room his last statement was, "Don't cancel my basketball schedule!" He really loved officiating whether it was basketball, football or baseball. It was an important part of his life. Like the saying goes, "He likes the unmistakable stink of the locker room!"

Many years later on our way to officiate a basketball game at a southern Minnesota high school, Jimmy told me, "Vern, I'm getting old and slowing down so I've decided that this will be my final game." I couldn't believe that this legendary official was hanging it up. I shared this information with the school athletic director and he was stunned as well. To my surprise, Jimmy was called out of the locker room at half time to return to the gym floor. The Athletic Director told the fans about Jimmy's amazing career and presented him with a trophy in honor of his many years of officiating excellence. The capacity crowd rose to their feet and gave him an extended round of applause. It was an honor for me to be present and share that special occasion with Jimmy. I have absolutely no idea where the trophy came from or what it said, but it was a wonderful gesture and brought both Jimmy and me close to tears. I was more than willing to take the heat on any tough calls that evening. In this instance I welcomed it!

We were throwing a big party at our home on Prior Lake with all the Schultz relatives invited. Without looking at the calendar, I had accepted a music gig on that same afternoon in Farmington, Minnesota. I figured this would be OK because I would be home about the time the party was to start. Not thinking, I had left all the preparations for this 'Schultz' party solely in the hands of my wife, Toodie. I should emphasize the words 'not thinking' because I failed to realize the amount of preparation and actual work this party required and I left it all in the hands of my capable wife. I arrived home when the party was going strong and had a wonderful time. I did notice that Toodie wasn't communicating too well with me during the party. When everyone left I was read the riot act as to what I had done. The light bulb went on and I realized that everything she was so upset about was true. I truly was an inconsiderate, @#%$# husband, and really did deserve to be hung by my fingers! I apologized, took the heat…and looked forward to better days! It's amazing what officiating has taught me! Be willing to take the heat… especially when you deserve it!

I could go on with hundred's of stories about my officiating experiences. This was the greatest part time job I could have ever picked. Actually it wasn't a job at all…it was a legitimate 'night out with the boys'. That glass of beer always tasted best after a ball game, a hot shower and sharing stories with friends. When I turned 58 there were signs that retiring my officiating garb was close at hand. I fell while working a football game at Winona University and I struggled on all fours to get up. This was not a good sign. I also noted that my basketball schedule was filling up with a majority of 'girls' high school games, which in the 1980's was a real soft touch…but not anymore. I think the 'Gods' were telling me something, and I know my legs were agreeing with the Gods. I must say however, that with advanced age I seemed to have gained more respect by the coaches. I felt I was hollered at less, and generally was treated in a more fatherly manner. Maybe being the same age as most of the coach's fathers was an advantage. After all, no one hollers at their dad!

I do miss the excitement, the tough calls, being hollered at, the coaches, the players and especially my partners in crime. I have the fondest memories of working with outstanding officials like Jerry Flathman, Billy Hafner, John Mauer, Jimmy Lee, Al Pieper, Lefty Yurek, Jimmy Griffin and so many others. The Officials Association gave me a nice plaque when I retired, and sent me off to find a hobby that was more sedentary.

My Music Career Awakened

From about 1955 to 1970 my musical career hit the skids. I packed my saxophone away and hung the tuba I stole from Wilson High School on the wall in our recreation room. Those wonderful evenings playing in local 'big bands' during and after high school became distant memories. I figured my music career was a thing of the past. Fortunately I was able to replace this sideline with another sideline; officiating football and basketball games. Making extra money was very important to our family and I quickly learned that I could do better on the football field or basketball court than playing in those smoke filled dance halls. In those days, my career in education was not a well paying occupation so this sideline money really helped keep our financial head above water. That $300 a month salary I received at St. Agnes and the $325 a month working for the State was close to poverty wages. On the other hand I loved the work and my job satisfaction rating was tops. Unfortunately a high score in 'Job satisfaction' doesn't pay the bills.

In the spring of 1970, Toodie and I attended a party at the home of our Prior Lake neighbors, Karl and Marilyn Mickus. This turned out to be a great party with live music. Jack Andrews, the local Prior Lake druggist was playing the piano and Wally Langhorst, the hardware store owner was on drums. They were playing lots of the old songs our big bands had played back in high school. I casually mentioned to Jack that in my high school and college days I played the saxophone. He told me to run home, take my sax out of mothballs and join them. Well, even after some 16 years of not playing, I got right back in the grove and we had a ball. For the rest of the summer I was invited to every local party in town along with Jack and Wally. I learned quickly that free music is apparently the key to a good party. We also became the house band for all the affairs held at the Prior Lake Sailing Club. Although these were freebee gigs there were some related benefits. I ended up making lots of new local friends and thrived on all that free potato salad, cole slaw, Pepsi Cola and hamburgers. (The beer flowed pretty freely as well) What a great way to conserve on the family grocery budget.

In mid 1972 I received a call from Don Seibold, leader of a band called the 'Dixie cats' out of Shakopee, Minnesota. His clarinet player had unexpectedly passed away and he was in desperate need of a replacement. They had a playing job on Saturday night and asked me to join them. Their uniform of the day was a stripped gabardine leisure suit. Don dropped off the suit worn by the deceased clarinet player. It was the most god-awful ill fitting outfit I ever saw. The pants came to the top of my ankles and the waist was about 6 inches to large. It became immediately apparent that the deceased clarinet player was short and slightly on the robust side. No matter how hard Toodie tried to stretch and stitch this suit, I ended up looking like a real rube! The band turned out to be great with some fine Dixieland musicians. Those leisure suits however made us look like a bunch of amateurs. Frankly we looked like 'hell frozen over.' Fortunately, a few months later, they abandoned the leisure suits and turned to blue blazers...what a wonderful change. I'm convinced the blue blazer even helped improve my playing

Playing with the Dixie Cats was really fun. Doc Johnson, a dentist from Farmington, was a terrific trumpet player who had a terrible habit of showing up about 30 seconds before the job began. George Jankowski, one of the trombone players, was a real showman. He played his favorite song void of hands on the trombone. It was a real crowd pleaser. Don Seibold, the leader and other trombone player, was the champion beer drinker of all time but had the uncanny ability to always remain sober. Like the saying goes, he must have had a hollow leg. Our accordion player was very talented with a large gay following. After about four years of playing with the Dixie Cats the band folded. The accordion player left to live with his gay friends in northern Minnesota and unfortunately, Doc Johnson, George and Don all passed away. I couldn't play alone so it looked like my budding music career had come to a screeching halt. I did manage to keep the blue blazer.

The word seems to get around when you're a musician and not playing. I received calls from a number of different bands to substitute for other musicians and to sit in on various jobs so I didn't totally retire. Then, in the early 1980's I got a call from Ben Baer, a good friend, who met a fellow in an electronics store that mentioned he was starting a band. His name was Norm Hall. In the course of their conversation Ben learned that Norm was looking for a saxophone player and Ben mentioned my availability. I called Norm that evening and was hired on the spot for a job that coming Saturday night. It turned out that Norm's band really was an old time polka band with a few country western songs tossed in. I'll never forget that first job. I knew only one song Norm played that entire evening, so I just faked the evening away. To my dismay, he said I sounded great and wanted me as a regular. I offered my services as a tuba player along with the Sax. He thought that would be perfect, especially for the polkas. The tuba I played in our high school German band had been hanging on my recreation room wall as a decoration for a number of years. I took it down, cleaned it up and was delighted to find it still worked. I figured I could 'fake' those old time songs on the tuba much better than I could on the sax.

After hanging on the wall as a decoration all those years the tuba had cobwebs, needed oiling and required a good cleaning. I proceeded to fill the bathtub and let the tuba soak in the tub for a full 24 hours. Toodie was furious that evening when she entered the bathroom and saw this grimy green scummy looking water in the tub with this old ugly tuba lying there like a dead fish. She might not have reacted so negatively if company wasn't coming that evening who obviously would need to use the bathroom. I tried to explain that cleaning that tuba meant a source of income for us. It didn't work…it was those guests seeing that filthy bathtub that had her fit to be tied.

Norm was an absolute 'wonderful' man who was a gifted salesman. In truth, we weren't the best band in town but Norm had a knack of convincing everyone that we were really good. Each year Norm would reserve a room at the St. Paul Hilton Hotel during the music tryout sessions held by the Minnesota Country Fair Organization. After our 20-minute audition, and wining and dining all the judges, Norm got us bookings for a number of County fairs. He sure knew how to schmooze!

Norm was a unique bandleader who would go to any lengths to get a playing job. He actually organized his own dances, publicized them, and used Opel, his wife, to collect tickets at the door. If he didn't make enough to cover band costs, he would dip into his own pocket to pay the band members. He also proceeded to make tapes and video's and sold them at our dances and at all of the polka fests. It was absolutely unbelievable how many of those videos were sold. Norm also got us booked each year at the Minnesota State Fair in the Farmers Union booth. There was no pay but we did get into the Fair free and got a parking pass. Money wasn't the big issue with Norm…he just loved to play!

Norm also was a dance instructor who specialized in teaching the Polka Hop dance. Toodie and I actually took his dancing course through the Prior Lake Community Education program. I must have been a slow learner because I never really caught on to the polka hop. My assignment at each playing job was to get on the mike and inform the dancers that Norm was a dance Instructor and would they like to see him perform. Of course they cheered him on and Norm and Opel would dance the Polka Hop to the applause of the audience. He also would invite some semi professional dancers to some of our playing jobs and have them perform to the enjoyment of those present. He was a true showman who lived for the applause and adulation of the dancing public. He, without question, was the P.T. Barnum of the old time dancing circuit!

Norm's band played for years at the Gibbon Polka Fest in Gibbon Minnesota. There was the main stage where the top bands played and a number of band stages in tents spread around the dance hall grounds for the lesser known bands. We always played in one of the smaller tents but Norm's dream was to play on the main stage. After three or four years Norm finally talked the manager into playing on the main stage. I remember it well. A big band from Wisconsin preceded our appearance on the main stage and they were outstanding. Following our appearance would be Carl and the Dutchmen, one of Minnesota's finest concertina bands. It was like playing between Lawrence Welk and Whoopie John. We were way out of our league but Norm didn't care, playing on that main stage meant he made it to the big time.

The best way to describe our performance on the main stage is to share my son Casey's comments. He had been working in Western Minnesota and stopped by Gibbon to hear us play on his return home. Unfortunately he had arrived after our playing was completed. He asked one of the bartenders how we sounded. The bartender said we were awful and didn't belong near the main dance hall. I think you can understand why I never shared these comments with Norm. You see, we violated a cardinal music rule. A rule that goes something like this, "When in the presence of other bands, never follow a better band than yours… and… precede an even better band." A similar cardinal rule in applying for a coaching job is, "Avoid following a winning coach!"

The final job I played with Norm was at a Polka Fest in Minnetonka. He had been diagnosed with cancer, and knew his days were numbered but that event was not going to go on without Norm. He passed away two weeks later. Norm was truly a unique individual. Here was a guy with a very meager education who struggled to make a living most of his life and ended up achieving every goal he went after. He actually had more 'street smarts' than most of the Ph.D's I worked with. He provided me with an education I'll never forget. He showed me that it isn't necessarily talent that gets you success, but how dedicated you are to your cause. He taught me that if you believe in something you have to go after it with all the energy and enthusiasm you can muster. I would classify Norm as one of the most "Unforgettable" persons in my life.

The 'Jolly Musicians' served as the town band in Prior Lake for many, many years. This band, comprised of Florian Blumberg and his brothers, played for every wedding, anniversary, and just about every event in Scott County. After two of his brothers decided to quit playing and when Florien retired, the band folded in the late 1980's. At about this same time the St. Michael's Church choir decided to have a music variety show. They contacted Florien asking him if he would round up some local musicians to play a few old-time songs in this show. He contacted me, along with Dick Cates on drums and a few others, to join him for this show. We were very well received and Florien asked us if we were interested in forming a new 'Jolly Musicians' band. The answer was a rousing "Yes!" I agreed to play with the understanding our attire would not require us to wear 'Stripped gabardine leisure suits'!

Florien was an outstanding trumpet player who was in his glory when the two of us would harmonize on some of those great old time waltzes. He was truly a musician's musician. In addition to his years of playing in the band, Florien also served as the bugler for the Prior Lake VFW for 57 years. This has to be a record! Our new 'Jolly Musicians' band played together well into the 1990's until Florien became ill. Our final job with Florian took place at the St. Michael Church 'April Festival'. He was quite ill at the time and wanted to play at least a few songs with us that afternoon. He called Dick Cates, our drummer, the evening before we played and asked if he had any Blackberry Brandy to bring to the job. He was looking for some good liquid support. Dick had none so he gave me a call. I fortunately had just bought a brand new bottle yet unopened. I brought it to the Festival for Florien who was quite weak and had to be helped onto the stage. To our complete amazement Florien played the entire afternoon while emptying that full bottle of blackberry brandy. He ended the day having a few more drinks at the VFW for good measure. What I learned from this experience is that Blackberry Brandy is truly the miracle drink. Florien passed away the following week after the healing effects of the blackberry brandy wore off.

The Jolly Musicians band. Left to right; Florian Blumberg, Dick Rosendahl, Vern Schultz, Dick Cates.

With Florian's passing, Dick Rosendahl, our accordion player, took over the 'Jolly Musicians' band. We continued to play for many years until Dick passed away. Dick was a recovered alcoholic and unfortunately had a heart attack riding his bicycle to the local AA meeting. I was in a real dilemma when Dick passed away because we had a number of bookings scheduled and no accordion player. In desperation I contacted Boots Johnson the accordion player from our high school German band that had disbanded over 50 years ago. Boots agreed to join forces with me because the members of the band he was playing with were all over 80 years old and as a result were close to calling it quits. We have been playing on a regular basis even at the time of this writing. I recently reminded Boots that we had both reached the 80 year mark and was it time for our music career to come to an end. He said, "Let's shoot for the 90's." I like his attitude!

Boots had been the accordion player in the very popular "Grumpier Old Men" movies. When the movie was completed he got possession of the band 'fronts' from the movie. A large 'H H' was stenciled on these 'Fronts' that stood for 'Handsome Hans', the band leader in the movie. We decided to get real clever by changing our band name to the 'Hi Hats' so we could continue to use these fronts. Hi Hats is certainly a better name then one a friend suggested, 'Hillbilly Hotheads!'

The Hi Hats -Vern Schultz and 'Boots' Johnson.

I retired from the St. Paul School District in 1993 and have continued to pursue my music sideline even till the time of this writing. Much to my surprise I find myself leader of the 'Hi Hats' band playing both Sax and Tuba and, believe it or not, am lead singer. My mother would have been proud to know that those music lessons paid off for her son Vernon, and that I made a buck singing her favorite song, "Billy Boy" at all the retirement centers and nursing homes south of the Minnesota River. I'll share more about my music career at completion of my retirement...well; maybe I won't, but just ask around.

SECTION VI
CHANGING ATTITUDES AND MOTIVATIONS

Mary Sweeney gave me some pretty good advice during the time she was training me in as a Vocational Rehabilitation Counselor. She said there were many things that would have to change before our community would be willing to allow people with disabilities to be equally accepted into our society. She stressed the point that it's the responsibility of us folks in the Rehabilitation business to convince government agencies, community resources, employers and the population in general that changes are needed. I didn't read this in my Vocational Rehabilitation Counselor job description so wasn't exactly sure what she meant; but I soon found out!

In my second week on the job she invited me (more like forcing me) to attend a meeting of the Minnesota Rehabilitation Association and directed me to pay the dues and join this Association. Members consisted of other Vocational Rehabilitation workers, Physical Medicine Doctors, Physical and Occupational Therapists, Speech Clinicians, Artificial Limb Company Representatives and other folks involved in rehabilitation related activities. I soon learned a key function of this Association was to present a united effort to improve conditions in Minnesota for people with disabilities. Mary explained that there was a Regional Association and a National Association as well. I must admit that at that early point in my career I was more interested in figuring out how to use the Dictaphone machine and learning what day my paycheck would arrive. I was mighty low on cash at the time!

It wasn't long before I began attending these MRA meetings on a regular basis and started getting involved. Mary kept the pressure on for me to attend. I joined a sub-committee at Mary's suggestion (ordered might be a more accurate term) and began making friends, and learning more about the broader field of Rehabilitation. As my interest grew I decided to attend the annual Regional Rehabilitation Association meeting in Kansas City and was given permission to participate in the National Rehabilitation Association meeting in Washington D.C. Attending these sessions brought me face to face with the many occupational, architectural and attitudinal challenges that individuals with disabilities had to face all over our Country. It was a real eye opener! I began to understand the message Mary was giving me, "Vern work hard on your Rehabilitation Counselor job, but also get involved in these organizations to help change the attitudes of our society. In the long run it'll make your job easier." I figured she knew what she was talking about so decided to take her advice.

I have to thank Mary Sweeney for opening my eyes to the importance of becoming an advocate at both the local and national level to help improve state and national employment practices, eliminate architectural barriers and to enhance equal opportunity legislation. I also found out that working toward change was exciting and offered a real adrenalin shot. Mary taught me that being a Rehabilitation Counselor was just part of my job responsibility. She would have been a great coach. I'll bet her half time talks would have matched anything Knute Rockne of Notre Dame could offer. What a great role model to have as a teacher. Looking back, it's hard to believe that in a short few years I became President of the Minnesota Rehabilitation Association and later President of the Regional Rehabilitation Association and annually participated in National Rehabilitation Association activities. I guess I really got hooked!

Rolling Up Our Sleeves

Gus Gehrke, Director of the Minnesota Vocational Rehabilitation program, was running for President of the National Rehabilitation Association in 1981. He asked if I would serve as his Campaign Chairman and I said it would be an honor. Our committee had the usual buttons and advertisements that all campaigns have but we held one unique event at the convention in Las Vegas that really put him over the top in this election. We organized an affair the evening before the election and called it, 'Gus's Minnesota Beer Fest'. We rented a ballroom at the convention site, purchased kegs of beer, had our Wisconsin friends donate some of their finest cheese and we offered live music. Dick Ramberg, a Rehabilitation Counselor in the Minneapolis office played the piano, Bill Gulbranson another counselor was on drums and I played the saxophone. No one had ever put on an affair like this before and everyone at the convention came to 'Gus's Beer Fest' and had a ball. After that party everyone voted for Gus and the election was a landslide! Someone said it was the free beer that turned the trick, the Wisconsin folks said it was the cheese, but we all know it was that great music! People just love a party with lots of free beer, cheese and music to dance by. When I returned home I told everyone that I played for a gig at the Stardust ballroom in Las Vegas. If that didn't impress them I don't know what would.

In the mid 1980s the National Rehabilitation Association Convention was held in Hollywood, Florida. Following one of the gala banquets was an evening of dancing and socializing. Most everyone was having a great time dancing except a few of us who were having a good time visiting. Lorraine Zeimer, one of our rehabilitation counselors confined to a wheelchair because of Polio, asked if I would dance with her. Years earlier I had been her counselor and over time we had become good friends. Frankly I had no idea what I was supposed to do with a wheelchair as a partner but I figured, "Let's go for it." I was amazed at Lorraine's rhythm and skill in manipulating that wheelchair to the beat of the music. We twirled around and she flew in every direction using that wheelchair like a corkscrew. I never had so much fun. To my surprise when the music stopped everyone attending this affair gave us a round of applause. It was almost like being in show business! We proceeded to dance a number of times that evening until I made one fatal mistake. As she was spinning around I gave her wheel chair a gentle jerk but maybe it wasn't so gentle because it flipped the wheelchair backwards and there were two loud 'bangs'. One was the handles of the wheelchair hitting the floor followed by the second bang... her head hitting the floor. For a moment I thought I killed her! Everyone on the floor immediately stopped dancing when they heard these 'bangs' and hotel security staff rushed to the scene from every corner of the ballroom. I took a sigh of relief when Lorraine finally opened her eyes and said she was fine but did have a slight headache. I apologized for having pulled when I should have pushed and that it might be wise to take a rain check on any more dancing. If the result had been more serious, who knows, I might have ended up in jail being charged with 'illegal dancing.' I discovered that playing my horn for a dance was much safer than actually dancing.

A Tough Decision

The year I was President of the Regional Rehabilitation Association, the Board of Directors decided to hold a Casino Night at the Hilton Hotel in St. Paul as part of the annual convention. A local company was contracted to handle and manage all the gaming tables while our program committee was responsible to decorate the hall, make all the banquet arrangements, handle registration and cocktail hour. As an inducement to guarantee full attendance, this committee was able to secure a grand prize of two all expense paid tickets to Las Vegas from a local travel agency. The evening was a huge success with an overfilled banquet hall. At completion of the banquet the drawing was held to determine the winner of the Las Vegas trip. Toodie and I were seated at the head table along with all the other Association officials when the drawing took place. To my astonishment my name was pulled out of the box as the big winner! What exactly was I to do? I was the President of the Association but had nothing to do with securing this prize or with the drawing…but I was the President. Would this look like an inside job? What would you have done? Did you know that Las Vegas is really beautiful at night with those millions of glittering lights?

When The President Called

In 1968 I attended the President's Committee on Employment of the Handicapped annual meeting which was held at the Washington Hilton Hotel in Washington D.C. This was a major meeting attended by many disabled individuals from throughout the country in addition to Rehabilitation staff and many employers. I decided to take my 14 year old son Tom with me so, in our off time, we could tour all those key Washington historical sites. The middle to late 1960s were difficult times in our Country and those attending this meeting were advised to stick close to the hotel in the evenings because the hotel was located very close to a troubled area of town. As we left the Washington airport Tom dropped his glasses and unfortunately shattered his right eye piece. Without glasses he would get headaches so when we arrived at the hotel I picked up a meeting program which had a black cover and proceeded to cut out a black circle and taped it in place of his right eye piece. With this black eye patch Tom fit right in at this meeting. We really didn't plan it that way however.

On the second meeting day I was scheduled to attend a 7:00 P.M. event. I made Tom promise to stay in our room, to definitely not leave the hotel and told him I would be back no later than 8:00. When I returned to our room Tom was gone. I figured he probably just went to the lobby and would return soon. At 9:00 he still had not returned and at 10:00 he was nowhere to be found. The hotel is one of the largest in Washington D.C. and I walked it from one end to the other. I remember asking the lobby desk and bellboys if they had seen a one eyed boy walking around. They gave me sort of a funny look and said, "No one eyed kids had come by that they remembered." At 11:00 I was truly desperate and in a panic state when

I walked by the Bar and saw a boy sitting with two ladies in wheelchairs. To my dismay it was Tom! I remember walking into the bar, holding back my temper and saying in a very normal voice, "Hi Tom." Before I could say another word one of the ladies said, "Are you Tom's father? What a fine boy you have. You should be so proud of him. He pushed us all over the hotel and we have had a wonderful time." Tom was smiling at me with pride and I said, "Gee, that's great, I'm glad he was of help to you." Actually I was really proud of him on one hand but could have killed him on the other. As we were walking back to our room he told me he had left the room just to get a coke when these ladies came by and appeared to need help and afterwards had bought him a coke in the bar. I said, "Tom that was really thoughtful of you." What else could I say?

A few years later I attended this same meeting with my good friend from the St. Paul Mayor's Committee, Dick DuCharme. Dick had Spina Bifida and was confined to a wheelchair. He was anxious to attend this meeting and to also see the Washington sights. He had pre-arranged a visit to the White House for Tuesday morning. As I was wheeling him to a cab outside the hotel, for some unknown reason, I slapped the back fender of the cab. I must have scared the cab driver because he flew out of the cab ready to attack both of us. I apologized profusely and he simmered down. I guess I was a little excited and when lifting Dick from his wheelchair to the front cab seat I dropped him. That's right I dropped him. I immediately picked him up and set him in the car seat. He grimaced when he sat down. I asked if he was OK and he said that he was fine. We proceeded to the White House and had a wonderful tour. The nice thing about a tour with a person in a wheelchair is that you see parts of the White House the normal tour group never sees and you also get lots of special attention. I previously had a couple of White House tours but this was the best tour I ever had. I told Dick that having a disability may have some benefits I never realized. I told him we should travel together to Las Vegas and maybe he would get us front row seats. Actually we did go to a meeting in Las Vegas a few years later. We didn't get front row seats but we didn't have to stand in line either!

I did notice that when we got in the cab to return to the hotel and also when I lifted him out at the hotel he grimaced in pain. I asked if he was OK and he said he was fine. We did check with the hotel nurse the next day and she said that it might be a good idea for Dick to check in with his Doctor when he returned home but she didn't think anything was wrong. We spent a wonderful week together but I did notice that grimace was occurring more frequently, but he always said it was nothing. When he returned home he visited his doctor and found out he had broken his leg! A whole week with a broken leg and he never complained. What a great traveling companion I turned out to be. It was not one of my finest hours.

Local Action for Equality

I joined the St. Paul Mayors Committee on Employment of the Handicapped in the mid 1960's and continued my involvement during the tenure of at least five mayors. It was an active committee that was formed to improve conditions for the handicapped in St. Paul. In 1974 under the direction of Mayor Lawrence Cohen a special project was undertaken to develop a comprehensive Guidebook that would list Accessible stores, restaurants and other facilities and resources in St. Paul. I was to serve as co-chairperson of this project along with Dick DuCharme another member of the Mayors Committee. Dick was confined to a wheelchair himself so he knew firsthand the myriad of barriers facing folks using wheelchairs in our community. Dick was a real go-getter and proceeded to attack this project with enthusiasm. As a result of his leadership a booklet titled, 'Wheeling St. Paul' was published and distributed from the Mayor's office. It's amazing what can happen when you get the right people involved.

Just after the 'Wheeling St. Paul' booklet was published, construction of the new Civic Center located on 7 corners in downtown St. Paul was begun. Our committee monitored this construction very closely and as a result this Center met every standard for accessibility. Dick and I happened to be driving by the front entrance of the building the day they were pouring the sidewalks and curbing. We immediately noticed that new concrete curbing was extended around the entire front entrance with no curb cuts for wheelchair accessibility. We rushed to the Mayor's office and confronted him with this problem. Mayor Cohen immediately contacted the Building Contractor and read him the riot act. It's amazing the clout a mayor has when his promises aren't kept. Jack hammers were soon out in full force and those curbs were replaced with curb cuts. This committee with the full support of the Mayor served as the catalyst for helping to make St. Paul a much more accessible city for all its citizens. I learned quickly that if you have the mayor on your side you just can't go wrong.

The best example of this committee's efforts is to visit the Minnesota State Fairgrounds. For years the fairgrounds was loaded with architectural barriers of every type. With guidance by our Mayors committee and other advocacy organizations, the fair management over the years has done a masterful job of eliminating barriers. I attend the Minnesota State Fair every year and am amazed to see the numbers of wheelchairs and elderly folks that are now able to attend any event without being turned away because of accessibility issues. My mother, who worked in her church booth at the fair for many years, said to me one day, "I don't ever recall seeing so many folks in wheelchairs attending the fair." It's interesting to find out that there are committees that can really accomplish something.

I was appointed chairperson of the Mayor's committee during the tenure of Mayor Charlie McCarthy. He was a character if there ever was one. He was blustery, loud, unpredictable and certainly controversial…and he was Irish! During his tenure we came up with an interesting idea for 'Employment of the Handicapped week'. We would have Mayor McCarthy confined to a wheelchair for the entire day including his speech at the noon banquet. He fully agreed to follow this plan. Well, the day started off OK with Charlie using the wheelchair in his office. He showed up at our noon lunch in the wheelchair and proceeded to give his speech from the chair. When he completed his speech, however, he proceeded to get up from the wheelchair and walked out of the building. Our plan went to pot! I guess the wheelchair just cramped his flamboyant style and he couldn't take it any longer. Frankly, he never did get the picture, which was probably one of the reasons he was just a one term mayor.

Being A Big Brother

Jim Griffin called me up one day and said, "Congratulations Vern, I've just nominated you to the Board of Directors of the St. Paul Big Brothers-Big Sisters organization." My first reaction was, "No, not another organization with meetings." Jim was already on their Board and he thought it would be good to have someone from the school district participate. The Superintendent of Schools was a Board Member but apparently seldom, if ever, attended. I ended up serving on this Board for over 20 years and was elected President in 1991. This was a great organization led by Bob Mitchell, Executive Director. Up to this time every organization I was associated with focused primarily on adults or youth with disabilities. This organization served all youth who found themselves without a father or a mother and in need of positive role models. It was enlightening for me to see so many young men and women in the community willing to help these young people without any thought of getting paid or the time it would take away from their own lives. You can't help but be stimulated and motivated when surrounded by so many dedicated individuals. During my tenure, I did try to stimulate interest in serving those disabled youth without a father or mother and did see some inroads in this effort. It's amazing just how many evening community activities you can get involved in that keep you away from home. Add these meetings to my officiating schedule and I began to wonder if my kids would be eligible for a big brother!

A Special Foundation

In the 1960s a gentleman named Nevin Huested passed away and left a fairly large sum of money in his will to be used for the benefit of handicapped children and young adults residing in Minnesota. Jim Geary was the State Director of Special Education at the time and he was asked to help determine how these monies might best be used. After a series of discussions it was decided that a Foundation should be formed with these monies used to provide grants to enhance services to children and young adults with disabilities in Minnesota. Since this Foundation was formed, more than 500 Grants have been approved. Jim Geary asked me to serve on the Board of Directors in 1964 and I have served ever since. I was appointed President in 1990 and continue to serve as President today. My favorite saying to St. Paul Special Education staff when an interesting idea or curriculum adaption surfaced and District funds were unavailable was, "Maybe the Huested Foundation has funds to help you implement that new idea." Although Huested Grants have been provided to organizations throughout the State, the St. Paul schools certainly have received their share. My experience on this Board has taught me one very important fact: "It's just as much fun to give money away for a good cause... then to receive it!"

Spending Time

Over the years I have served on numerous other Boards of Directors, Councils, Advisory Committees, and Associations. Toodie will vouch for my absence from the dinner table for as many as two to four evenings a week (or more) attending these meetings plus my time away from home officiating. If I could remember the names of these committees I'd list them here but you're probably not interested anyway. Apparently I got hooked in joining community action groups when I became a member of the Minnesota Rehabilitation Association and saw what organized efforts could actually do to improve conditions for the disabled in our community. Before I knew it I was over my head in various community activities and enjoying being a part of the action that goes along with making change. Who knows, without Mary Sweeney's initial push I would have probably found myself spending more time lounging in front of the TV at home instead of in those smoke filled meeting rooms. My family was always supportive of my work and never complained that I was so frequently an absentee father. Toodie understood that my officiating put bread on the table and that my community participation was a key part of my work. With this support I found it far more palatable to down all those hamburgers at McDonald's for dinner while I waited for those all to frequent 7:00 P.M. meetings to begin. Every once in a while I found it necessary to remind myself that it was my decision to live 25 miles away from work...and it was worth a little sacrifice. Anyway I like McDonald hamburgers!

I get a thrill every time I see a wide stall in a restaurant restroom, curb cuts on every corner in downtown St. Paul, learn of a successful Big Brother/Little Brother match, observe a paraplegic driving, see a car with a lift in a handicapped parking spot, observe a barrier free playground, see kids with disabilities horseback riding, reading about a disabled Boy Scout making Eagle Scout, observe Braille numbers on elevator pads, or having my restaurant table cleaned off by a young man with downs syndrome. Maybe I wasn't the key figure in helping make these things happen, but I get a great deal of satisfaction knowing I was at least a part of the movement that broke down the barriers allowing equal opportunity for all; not just the able bodied. I'm reminded of a client of mine who as a result of a severe car accident was paralyzed from the neck down. Dan Fitzpatrick spent eight long years just looking at the four walls of his living room. In time and with support, Dan secured vocational training, got a job, purchased a home, got married and traveled anywhere he wanted to go in his electric wheelchair and adapted van. What bigger kick then to see the changes society has made to make this type of rehabilitation effort possible? Mary was so right when she urged me to work beyond my job description and do something at a greater activity level… to make a difference. Thanks Mary, you made my retirement much more enjoyable!

SECTION VII
LOOKING BACK

In 1993 I retired from my job with the St. Paul School District. I really planned to work till that magic retirement age of 65 but as it turned out there were four pretty good reasons why I hung it up at 63. I was attending a Christmas party in our school district administrative office building December 17th 1992, when I received a phone call from my doctor telling me, "Congratulations Vern, you have prostate cancer." It sort of threw a damper on that party for me. Not knowing the outcome of that diagnosis, I figured early retirement might be a wise move. The second reason was more of a practical issue. I had reached the 100% level of my pension so working beyond 1993 didn't affect my retirement income to any degree. The third reason might best be classified as 'burn-out'. I was really tired of attending those two to three evening meetings a week dealing with so many issues that had already been discussed in the 1960s, again in the 1980s and here they were popping up again in the 1990s. I caught myself telling folks far too frequently, "Yeah, it's a great idea but you should know we tried it in 1966 and again in 1978 and it didn't work." No one liked hearing that and I probably should have kept my mouth shut. The fourth reason had to do with paper-work. It seemed that the ever increasing volume of paper going across my desk was turning me into a sedentary paper jockey. Now don't get me wrong, there were many things I really did love about my job. Looking at the big picture however, I felt it was the right time to leave. I almost forgot to mention another reason...I kept falling asleep in those staff meetings. Unfortunately, the sleep clinic couldn't come up with a solution to that problem!

Actually I didn't really leave my job in 1993. I was asked to serve as a consultant for the school district and continued to assist the vocational services program operation. I served in this capacity for a year and a half. When the Superintendent asked me to help identify a million dollars in cuts to this program, I figured maybe it was time to officially retire. Remember…timing is everything! I've been retired now for the past 18 years and hope there are many more exciting years ahead. I usually start my day by attending Mass, head to the Dakota Health and Fitness club for a little exercise and socialization, come home for a brunch and read the paper. Now its noon and I've killed the morning. I have no problem finding something to keep me busy every afternoon. I watch absolutely no TV during the day until the 6:00 o'clock evening news comes on. I love playing in my 20 acre yard, keeping my eye on the horses or cattle that roam the field, playing that great music of the '40's in my 'Hi Hat' band, managing the Huested Foundation, helping with family projects, vacationing each winter in Mexico, and doing whatever Toodie asks me to do. What I do for the years ahead is certainly up for grabs. I can hardly wait to find out what's in store for me!

Writing these memoirs, in addition to stimulating a little brain activity, has offered an excellent opportunity to look back over my life and remember fondly some great moments, wonderful friends, and a few memories I'd like to forget. Retirement leaves plenty of time to ponder and review the many decisions and directions one has taken in 80 years of living on this earth. I've spent lots of time during these retirement years asking myself if I made the right decisions in my life. Did I learn anything worthwhile that might benefit my grandchildren or their children, or as a matter of fact, anybody? Well, I'll take the leap and offer just a few thoughts that are absolutes…no chance for error!

1. **Don't give up on yourself before you try –**

I often wonder what would have happened if my Dad hadn't insisted that I try out for the St. Columba baseball team way back when I was in the 6th grade. I just knew I wasn't good enough to play on that team, and if left up to me, I wouldn't have gone anywhere near that ball field. Not only did I make the team I ended up a starting player. It was quite an eye opener for me to realize that maybe I was just as good as the other guys. I was encouraged to enter a music contest when I was 9 years old. I wanted nothing to do with it because I wasn't good enough, but my folks saw it different. I never dreamed I would win top honors and a nice gold medal. For some unknown reason, as a kid, I seemed to lack a sense of confidence, a reluctance to compete with others and frightened to death to be in the spotlight. I felt like crawling under the bed when my mother would say, "Vernon, get your horn and play that pretty song for our guests."

I thank my folks over and over again for pushing me forward and not letting me crawl into a shell to avoid some of the challenges of life… to play it safe. As I grew older I found myself faced with new challenges in every facet of my life; in school, at work, in sports, refereeing, in my music and in community activism. The lessons my folks taught me, in those early years of my life, provided me with the confidence to face these challenges head on. They simply wouldn't allow me to put myself down…to take the easy way out. Their advice was always, "Go for it!" My advice to any young person today is to set your goals and "go for it!" Don't wait for someone else to push you into action like I did. In time, I found that the challenges we face in life really offer the stimulant that makes our lives exciting and meaningful. You may not be as fortunate to have such astute parents as Art and Fleurine Schultz. Take the chance and do it on your own!

2. **Give God a chance to answer your prayers** –

I've come to the conclusion, over all these years, that every single one of us at sometime in our lives comes face to face with one (and maybe more) personal crisis that will test our faith in God. This crisis may occur early in life, for some in the prime of mid-life, and for others in the twilight of their life. I honestly don't think anyone 'gets away free.' The way I have it figured out is that God uses this crisis to sort of test out the depth of our faith. In a way it's his test to see if our faith is of a superficial variety or if it's truly 'beneath the skin'. In other words, is our faith in God only strong when life is treating us great!

My test of faith came in the 1950's with the death of our three children. Remember, I said earlier that this was the lowest point in my life. I called it 'the pits'. The very roots of my faith in God and in the church were truly challenged during that time, but fortunately Toodie and I never lost sight of God's love and concern for us. He tested our faith and I would like to believe we achieved a passing grade. As a result we have been rewarded over these past years probably more than we ever deserved. My mother's advice was right on target, "Get on with your life. Have faith in God, and time will eventually heal the wounds." She knew exactly what she was talking about. As I look back now, it almost seems like our lives have been blessed over and over again well beyond my expectations. Here's how I see it. Toodie and I had wanted a family desperately, but it appeared that this was to be just a dream. Father Curtain, Director of Catholic Charities, listened to our story and when he said, "Don't worry, you'll have your family," he wasn't kidding. In just a few months, we picked up our first adopted child, Thomas. A year and half later Casey entered the picture, and in two years we were holding our beautiful daughter, Patricia Marie. Our lives have been enriched over and over again by our three 'exceptional' children and five wonderful grandchildren.

If our three biological children had not been ill I would most likely have continued my career as a teacher and coach without interruption. Actually, it was our children's illness that indirectly opened the door to an entirely new career in the field of Vocational Rehabilitation. This turned out to be a career even more challenging and exciting than teaching and coaching. My promotions came fast in this new field, and from a monetary standpoint, I benefited much more than if I had continued to teach. From the mid-1950s on everything I touched seemed to meet with success; in my work, in officiating, in my music and in terms of our life in general. Most of all, after going through these emotional challenges together, my relationship with Toodie flourished and strengthened more than ever.

I must have been too busy during those years to realize all these wonderful things that were taking place in my life until one day, after my retirement, while sitting on the beach in Mexico the light bulb suddenly went on! At that moment, I came to the full realization that my prayers had been answered and over those many years I just never realized it. There had been no miracle lightning strike from God that suddenly erased our problems. Without any fanfare it all just seemed to come together. We must have passed God's test. The lesson I learned and would like to share with others is simple. Don't give up on God when life appears to treat you badly, and don't expect your prayers to be answered immediately or in the way you might expect. Give him time…he has an interesting way of answering prayers. I'm almost embarrassed to say that I didn't realize how well my life had changed and my prayers were answered until that day in Mexico. In those difficult years God wasn't punishing me, he was simply testing my faith! Remember this when the time comes for you to face your crisis!

3. **Be willing to face a challenge…don't run away-**

Jim Griffin, my long time friend and Referee partner told me, "Vern, as a black man in the 1950s it was up to me, and me alone, to convince the Civil Service Board that I could be just as good a Deputy Chief of Police as those white applicants. There was no one else fighting for me." As it turned out he passed highest on the Chief of Police Civil Service test and found himself number one on the list. It looked like he had the job in the bag but to his dismay the number two man on the list ended up getting the job. The day after he was turned down for this position he told me, "If I have to mortgage my house and go up to my neck in debt to pay my lawyer, I'm going to become Deputy Chief of Police." You guessed it; he did win his court case and became St. Paul's first black Deputy Chief of Police. He made up his mind to achieve his goal and was willing to sacrifice everything to get this job that was rightfully his. There is a message in this example. Once you set your goals, be willing to go full throttle to achieve them. Don't give up easily or decide they really aren't attainable or expect someone else to help. If you aren't willing to sacrifice and fight for what you believe or are willing to let the other guy do it, then just forget it. Remember, in the ballgame of life, the ball is in your hands. Don't rely on your parents or friends or support from your drinking buddies to achieve your goals!

Ken McGonagle and I had just finished officiating the preliminary game before the Minneapolis Lakers vs. College All Star Basketball game at the Minneapolis auditorium. When our game ended the Lakers General Manager came up to us and said, "The officials for the Lakers game are snowed in at the Chicago airport, so you two are going to officiate the game." We never changed our clothes or showered and went right on the floor and officiated one of the top games in the country involving the Minneapolis Lakers Professional World Champions. The game went smooth and the Lakers won handily. They gave each of us 4 dollars and said we did a fine job. We had no time to think about the magnitude of this game or to worry if we were qualified or not. If I had known two or three weeks a head of time I would have worried myself sick and, who knows, maybe found an excuse to avoid this challenge. This experience really helped build my confidence as I moved up the ladder in officiating. I figured if I could officiate the professional world champions successfully, I certainly could handle any game assigned to me and any other challenge life has in store for me.

Moving from a safe secure Civil Service job with the State of Minnesota to a far less secure position as Director of the Vocational Services Program at Kenny Institute was a decision I came within a hair of turning down. After days of anxiety and fear, I took a deep breath and accepted the challenge. To my surprise, I found that I was fully capable of handling this position and our vocational program blossomed. Taking this plunge into the unknown and succeeding gave me that added confidence to seek out other more responsible leadership positions in the future. I realized that

I was just as good as the next guy and, who knows, maybe even better. I believe the formula for achieving success in life goes something like this: **(Avoiding challenge + status quo = mediocrity. Facing challenges + hard work = confidence & success.)** I recommend that you follow the formula leading to 'confidence and success'. In life you must be willing to take a chance. Remember, no one ever wins the lottery if they don't buy a ticket.

4. **Show your appreciation for good deeds –**

One of the School Psychologists who worked with me did a really nice job of presenting a case study at a family conference. I wrote a short note complemented her on the presentation. She stopped by to see me a few days later and said, "I've been working for the school system for 20 years and no one in all those years has ever personally complemented me on my work. Your note really meant a lot to me." All of us can benefit from a little pat on the back, or a thank you, or just a friendly word of gratitude. Unfortunately, it's so easy to go about our job each day and overlook some outstanding work by our peers or employees. Take the time in one way or another to say, "You did a really nice job." Not only will the person you've complemented feel better, but so will you. Actually I learned the value of a 'thank you' from my wife, Toodie, who makes a real point to send cards, make a phone call of 'thanks', or a note of congratulation on anniversaries and special events to relatives and friends. I've found out over the years that a 'thank you' or a 'pat on the back' reaps real dividends in increased performance and having a more motivated worker. It's so easy to do, but just as easy to forget. Just do it without expecting anything in return.

5. **Listen to others—there's always a better way-**

My son Casey would frequently get upset with me when I'd ask for his opinion on a project or issue we were working on. After getting his opinion I would usually ask others for their opinion on this same issue. I remember him saying, "Why do you ask my opinion if you're not going to listen to me." I said that each person I talked to gave me a different answer, so how do I know you're right? Loren, my brother, wrote a book entitled, 'The Arthur Young Business Plan Guide.' The book provides an excellent guide as to how to write a 'Business Plan' before you start a new business. He would say, "You just can't start a new business on a 'good idea, and anyway the bank won't lend you money on your 'enthusiasm." You plan, brainstorm, use models, and talk to experts before building your 'plan.' The only time I can think of making a decision on the spot without consultation from others is in Officiating. Once you blow your whistle, you are always absolutely right, no matter what those coaches or fans might think. I'm sure glad they didn't have instant replay during the period I was officiating.

Don't be bashful, think you're wasting time, or feel stupid if you consult or share ideas with others before you jump into action. What I've learned in my lifetime is that someone, somewhere, always has a better way of skinning a cat than I do. I want to learn his/her way. Remember, it's a sign of intelligence to listen to others. By the way, there's nothing wrong with asking a parent or friend what they think of your girl friend. They may see something you overlooked. Remember Love is blind!

5. **Associate with winners –**

I received a wonderful education at the University of Minnesota and over the years gained considerable knowledge by attending hundreds of workshops and seminars to enhance my skills. When I look back, however, I must confess that my real education came right on the job, the athletic field, the dance hall and with associates sharing experiences, ideas and theories over a drink or two. I had wonderful mentors in each of my life experiences that taught me the value of dedication to the cause. They also shared techniques and skills to do a better job, with practical aids to achieving success. I've named just a few of my key mentors in this book. In addition to my folks, these were the folks who influenced my life and guided me in the right direction. There were many additional people I could have mentioned that would fill the pages of this book. I will be eternally grateful to Bill Fitzharris, Dick Seibert, Mary Sweeney, Gus Gehrke, Norm Hall, Harry Bealke, Jim Geary and the hundreds of other co-workers, referee partners, musicians, supervisors, and community activists whose advice and encouragement have been priceless. They were my mentors who kept me on target. These folks were all winners. I tried to emulate their many positive qualities. I'm not sure I was always successful!

During my lifetime, I've come in contact with a number of special individuals who were dedicated exceptional workers; many mentioned in this book. I also remember those many folks who were very good at what they did and also those individuals who spent most of their energies just getting by. Some folks are just comfortable to stay within their box, avoid joining a cause, but willing to reap the benefits of the job. Most of these individuals were good people but not particularly willing to go the extra mile. I learned that the world is full of these 'good' people but it doesn't take a Philadelphia lawyer to sort them out from the dedicated exceptional worker. Join forces with the very best and you will have a better shot at being a winner yourself. The best advice for success I can offer is to hitch your wagon to winners...let the losers wander by themselves toward mediocrity!

7. Convert disappointments and obstacles into success –

Let me remind you again of Gus Gehrke's advice when I went to his office and told him I had this big problem. He said, "Vern, you don't have a problem, you have an opportunity!" I have always remembered that statement. Problems, disappointments and obstacles force us to become innovative and think out of the box. I've had an architect tell me that some of his best designs took place when he was faced with what appeared on the surface to be an insurmountable obstacle. Have you ever left a football stadium with two minutes left in the game because your team was behind and didn't have a chance to win? When you arrived at your car, you heard the roar of the crowd and to your dismay discovered that your team scored in the final seconds to win the game. You succumbed to your disappointment and gave up, only to find out you missed the game's real excitement!

If you think life is going to be perfect with no disappointments, frustrations or losses you are living in a dream world. Its how you deal with these 'challenges 'that will set the tone of your life. If you succumb to them, give up, throw in the towel, cry in your beer, quit, punch out the boss, shoot everyone in the office, or go home and cry your eyes out, you are heading down the road to being a loser. None of the folks I've mentioned in this book were losers. When faced with obstacles, they fought back, worked harder, got clever, tried a new approach, figured out a new technique, practiced more, changed their ideas or hired a lawyer. None of them gave up...and for gosh sakes, don't you give up either!

www.ingramcontent.com/pod-product-compliance
Lightning Source LLC
Chambersburg PA
CBHW022246290526
45785CB00015B/257